C. Boyd

# THE
# PRACTICAL
# FISHERMAN

# THE PRACTICAL FISHERMAN

*by*
*C. Boyd Pfeiffer*
*and*
*Irv Swope*

NICK LYONS BOOKS

To my wife Jackie who serves as an inspiration for everything I do.

Boyd Pfeiffer

To Nancy, who allowed me enough time with Boyd to complete this project.

Irv Swope

Though every effort has been made to secure the best information from the most reliable sources, the authors are not medical doctors and neither represents himself as such in offering various practical tips related to safety.

**Library of Congress Cataloging in Publication Data**

Pfeiffer, C. Boyd.
    The practical fisherman.

    1. Fishing.   I. Swope, Irv.   II. Title.
SH441.P48         799.1'2       81-21982
ISBN 0-87691-348-6 (paper)    AACR2
     0-941130-01-0 (cloth)

NICK LYONS BOOKS
is a division of
BENN BROTHERS, INC.
212 Fifth Avenue
New York, New York 10010

# CONTENTS

Both of us have gained over the years from our own experiences and from the experiences of various anglers, guides, charter-boat captains, boaters, outdoorsmen, and tackle tinkerers. Without the generosity of other anglers, who shared tips, techniques, helpful ideas, and their good and sometimes bad fishing experiences, such a book as this would not have been thought of, much less begun or completed. To those unnamed legions of anglers, our thanks.

Our thanks also to members of the fishing and boating industry who provided information and in some cases photos. We are especially grateful to Burke Fishing Lures, Grumman Boats, Johnson Outboards, Boating Industry Association, The Coleman Company, Evinrude Motors, Lowrance Electronics, Mercury Marine, Ranger Boats of Arkansas, Shakespeare Fishing Tackle Division, Techsononic Industries, and Vexilar.

Fishing friends have also helped with ideas and comments. Joe Zimmer, Walker Zimmerman, and Chuck Edghill put in extra effort and time by posing for some of the photos.

Special thanks also to Craig Woods for his thoughtful and thorough editing, Birdie Wright for typing much of the manuscript, and Jackie Pfeiffer, both for typing and for her constant encouragement.

# Introduction

When one starts a book project, interested acquaintances always ask about the subject matter. Answering such questions and trying to come up with a suitable title for this book has been difficult for us. It's not that we didn't know what we were writing about or how to go about it; the difficulty was in describing a book that doesn't tell the reader how to fish for a certain species of fish (such as trout or bass) or with certain tackle (such as fly tackle). This book is designed to aid all fishermen.

About the best answer we could come up with to such questions was to describe the book as one that tells you how to have more fun while fishing, how to stay out of trouble, and what to do about it if you get into trouble. And since this means that this book is full of practical information, we titled it *The Practical Fisherman*. We can't recall any modern fishing book among the thousands published to date that deals specifically with how to get more out of your fishing without dealing solely with one method of fishing or with one certain fish or group of fishes. We feel this book fills a need.

Most fishermen just start to fish with the feeling that anyone can do it, that no practice is necessary, and that any type of tackle can be used in any situation without danger to the angler or others. Yet this is not so if you want to get more out of your fishing safely and efficiently.

Sports need practice and precaution to get the maximum out of them. Golfers spend hours practicing putting or hitting balls on the driving range; tennis buffs play with the club professional, hitting balls just above the net or practicing corner shots. Sand-lot ballplayers wear batting helmets to protect against a wild pitch or foul ball; skiers wear special boots to protect ankles on a downhill run. Yet fishermen are often oblivious to the benefits that can result from care and forethought.

Some may scoff at the thought of danger in fishing, yet a recent news release from the Michigan Department of Natural Resources lists an average of 45.6 fishing-related fatalities annually in Michigan from 1962 through 1977, while hunting fatalities in the state for the same period averaged only 15.5 annually. And minor accidents occur constantly, for example, with hooks, lines, gaffs, and when handling fish. But most accidents while fishing can be avoided.

We like to think that safe, efficient, and enjoyable fishing can be aided by physical and mental organization. Physical organization in your home workshop, in your vehicle, or in your boat will make your fishing safer and allow you to get the tackle you need when you need it. Mental organization helps, too. For example, learning more about the fish you handle and the potential dangers of teeth, tails, fins, and gill plates will help you avoid cuts and bruises when landing or releasing your catch; and a constant awareness of your partner's position in a boat or the movements of other anglers on a crowded beach or stream will eliminate casting accidents.

This book is especially geared to the angler afoot and the small-boat fisherman. In the section on first-aid, for example, you will find methods of removing hooks along with information about sunburn, insect bites, scrapes, cuts, and minor burns—all injuries that are unfortunately too common among fishermen. But you won't find information about heart attacks or splinting broken limbs and other such emergencies. Our reasoning for this is twofold: first, even though there is no question that anglers do suffer from these problems, there is little likelihood that they will need this information with the current availability of paramedics, ambulance services, and civil servants well trained in first aid; second, there are many excellent first-aid manuals and courses available for those going into wilderness situations or interested in complete first-aid training. Thus, we have taken the approach of dealing with those problems most likely to be encountered most often by anglers and easily dealt with in the field.

We've taken a similar approach throughout the book. For example, since most boat anglers use anchors at some point in their fishing, there is extensive coverage of anchor types, accessories, and techniques for use. But because most anglers fish from small boats that can be trailered or carried on a car top, there is no mention of offshore radio systems, offshore boat rigging, and so on. Here again, there are numerous excellent manuals available covering such topics.

Our approach is to cover those situations and those items directly related to fishing and to suggest ways in which all types of fishing can be more fun, less trouble, and safer. We would like everyone to bring home only good memories of pleasant days on the water—preferably memories that include a fish or two on the end of the line.

C. BOYD PFEIFFER
IRV SWOPE

# PART ONE

# 1
# Casting

Fishing should be a pleasant experience, but it involves equipment and situations that can sometimes spell trouble. Fortunately, all it takes to eliminate problems in fishing is forethought, common sense, and some knowledge of equipment and fish handling.

Much fishing involves casting a hook or a lure equipped with several hooks. We occasionally hear of an experience in which an angler has hooked himself or his partner in a hat, shirt, or pants. Sometimes the hook ends up in someone's flesh. We recently heard of an offshore experience in which a trolling boat ran out of bait and signaled over the radio to a companion boat for some extra bait. The boats approached each other from opposite directions. The boat needing the bait had its outriggers stowed vertically for the transfer; the other boat still had its outriggers extended with trolled lures in the water. The bait transfer was easy, but as the boats continued a trolled line with a lure was dragged over the other boat. A large single-hook lure was dragged over the bow and across the neck of one of the fishermen. The captain grabbed the lure and jerked it to pull it out of the outrigger pin—and in doing so drove a 10/0 hook through his finger.

The episode ended the fishing with a trip to the hospital after the three-hour run back to the dock. Had the outriggers on both boats been up, the lures tripped and reeled in, or had the boats been going in the same direction, the accident wouldn't have happened.

Such an experience is rare, but it points out the constant care that must be taken while fishing. Most accidents with hooks probably happen while casting, and most probably happen while casting sidearm or without an awareness of the positions of other anglers.

The best basic casting rule is always cast straight overhead. This applies to fishing with fly, spincast, spinning, bait-casting, surf, or any other type of tackle. (There are some exceptions to this, which we'll cover later.) But even with a straight overhead cast it is still necessary to watch behind you—this must be done continuously in popular fishing areas, such as along crowded streams, piers, shorelines, catwalks, and all other places where anglers might be moving around constantly.

## CASTING FROM SHORE

Watch for anglers in back of you and around you at all times. Occasionally, you might find situations where you can't cast overhead because of an overhanging tree limb, overhanging brush, bridge support, boardwalk, or other such obstruction. In this case, cast sidearm, but take particular care that you don't have any anglers within striking distance on either side of you.

## SURF FISHING

Cast overhead in crowded situations, such as those that occur when the bluefish are running on the Outer Banks of North Carolina. If you are fishing without other anglers nearby, you can use the side-angled cast favored by experienced surf casters. Keep in mind that with surf casting you often will have up to six or eight feet of line between the rod tip and the lure or sinker. This, coupled with the 9- to 12-foot or longer rod that you will be using, requires at least 20 feet of clearance around you as the cast is made. Double this distance to insure safety.

## PIER FISHING (INCLUDING CATWALKS, JETTIES, DAMS, AND SO ON)

These places pose the same problems as fishing from shore under crowded conditions. You will have to watch behind you for any other anglers. Bridges require even more care; on a bridge you must watch not only for other anglers but also for pedestrians and cars. Some bridges have catwalks alongside the main bridge; some are separated by a chain-link fence from the bridge traffic; some have catwalks on a lower level. However, because of the nature of a cast, often the bait, sinker, or lure will swing behind the fence or catwalk (particularly with long rods) so that you must be careful.

## BOAT FISHING

Small-boat fishing has its own set of casting problems, basically because two and sometimes more anglers are confined to a relatively small space. As a basic rule, always cast at right angles to the length of the boat; that is, cast off port or starboard. Some time ago one of us was fishing with a companion who turned to make a quick cast off the bow—and took the author's cap off with a large, two-treble-hook bass plug. Without the cap (or even with it in some circumstances), the plug could have just as easily taken a piece of scalp.

The companion just didn't realize how close he was to the author. This isn't uncommon. Most anglers think of the typical 14-foot fishing boat as having plenty of room. But in most fishing boats and in most fishing situations, each angler will be about three feet from his end, reducing the space between the anglers to eight feet. With a 6½-foot spinning rod and a lure hanging down 18 inches from the tip, you have closed up that 8-foot distance considerably.

If you ever have to make a cast directly ahead or astern, warn your companion so that he can move or duck low in the boat. There are other things that you can do to help increase the distance between the anglers and thus increase the safety factor when casting from a small boat. One is to buy, rent, or use a boat with seats far enough apart to eliminate any accidents when casting. Many boats have seats near each end but not touching the bow or transom. Others will have seats that butt the ends of the boat, providing more deck space for anglers to move around in and to stay apart from each other during casts.

Some freshwater boats of 14 to 16 feet or more have four seats, which brings the anglers closer together and reduces the amount of usable space. We strongly feel that three anglers in a freshwater boat of less than 16 feet not only makes fishing difficult but also dangerous if casting is the method of fishing. Of course, this problem is greatly reduced when still-fishing with bait. Provided that the boat is anchored in a pond, lake, or across current in a quiet section of a river, still-fishing with bait by three persons can be comfortable and easy. In this case, the important factors to consider are the total load range and the stability of the boat for three anglers, their tackle, and the engine (if any) for the water fished.

Larger boats, such as those used in large lakes and inshore saltwater fishing, have some of the same problems for angers as the small boats. For example, many of these boats range in size from 17 to 23 feet, and while some of the 23-foot boats can accomodate three anglers without much trouble, care must be taken by all three in moving around to watch out at all times for the positions of others.

Many large boats have special problems when it somes to casting. First, you must look out for rails, windshields, antennae, and similar accessories that can catch a line or lure on the backcast. Second, boats differ in construction, which makes a difference in the position of anglers as they cast. For example, center-console boats are pretty good because the console tends to separate the bow from the stern of the boat, which allows two anglers to separate, one casting from the stern and one from the bow. Bow riders tend to do the same thing, but the bow angler will have the added obstruction of the windshield on a backcast when casting directly off the bow.

On any boat, rigs with long terminal tackle will greatly increase the possibility of hitting something or someone. For example, when casting lures only about six inches of line will be hanging from the tip-top of the rod until the cast is released. But if you are using a bait rig with a sliding egg sinker or a single- or souble-hook bottom rig, as is popular in many coastal areas for inshore bottom fishing, the line will be extended about 18 to 24 inches. Freshwater anglers will have the same problem with sinker and bait rigs for carp, catfish, bass, and tandem-lure rigs for fish such as shad and crappie.

## FLY CASTING FROM BOATS

Fly casting presents by far the greatest problems in fishing from boats. First, no boat is suitable for more than two fly casters, and wind conditions often demand experience and expertise for even two fly casters to work well in a boat.

Some boats are completely impractical for fly-fishing. Examples of impractical boats would be those with a cluttered interior, rails, antennae that can't be lowered, cleats, windshields, or deck chairs. A boat almost has to be designed from the bare hull up to be suitable for serious fly-fishing.

The nature of fly casting requires stripping line from the reel and coiling it on the deck before making a cast. The line is also stripped in during a retrieve to lie on the deck. An experienced boat fly rodder will swear that fly lines seem to have a natural affinity for cleats, tackle-box handles, rod tips, reel handles, gaffs, landing nets, or anything else that might catch a loop of fly line. Thus, the first problem is to make it possible to cast and get all the line out of the boat. A good example of a boat that is specifically designed for fly-fishing is the Florida guide boat, in which there are fly casting platforms at both the bow and the stern. On most of these boats, cleats are below hawseholes, under gunwales, or flush to the deck to prevent or reduce the chance of a fly line catching on them. If you lack a boat designed in such a way, there are several ways to deal with exposed cleats and other accessories.

You can carry a roll of one-inch-wide masking or duct tape to run over cleats, anchor brackets, and similar obstructions. Cover the points of the cleats or any overhanging part that will catch a line. Also, you can carry a lightweight fine-mesh (about one-inch mesh) net, five to six feet square, to throw over everything before stepping onto the casting platform. This also covers other rods, tackle boxes, coolers, and so on which might be nearby. This helps even when rods are stored under overhanging gunwales.

Wind is a problem; it will tend to blow around coils of fly line on a polished deck, causing tangles. It can also blow a cast off course, causing the fly to hook things or people. Avoiding tangles on the deck is a must, especially when fishing for such large fish as amberjack, tarpon, and sharks, which will take out a line on the strike whether or not there are any tangles or knots in it. One solution is to use carpeting of artificial grass onto which you drop the fly line. The "teeth" hold the fly line in place as you strip it in during a retrieve.

The act of casting with a fly rod from a boat has some inherent problems. First, since a lot of line is in the air during casting, you shouldn't ordinarily cast along the axis of the boat. If you do, the danger to your fishing partner is great as well as the possibility of

*Dangers exist when proper precautions are not taken while fly casting in small boats. Walker Zimmerman has to duck as the author casts over his head. Note: no hook was used on the end of the line to take this posed picture.*

fouling on an antenna, windshield, outrigger, console, or rods in vertical rod racks. Since two fly casters are the maximum in any small fishing boat, it is always best to position the boat so that both of you will be casting off the side.

In a small boat you might have to modify your fly-casting technique. For example, instead of using a straight overhead cast, it is better to use a slightly angled cast to keep the lines as far away from each other as possible when two anglers are fishing. If you are in a small boat and casting toward the side, both anglers would angle their casts so that the lines are over the water ahead and astern of the boat instead of over the boat. And, if one of you is left-handed and one right-handed, it is best to keep the right-hander at the bow and the left-hander at the stern when both are casting toward the port side, reversed if casting toward the starboard side. The reason is that the rod hand of both anglers will be outboard of the boat.

## FLY CASTING FROM A BOAT IN THE WIND

Wind is always a problem for boat fly casters on a large body of water. Knowing how to cope with it properly can markedly increase the possibility of getting fish as well as the safety for all on board.

With the fly line in the air during the cast, any wind will blow the line off course unless the cast is made to deal with the wind. The wind can come from any direction, which means there are four basic situations to deal with.

**Wind blowing into the cast.** In this situation, the backcast won't be any problem, since

*Standing up in a canoe to fly cast is possible only when both anglers are experienced and the water is calm.*

the wind will blow it back and high. The problem is with the forward cast, which the wind will catch and blow down.

The solution is to make a high backcast, perhaps with a little more force than necessary, to load the rod well for the forward cast. Then come forward with the cast, but make the forward cast with a tight loop and as low as possible. The line will drive under the highest force of the wind, since there is less wind the closer you get to the water's surface. This forward cast will have to be made with far more force than normal while at the same time driving the rod low. Loop control is essential—a tight loop will provide less surface area for the wind to catch.

**Wind blowing from behind the angler.** Here, the backcast will be blown down, which will make a proper forward cast impossible even though the wind is blowing in that direction. The solution is to take advantage of the fact that the wind decreases closer to the water's surface.

To make a cast with the wind at your back, angle your rod and cast to the side (outside of the boat and away from your partner). The result will be a sidearm, tight-loop backcast that will be only one to two feet off the water.

Make the backcast harder than normal so that it will straighten out properly. As soon as the backcast is straight, bring the rod up and make a higher-than-normal forward cast. The wind will catch the line to give you as much or more distance than you would get if there were no wind. You'll probably find that the backcast will have to be shorter than normal, but the wind assisting the forward cast should make up for any distance that you would otherwise lose with a short backcast.

Wind blowing from behind is an especially difficult problem for the caster whose backcast goes over the boat. One solution is to turn completely around and make a low forward cast, then turn immediately back to make a second, high forward cast to the target. The only alternative is to make the low backcast and high forward cast using a cross-body cast—something extremely difficult if not almost impossible to control in a strong wind.

**Wind from the left (for a right-handed caster).** In a strong side wind, only one (the downwind) fly caster should cast, since the line from the upwind caster will at all times be blown toward the other caster. In this case, if you are casting so that the line is carried over open water, the wind will not present too much of a problem. True, you will probably have to increase the force of the cast and alter the direction as necessary to overcome the wind and to gain some degree of accuracy. If the wind isn't too bad, both casters can cast, provided that both are accomplished in dealing with wind and that they take turns in casting to stay out of the way while one angler's line and fly are in the air.

An alternative is for the upwind caster to make a cross-body backcast to keep the fly line and fly away from the boat and the other caster.

**Wind from the right (for a right-hand caster).** For a right-handed caster, a wind from the right will blow the line over his body as he casts, creating a dangerous situation if normal casting technique is used.

One way to overcome this is to make a sidearm power backcast so that the fly is thrown well to your right by the force of the cast. As soon as the fly has passed you, roll the rod up and to the left, and as the backcast is completed make the forward cast with the rod tip angled over your left shoulder. This will carry the fly line to the left of your body and keep the fly from hitting you. If you have a fishing partner to your left, check that the wind isn't strong enough to blow the fly into him, or to require taking turns in casting to prevent an accident.

The downwind caster should not cast if casting in the same direction as the upwind caster, since the fly and line will have to be brought low over the boat, endangering the other caster. An alternative is to cast in the opposite direction, or to use a complete cross-body cast to keep the fly over open water and not over the boat and other caster.

# 2
# Hooks and Hooking Bait

Bait for fishing can range from a garden worm or doughball up to madtoms, live pinfish, eels, and rigged baits such as ballyhoo and mullet. Fortunately, there isn't much danger with most baits, except that most of them are being placed on a hook. Accidents are likely to be small, usually nothing more than a prick from a fish's spine or a hook point. All can be avoided.Ironically, one of the best ways to avoid hooking problems is to make sure that your hooks are extra sharp.

If you have a dull hook, it is going to take more force to push the point through even a worm and especially through the skin of a fish or cut bait. If you miss, the force that you use to push the dull hook through can direct the hook into you. Good triangulated hook points make it safe and easy to hook any bait.

Usually the best way to hook a bait is to hold the hook in your dominant hand and the bait in the other hand. This allows better control of the hook. We also find it best to hold the bait stationary and thread the hook into the bait.

Some baits that can cause problems include any live fish with sharp gill covers and sharp spines on their fins. Night crawlers squirm, making hooking difficult.

Obviously, hooks must be handled with care while fishing. You should have a specific spot for them in your gear. Possible choices include a special compartment in your tackle box, a special box for terminal tackle including hooks, sinkers, snaps, and the like. Other alternatives are to tape hooks onto cardboard with clear plastic tape or string them through the hook eyes by size and type on a safety pin or paper clip. Other small items can be kept the same way. Snaps, swivels, snap swivels, and so on all lend themselves to this type of storage. The big advantage of using a system is that you can get at these often-needed parts in a hurry and without spilling out a miscellaneous assortment to dig through when the fish are biting.

Do not leave hooks and lures lying about the boat. At best, you won't know what you have out or what you might need at any given time. At worst, you can end up with a hook in you when sitting down or grabbing at the boat for quick support in a sudden roll or you could turn you ankle or suffer a bad fall from a plug left on the deck.

# 3
# Playing, Landing, and Releasing Fish

Playing fish is an art in itself that can only be learned through time and experience. It will vary with fish species, since each type of fish acts differently when hooked. While tackle may be designed to control the fish through reel-drag systems and other features, there are skills required to use the tackle correctly.

## BAIT CASTING

Today's bait-casting gear usually features a star drag to control the run of a big fish, and if the drag is set properly it will do the job.

If it is set too loose there is the danger of the line over-running the spool, which results in backlash. Also, if it is set too loose you might try to clamp down on the spool with your thumb to control a running fish—but except for a very light touch for a very short period of time, you can burn your thumb quite badly. You may burn it enough to be uncomfortable for the rest of the fishing day or perhaps even for a few days after.

If the drag is too tight there is the danger that you will break the fish off or that you will suddenly loosen the drag too much.

The solution, of course, is to have the drag set properly for the fish you are after (about one-quarter to one-third of the line test in most cases) and to allow the drag to do its job when a big fish takes line. When the fish stops, you might want to add pressure to the drag to pump the fish toward you. Pumping is raising the rod to gain line and then dropping the rod while cranking in line for the next pump. You can put your thumb on the reel as you raise the rod to keep the drag from slipping, but be ready to release it in a split second and drop the rod should the fish take off on another run. At this point the drag would take over again to slow and control the fish.

## SPINNING

The same pumping technique used for bait casting can be used in spinning. Here you use your reel hand to hold the spool to prevent the drag from slipping. The main danger here is to not get your fingers under the line or around the bail where they could get caught on the run of a big fish.

In spinning it is essential that you do not crank in line with the fish running out or with the fish stationary in the water. To do so will only twist the line, giving you problems when subsequently fishing with that line if not with the fish that you are fighting. This is the purpose of pumping in a large fish: to gain line with the leverage of

17

the rod without twisting the line, straining the reel, or packing the line on the spool too tightly.

## FLY CASTING

The pumping technique requires modification with fly tackle since most reels are direct-drive (the handle turns while the spool turns). In this case, you can keep your hand on the reel handle, or better still, hold your fingers or palm against the edge of the reel if it is a flanged spool, or inside the reel spool and against the side plate if the spool is not flanged. To control the runs, this same palm or finger pressure can be used with care to increase the reel drag if you are using heavy tackle with a reel in which the drag is too light to effectively control the run of the fish.

There is an additional important consideration immediately after striking a big fish with a fly rod. Because of the nature of the tackle, line is stripped in and coiled on the deck of a boat or held in your hand when wading. A big fish will immediately take out line on a long run. Thus, the line must be clear and untangled to allow it to go through the guides easily. A tangle in the line, a knot, or a coil around your feet will break the tippet or strip the guides off the rod when the fish runs.

## TROLLING AND BIG—GAME TACKLE

Basically the same rules that apply to casting tackle also apply to big-game tackle in terms of handling the gear. Let the drag do the work and don't try to thumb the reel when a fish is taking line. Anglers usually fight fish with their rod hand on a foregrip above the reel. One way to add a little pressure while pumping a fish is to press down on the line to hold it between thumb and foregrip. You will gain a little advantage this way, and can instantly release any pressure if the fish starts to run.

## RULES FOR HANDLING ANY TACKLE

The basic method for tiring a fish is to keep the rod tip up and make the fish fight the bend (power) of the rod and the drag of the reel. This is a primary purpose of the rod and of the reel drag. Don't try to fight it out with the rod pointed at the fish, the drag cranked tight and the antireverse on. Even if you don't tire out and give up, the tackle will suffer and probably break.

Make sure that you have a clear area in which to fight the fish. If you are on shore, make sure that there are no overhanging limbs above you. On a boat, watch out for any such overhead obstructions as canopy supports. If you have a big fish on and the line breaks, you could break the rod if it comes back and hits something. For the same reason, watch out for other obstructions, such as a boat gunwale.

Make sure that other anglers are clear of you as you play a fish. If you are watching another angler play a fish, stay clear of him. If a line should break or a hook pull out, anyone close to an angler could get hit with the rod, lure, hook, or sinker.

## BOAT HANDLING WHEN PLAYING FISH

Boat handling is extremely important in playing fish. Admittedly, in many cases, fish are small enough to handle without any particular regard for the position of the boat. In other cases, it is a must to be able to maneuver the boat to allow the angler to play the fish properly. For example, on the Florida flats, in the Great Lakes, or a similar area where large catches are possible from small boats, a big fish might require chasing with the boat to keep the angler from running out of line or to keep a light line from breaking due to the drag of the line through the water.

The wrong way to chase any fish is to follow directly behind it with the boat. It is difficult if not almost impossible to match the speed of the boat to the speed with which an angler can retrieve line or the speed of the fish. As a result, if the boat slows appreciably, the fish might take all the line off the reel, the fish might break a light line from the water drag, or if the reel drag setting is too tight the fish might break off.

If the boat goes too fast, the end result is that the slack in the line will be run over, which might allow the fish to shake off. Running over the line might cut it with the propeller of the boat or abrade and weaken it on the hull. Also, the line can wrap around the propeller, ruining the seals and resulting in a costly repair job.

An additional reason not to follow directly behind a running fish is that the gill covers, fins, or tail (and on sharks even the skin) can abrade the line or leader enough to cause a breakoff.

The proper procedure is to run off to one side of the fish as much as possible. This will keep the line away from the fins, skin, and tail while at the same time pull the fish to its side and off balance, which will help to tire it quickly.

## LANDING FISH

If you plan to keep the fish, your options are wider in terms of tackle, length of time you play the fish, and how you handle it once it is in. However, the longer a fish is in the water the better the chance it has to get away from you. The hole in its mouth from the hook can work larger; sharks can attack a saltwater fish on the end of your line; or a fish might cut off or break off by running the line against an underwater obstruction.

In some cases you might have a fish come to a boat in record time and be tempted to gaff or net it. Don't do it, especially if it is a big fish. Many fish don't really come to life until they are near the boat. Cobia, dolphin, and tuna are examples of such fish—and big cobia, for example, can wreck a lot of tackle. Thus, unless you are absolutely sure that you can handle the fish once it is on a gaff or in a net, try to play it some more. Use some tactic such as hitting the water with a paddle or gaff to convince the fish that it should run away from the boat.

The importance of not trying to boat large fish before they are completely tired out (such fish are called green fish) can't be overemphasized. The tremendous strength of a large fish in a boat can and has crippled anglers, destroyed boat cockpits, and ruined lots of good tackle. Examples of fish that can cause such destruction include but are not limited to large tarpon, sharks, billfish, amberjack, and cobia.

When fish get near the boat, you only have a short line out, which reduces the shock absorbency of violent action (less line out means less elasticity), and it is easier for a fish to break off.

Loosen the drag so that if the fish does decide to make one more break for it, there will be less initial reel drag to overcome, resulting in less shock on the line. Keep the rod tip up. Lowering it when a fish runs will reduce some of the initial line shock. Of course, if you want to release the fish, keep any such action to a minimum since the longer that you play a fish, the less likelihood that the fish will survive, even if it looks in good shape as it swims away. Fish put everything they've got into a fight, and during this time lactic acid builds up in the muscles. If there is too much of a build-up from too long a fight, the fish will die.

## GREEN FISH

Problems with green fish include the following:

• They can suddenly bolt from the boat and break off the line or leader.

• If you gaff them they can twist the gaff (sharks are well known for this) and make it difficult to get the fish into the boat or even for the person with the gaff to hang onto the gaff.

• If you get green fish into the boat they are still strong enough to break up tackle, injure people, and damage the boat. Toothy fish are often a problem in a boat, since they can bite people and anything else, including tackle and deck fittings. Their strength and bulk can also scatter plugs like shrapnel if they move violently.

• A large green fish at the side of a boat may suddenly jump and end up in the boat, which creates the problems mentioned above. Also, if you are fishing from a small, lightweight aluminum boat it is possible to pull on a fish while the fish is in the air and pull the boat under the fish when it comes down.

• green fish can pull an angler out of a boat. Hand gaffs with wrist loops are particularly dangerous because if you have the loop around your wrist and the fish takes a sudden lunge, you can't let go of the gaff and you will end up in the water.

## METHODS OF LANDING FISH

**Hand landing.** If fishing for such species as largemouth bass, pike, small barracuda, or striped bass, one way to land them with a minimum of fuss is with your bare hand. How you handle them will depend upon the size and type of fish.

For bass, the best and simplest way if the fish is exhausted is to slip your thumb into the mouth, run your index finger under the jaw, clamp, and lift. This action tends to paralyze or at least stabilize the fish. It will move when you first stick your thumb in its mouth, so this technique is best when fishing with single-hook lures such as spoons, spinner baits, and flies. With multiple-hook plugs, take extra care since the fish could shake violently before you have a good grip and drive a hook into you. Catfish can be dangerous due to the spines on their dorsal and two pectoral fins (see Chapter 4).

For trout, one good way to land them is to find a balance point under the fish's belly and lift straight up. Usually the fish won't move, and you can unhook it and release it or slip it into a creel. This only works on small trout. For big trout, use a net.

For pike and barracuda, the best way to avoid their teeth and still handle their long shape is to grab them directly behind the gills and squeeze. This will tend to paralyze them so that they can be lifted into the boat. It won't work on very big fish, but for anything with this long shape up to about five pounds, it allows a quick and easy landing. Cotton gloves help to give you a good grip, particularly on barracuda.

**Netting.** Netting fish is simple once you consider the basics. For example, if you chase after a fish with the net and hit its tail or side, the fish will react violently, possibly breaking the line, and certainly making it more difficult the next time you bring a net near it.

If possible, use nets with a dark green mesh that won't show up in the water and a dark frame and handle that won't stand out or cause glare that will alarm a fish. If you have an aluminum net with a white mesh, you can remove the net, dye the mesh in Rit or Tintex dye and paint the frame with flat-black paint before replacing the net.

To net a fish properly for a fellow angler (you can do it yourself, although it is easier and better to have someone else do it if possible), submerge the net and make sure that the mesh is soaked so that it will sink. Some polypropylene nets will not sink; in this case, you might want to add a couple of pinch-on sinkers to the bottom of the net bag to sink the net for better landing. If possible, move the net toward the fish, which should be led into the net head first. Moving the net, or allowing the net bag to flow out with the current or tide will help to belly out the net bag so that the fish will be well into it before it touches the net and reacts.

Once the fish is in the net, bring it up swiftly, surely, and into the boat if you are fishing from one. If the fish is a big one, fold the net over the fish so that it can't get out to break tackle or escape.

**Gaffing fish.** Gaffs are usually reserved for big fish that are too heavy to handle with a net. They are used on most saltwater species and some freshwater species when the fish are over about 15 pounds. To gaff a fish properly, bring it alongside the boat so that the

*Lip landing some species of fish is particularly effective when the fish has no teeth, a large mouth, and single-hook lures are used. An excellent example would be this largemouth bass caught on a spinnerbait.*

*Leon Martuch holds a Florida-caught barracuda behind the gills to paralyze it. Note the glove used for added gripping power.*

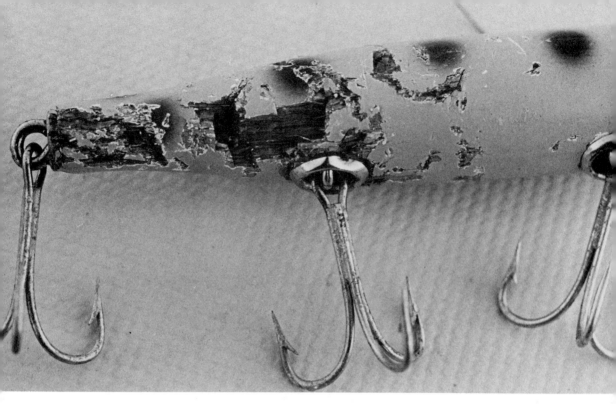

*Just how dangerous can a fish be? This wood plug, chewed up by a barracuda, gives one answer.*

fish is parallel to the boat. Strike the fish with the gaff using an upward motion. Some anglers like to strike from the outside of the fish and over the back, while others like to bring the gaff up into the belly with the gaff between the fish and the boat. Regardless of the method, it helps to gaff the fish in the middle of its weight distribution, usually somewhere just behind the pectoral fins. Gaffing at either end of the fish leaves too much of the fish's length to thrash around and cause damage.

Once the fish is stuck properly, bring it up and into the boat. If possible, drop the fish immediately into the fish box. This will reduce bleeding in the cockpit and reduce the risk of broken tackle. The important thing to remember about gaffing any fish is that it takes a positive action. Once committed to the job, stick the fish as solidly and hard as possible and continue right up and into the boat with one smooth motion.

If you miss the fish or only prick it, don't swing after it wildly—you may miss and cut the line. Wait until the angler can bring the fish around again and make a second attempt.

You can gaff a fish and still release it, as is done in lip gaffing tarpon. You can never release any fish, however, that has been gaffed in the body. To lip gaff a fish, run the gaff through the lower lip. This will not hurt the fish and will allow you to reduce thrashing and to remove the hook more easily at the same time. A standard method for tarpon releases is to pin a lip-gaffed fish to the side of the boat while unhooking it.

A gaff is nothing more than a hook on a handle to allow you to pull big fish into a boat or to shore. But there is a wide range of gaffs and gaff styles for a wide range of fish and fish-landing purposes.

**Hand gaffs.** These short gaffs come with either a two-inch hook-gap for most surf-fishing situations or in larger, stronger stypes with a three-inch hook gap for lip gaffing large tarpon for release. Some come with a wrist loop attached to the end of the handle. This should be cut off or not used, since any large fish could pull you out of the boat.

Surf fishermen often use small gaffs such as these carried in a holster on a surf belt and attached to the belt with a coiled elastic cord similar to the cords on telephones. The cord

*One way to prevent a fly line from tangling in a small boat is to use an open mesh plastic laundry basket to hold the retrieved line.*

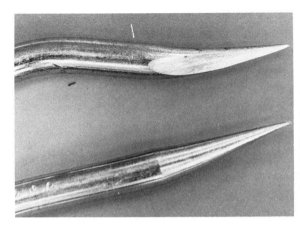

*To land fish properly, gaffs must be sharp and their points must be triangulated. Top: this triangulated point will penetrate easily due to the three cutting edges. Bottom: the factory round point will not penetrate through a fish's scales easily.*

prevents loss if the gaff is knocked from your hand in the surf, but the cord should have a breakaway feature to prevent a big fish from knocking you over and pulling you under should it prove too green or powerful for gaffing this way.

**Short gaffs.** These come with two- to four-foot-long handles and two-to four-inch hook gaps. They are ideal as standby gaffs for surf fishing, as boat gaffs for large freshwater fish such as muskie, big catfish, coho salmon, and such inshore saltwater fish as sea trout, striped bass, bluefish, redfish, and barracuda.

**Long gaffs.** These are six- to eight-feet-long and often with three- to six-inch hook gaps. Most have a plastic grip about halfway down the shank of the handle (in addition to the grip at the end of each gaff) to help in gaining a firm grip when landing a big fish. Gaffs such as these are necessary for big fish and are primarily found on big-game fishing boats for landing billfish, large wahoo, dolphin, swordfish, tuna, and sharks (although a spescial shark gaff is available).

**Flying gaffs.** Flying gaffs differ from regular gaffs in that the large hook end has a special eye for attaching a rope and a special socket for fitting onto a long handle. In use, the hook is fitted onto the flying-gaff handle and the rope pulled tight to hold the gaff head in place. The handle allows a long reach over the back of a big-game fish. The handle while the rope retains the tension necessary to strike the fish. Once the fish is struck, the pole is pulled out and back into the boat and the fish is controlled by the rope. The advantage of this system is that the thrashing of a fish can be controlled with the rope, whereas a long handle would swing wildly and prove dangerous to those on board landing the fish. Usually, flying gaffs have a barbed hook similar to a fish hook. Smaller gaffs have plain (or barbless) hooks to allow them to be removed easily from the fish once it is landed.

**Shark gaffs.** Some companies have recently been making special shark gaffs to cope with the tendency of large sharks to twist around on a gaff and twist it out of the gaffer's hands. These are similar to long gaffs in that they have about a four- to six-foot-long handle and a three- to five-inch hook gap. They differ in that the grips are made so that they rotate on the handle. Thus, when landing a shark it is possible to hold the shaft to sink the gaff hook and switch to the grips while the shark twists, preventing the gaff from being ripped from your hands.

**Tailing fish.** You can land some fish by tailing them with your hand. Salmon are the most common gamefish landed this way, although the tuna, bonitos, and other hard-tailed species can be handled this way. Atlantic salmon are hand tailed to prevent damaging them (when you wish to release the fish) or wire tailed (when you wish to keep it for a trophy or food).

Wire tailers consist of a length of braided wire on a spring shaft that holds the wire in a loop while you slip it over the tail of the fish. Pulling the tailer shaft tightens the loop to secure it around the fish's tail.

To hand tail a salmon or grilse, the secret is to use your thumb and index finger and to

*C.B.P. gaffing a dusky shark caught on a fly rod in the mid-Atlantic. Sharks must be handled carefully since they can twist gaffs and wrench them from your hand.*

hold the fish securely right at the wrist of the tail with pressure directed across the dorsal-ventral plane of the fish's tail to prevent the rays of the tail fin from collapsing. This is more difficult on a grilse than on a mature salmon, but it will work on grilse if done properly.

Saltwater fish such as jack crevalle, bonito, albacore, and tuna can be easily landed this way. Care must be taken with tuna to keep the fish from beating you while you do it. All these fish have extremely strong tails and all the muscle of their football-shaped bodies is directed into the tail. For fish up to about 20 pounds this method is fine; for fish above that size revert to beaching the fish if on the shore or gaffing the fish if in a boat. Also, never hand tail a shark. Any shark, large or small, can twist completely around to bite anyone hand tailing it.

**Beaching fish.** If you are fishing from shore, usually your best method of landing any fish is to beach it. This applies to fishing the surf, along muddy riverbanks, river sandbars, and rocky shoals—virtually any spot that has a slope not exceeding about 20 degrees. The method for landing the fish is to play the fish out, and then gradually lead it into the beach and up on the bank. If you are going to do this, you obviously are going to keep the fish anyway, so be sure to play it out as completely as possible.

If possible, try to lead the fish to some quiet water—for example, a small cove, a backeddy in a river, or the shallow slope of a sandbar. Play the fish out so that it is on its

*C.B.P. with a tailed salmon caught in Labrador. Tailing is effective on certain fish, does not harm the fish, and permits an easy release.*

side. Since most fish are thicker through the belly than across the shoulder, this will allow you to lead it into shallower water before it realizes where it is and starts reacting. Because the fish will be on the surface of the water, use side pressure of your rod to pull the fish into as shallow water as possible. (Make sure that no anglers are behind you in case the hook pulls out.) In many cases, you can pull the fish right up onto the beach this way. If fishing the surf, you can time your pressure and use the waves to help you get the fish up on the sand.

If it is a really big fish, you may have to grab the shock leader or get some help (or both) to get it safely up on the beach. If you are careful of the gill covers (on some fish they can be sharp) and of any hanging hooks in its mouth, you can grab it under the gills and drag it up on the beach. With some toothy fish this is not recommended and you might have to gaff them in the surf or shallows after playing them out and in close enough to handle.

**Big-game fish.** Big-game fish such as marlin and sailfish are always caught from a boat, usually a large ocean-going sport-fishing boat with a large cockpit from which the angler and mate work.

Landing big fish takes the teamwork of the captain, mate, and angler. There are certain dangers involved with any large fish that must be avoided at all costs. But before considering specific dangers, let's discuss how landing a big fish would occur under ideal circumstances.

First the angler plays the fish until it is exhausted. This is only if the fish is to be kept; if the fish is to be released it should be brought to the boat as quickly as possible and the hook removed or the leader cut while the fish is still in the water. (The same would apply if the fish were to be tagged, with the tagging usually taking place by an additional person or the angler or captain leaving their post while the mate holds the fish and unhooks it, or before unhooking if it were a very big billfish.)

Once the angler has the doubled line through the guides and on the reel and the leader up to the tip-top of the rod, the mate takes over. This does not end the angler's responsibilities, however, since it is important to keep the rod at the ready and the leader in loose coils on the deck, free of any hands, ankles, or other obstructions should the fish in a sudden burst of energy take off again. An alternative, practiced on some boats, is to leave the leader over the side of the boat. The mate grabs the leader and carefully brings the fish alongside the boat, gaffing the fish with a long gaff and grabbing its bill. Usually the gaff is used first, especially on large fish, and then the bill grabbed at an opportune moment.

Often at this point an additional gaffer or two is required to get the fish into the boat. Once in the boat, all the danger isn't over, since such big fish are so active and strong. A priest or billy is required to dispatch the fish properly. Relatively small fish caught on big-game trolling trips should be dropped right into the fish box, which is usually located along the transom of the boat. Dolphin, cobia, wahoo, and amberjack are examples of such species where one gaffer, moving positively and quickly, can stick the fish and have it in the box before the fish reacts.

Cotton gloves are a must for anyone handling the leader of any big-game fish. They make it easy to handle wire or monofilament, and provide some protection, particularly since your hands will be solt from being exposed to water or spray for most of the trip and will cut easily.

# LANDING DIFFICULT FISH

If you are landing a big fish such as cobia, amberjack, or tarpon that can cause complications, the best solution is to have the fish box open and the rest of the deck clear before you get ready to gaff the fish. Once you stick the fish, bring it up with one smooth motion over the gunwhale of the boat and directly into the open fish box. Slam the lid on

*It's easy to beach a nice fish, like this Atlantic salmon grilse, when you do it properly.*

the fish box and wait for the fish to die or slow down before trying to remove the hooks.

In any case, big fish and all sharks should not be brought into the smaller boats. This rule applies almost exclusively to saltwater fishing, although considerations of boat size and fish size might make this rule applicable to freshwater fishing. A big muskie in a canoe might be a problem, for example, if it were still green.

Sharks, even little ones, are so slow to die and often "come to life" after hours of appearing dead, that it makes sense to leave all of them outside the boat, if at all possible.

## SPECIFIC DANGERS IN LANDING BIG FISH

There are several dangers in handling all big fish:

When grabbing the leader with cotton golves, never wrap the leader or line around your hand. Hold the leader so that you can release it instantly. Big fish are powerful and if they want to swim off, they will swim off—whether or not you have the leader wrapped around your hand or fingers. It is too late to unwrap leader when the fish decides to move.

For the same reasons as above, watch the wire on the deck as the mate brings the fish in

*This five-photo series of a cobia being landed by Ken Lauer after being fought to the boat by Joel Arrington shows how to handle big fish to prevent boat and tackle damage. Lauer gaffs the Pamlico Sound cobia and in one smooth motion brings it over the gunnel and drops it into a previously opened fish box. No damage and little mess.*

toward the boat. The best position for the angler is toward one side of the cockpit, rod in hand, watching that the wire doesn't get wrapped around the tip-top of the rod. Also, make sure that you don't step on or into a coil on the deck.

When billing a fish (grabbing a marlin or sailfish by the bill), do it with extreme care. Use deliberate and positive movement once you decide to move. Billfish have been known to try to stab with the bill. Whether it is conscious behavior by the billfish or not, boats, transoms, anglers, and mates have all been attacked this way. Similarly, toothy fish, although not in the big-game category, seem to snap at anyone handling a leader or trying to gaff or unhook them. A basic word to the wise is: watch out for the front end of any fish, large or small.

## UNHOOKING FISH

Whether you want to release fish or keep them for the table, you still have to unhook them from the lure or bait. You can do this when you land the fish by holding the fish in back of the gills (barracuda, pike, pickerel, and other long, slim species), when lip landing them (bass, when the hook is a single hook such as a spinner bait or spoon), or when you are lip gaffing the fish (tarpon, large barracuda, and pike). But the importance of properly and safely unhooking fish can't be overemphasized. There is usually only one way to do it right, but do it wrong and you'll have a fish with one set of hooks still in him, and the other set of hooks in your clothing or flesh.

If the fish is small, hold it behind the gills with pressure against the gills and head to partially paralyze it, and work the hook out.

If you plan to release the fish, unhook it if at all possible while it is still in the water. Unless it is a very small fish caught on a single hook, be sure to use pliers or an

*Note the cotton gloves worn by this angler billing a white marlin. Billing is dangerous under any circumstances and must be carefully executed.*

unhooking device to keep the fish from driving a second hook into your hand in its effort to escape. If the fish is hooked deep and you still wish to release it, the best way is to keep the fish in the water and cut the leader. Cut as close as possible to the fish's mouth.

Use pliers or an unhooking device on all large fish and all fish with teeth. Unhooking devices include a forked stick or rod, needle-nose pliers, commercial (the Baker De-hooker) or homemade disgorgers, the latter consisting of a long, heavy, J-shaped piece of wire that can be slid down to the end of the hook, which allows the fish to be shaken off into an ice chest or into the water.

On some large fish landed with a net, it helps to hold the fish in the net mesh while unhooking it. The mesh of the net will help to give a good grip on the fish until it is free of the hook. To remove treble hooks and plugs, work from the net opening to keep the hooks from tangling in the mesh.

Lip-gaffed fish can be held against the gunwhale of the boat or another secure spot on the boat and the hook worked out with the gaff still in place. This method is commonly used for tarpon as well as for many toothy fish.

Sharp hooks are a necessity in hooking any fish, but the same sharp hook that drives easily into a fish will just as easily drive into your clothing or flesh. For this reason, it is best whenever possible to fish with single-hook lures. Plugs with two or more sets of trebles are particularly dangerous in this regard. For safety in dangerous or big-fish situations, remove the trebles on your plugs and replace them with single hooks, using an open-eye Siwash-style hook or regular hooks attached with split rings to the hook hangers. If you are after big fish, be sure that you use a strong enough split rihg or that you weld or solder the split ring for added strength.

*Deeply hooked fish are best released using a special hook-out tool or surgeon's hemostats. Here Chuck Edghill uses hemostats to release a small bass that hit a shallow-running plug.*

When you do not intend to release a large fish and wish to reduce potential dangers when the fish is brought aboard, open the fish box and drop the gaffed fish right into the fish box. Slam the lid and wait for the fish to stop knocking around. Only after the fish is dead or calmed down should you reach into the box and remove the hook. In some cases of hooking deeply you might have to cut the leader, rerig and wait until you are at the dock to get at the hook. Rocking boats are no place to be fooling around with knives trying to cut a hook out of a deeply hooked fish.

## RELEASING FISH

Landing a fish actually begins long before you have the fish nearby. If you plan to release the fish, you should decide early in the fight to bring the fish to you as quickly as possible to unhook it or cut it free.

The following tips will help to increase the chances of a fish's survival if you plan to release it:

Use barbless hooks to aid in unhooking small fish such as trout, bass, and the smaller saltwater species. Barbless hooks are available in trout sizes, while any hook can be made barbless by forcing down the barb with pliers.

Don't fish with tackle that is overly light for the size of the fish. This will prolong the fight, which exhausts the fish and makes survival of the fish unlikely, even if the fish is otherwise unharmed.

Avoid any excess handling of the fish. If at all possible, try to release it without removing it from the water. If you must pick up a fish to get the hook out, grab large-mouthed fish such as bass by the lower jaw. Lift trout from underneath by balancing

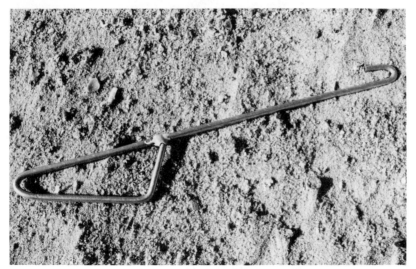

*Details of the steel J-shaped hook remover used with larger or toothy fish to remove the hook and simultaneously release the fish over the side, or drop it into a fish box.*

*J-shaped hook remover in use. The fish hook in this bluefish (held in the left hand—on the right side of the photo) is held by the bend of the hook with the J-shaped hook remover (in the right hand, on the left in the photo) ready to pull the hook free by pulling down on the hook and up on the hook remover.*

them on your hand. Hold other small fish with your hand over the back and behind the gills. Use a net on large trout to reduce the chance of injury to them. Larger saltwater fish should be released without removing them from the water; if the hook can't be removed, cutting the leader is the only way for a quick and easy release that provides the optimal chance for the fish's survival.

Don't grab any fish by the eye sockets or run your finger into the gills. While these are acceptable methods to land fish if you plan to keep them, either of these actions can kill the fish. If you drop the fish, don't release it. It is likely to have suffered internal injuries that will kill it later.

Don't jerk a hook out, particularly if it is deep in the fish's mouth, touching the gill plates or rakers, or in the stomach or throat. Jerking out the hook will fatally injure the fish. The best way is to back the hook out using some sort of hook-removing device.

Don't try to remove the hook from deeply hooked fish. Instead, cut the line or leader as close to the hook as possible. Most hooks will rust away or be dissolved by stomach acids. For this reason, saltwater anglers using bait who wish to release fish should use corrodable hooks of plain steel, not the higher-grade stainless steel hooks or VMC Perma Plate hooks.

# 4
# Dangers from Fish

Even after fish are played out, landed, and in the boat, they present a wide variety of dangers if handled improperly. Most of these dangers are not severe. At best, they may make a pleasant fishing trip a little less pleasant. If you have to fish with a cut finger or a minor puncture wound from a fish's spine you will be uncomfortable. However, some accidents can bring a fishing trip to a hasty stop while help or medication is sought. These more severe dangers fall generally into the areas discussed below.

## TEETH

The front end of any fish is usually the most formidable, and those with teeth even more so. Teeth of fish will vary widely, but most can cause cuts that can either annoy or disable you for the rest of the fishing trip.

Types of teeth vary from those of mackerel, bluefish, and sharks, which are a series of triangular, razor-sharp teeth around the edge of their mouth, to those of pike, pickerel, and barracuda, which are present on both the roof and floor of the mouth, to those of sea trout, which are a few incisors around the front edge of the mouth. Regardless of the type of teeth, stay away from them. Don't put your hands in the mouth of any toothy fish, including dead ones.

Several years ago, while fishing the Turneffe Islands off Belize, we caught some barracuda that the barefoot cook was going to fillet while we were out fishing. When we returned, we found the cook hobbling around the cabin with his foot in a blood-soaked rag. It turned out that while starting to fillet one of the dead barracuda, it slipped to the deck and its open mouth ran across the cook's big toe, slicing it to the bone. It required the better part of the evening to fix up the cook temporarily with butterfly bandages.

Bluefish, before they are dead, will actively jump at you from a cooler when you try to add another one to the box.

Be especially careful with sharks, since they can seem to be dead for hours then spring to life when a hand or foot gets too close to their mouth. Also, never try to hand tail a shark or hold a small shark up by the tail for a picture because they can twist around to their tail and bite you.

Some fish have teeth that won't hurt you. The small teeth of bass and the vomerine plates of small trout are examples. They are a little like rough sandpaper. Even if you lip land a big bass and hold him that way for a while, you won't have anything more than an abraded thumb.

## CRUSHERS

Some fish, including bonefish, permit, pollock, tarpon, and grouper, have crushers in the back of their throats that could hurt if you get your hand or fingers into the fish far enough when removing a hook. On fish such as these, use pliers or an unhooking tool to get out any deeply imbedded hooks.

*The small teeth of a largemouth bass will abrade line.* Berkley and Co.

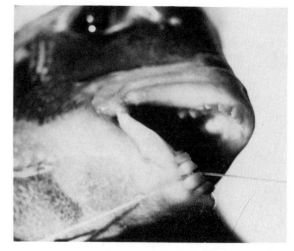

*Toothy fish like this sheepshead will damage line so that it must be cut back before fishing again.* Berkley and Co.

Teeth on a bluefish must be avoided at all costs since blues will try to grab you and can shred the flesh from a finger.

The proper way to handle small catfish is to grasp them just behind the gills and in back of the dorsal fin spine. Dorsal and pectoral fin spines are especially sharp and dangerous.

## SPINES ON FINS

Almost all fish have spines on the leading edges of their dorsal and pectoral fins, and sometimes even on the pelvic and anal fins as well. This applies both to freshwater and saltwater fish. The list of fish with damaging spines would be long, but it includes common species such as the largemouth bass (forward dorsal fin), crappie, sunfish, white perch, pinfish (used as bait), catfish (sharp spines in dorsal and pectoral fins) striped bass, and sea bass.

Catfish deserve a special mention, since they have sharp spines on the pectoral and dorsal fins. Catfish will often cock up these fins, making the fish difficult to handle. The sharp spines easily penetrate skin, and when they do the sheath of the spine is damaged, exposing venom glands peculiar to the catfish family. The toxic venom enters the puncture wound, which in some cases causes severe pain, swelling, inflamed lymph glands, and other reactions. One species of marine catfish was found to have a venom that had both neurotoxic (nerve-poisoning) and hemotoxic (blood-poisoning) properties. While the symptoms usually subside in a few hours, the only sure way to avoid this unpleasantness is to handle catfish carefully and avoid the toxic spines.

Dead fish that are handled carelessly can often cause the same symptoms, since the slime on the fish will become toxic and will enter the skin with any kind of puncture wound from a spine. Alcohol or an antibiotic salve administered to the wound will usually help alleviate the pain and prevent or reduce swelling.

## SHARP GILL COVERS

Some fish (such as snook) have a very sharp edge to the side of the gill covers that can cause a razorlike wound. Many other fish have a similar cutting edge that is smaller and more protected, even though still dangerous upon contact. Avoid these areas on all fish. A similar sharp edge can be found near the anus of the jack crevalle.

*Many fish, especially salt-water species, have razor-sharp edges or projections on their gill covers.*

## ROUGH OR SHARP GILL RAKERS

One of the time-honored ways of landing and handling caught fish is to lift them under the gills to hold them securely. In addition to the danger of cuts from the sharp plates alongside the gill covers, fish with rough or sharp gill rakers can cause cuts or abrasion to your fingers when lifted this way. Examples of such fish would include large striped bass, channel bass, black drum, grouper, and big largemouth bass. Since gill rakers under the gill covers are sharp, toothlike projections, a large specimen of virtually any species can cause some damage to your hands. Unless your hands are actually cut, a little hand lotion will help to smooth them again.

## BILLS ON MARLIN, SAILFISH, AND SIMILAR SPECIES

Billfish will sometimes seem to make a concerted effort to do damage to anglers, mates, boat hulls, and so on with their bills. Take care when handling any big billfish, and always stay to the side of a billfish when landing it so that a sudden thrust of the fish won't put its bill into you.

## SIZE

Big fish can do considerable damage in a boat to people, tackle, and equipment from their sheer size and strength alone. Just because they have been landed doesn't mean that they are going to like it. Usually this applies only to saltwater fish, although big pike, muskie, catfish, carp, and the like can create similar problems for the freshwater angler. On almost any dock where large fish are being checked in with regularity you can find one or more tales of boated sharks eating tackle boxes, big tarpon making kindling out of the interior of a small boat while crippling anglers and guides, and big billfish or tuna wrecking fighting chairs and gaffs in the cockpit of an offshore sportfisherman.

Make sure that the fish is incapable of such destructive behavior or make plans before the fish is in the boat to dispatch it as quickly as possible.

## FISH LEAPING NEAR A BOAT

Closely related to the above is the danger of a big fish being played to the boat and then leaping alongside. The fish might come aboard or might create enough of a splash to endanger seriously a small boat or its occupants. Any such splash might ruin cameras recording the event as well as making it tough to keep the fish on the line once it is back in the water. There is no way to prevent this when it does happen, except to try to plan ahead and keep green fish well away from the boat until they are exhausted enough to land properly.

An additional danger with small, lightweight boats and a big fish in the air is that some anglers might make the mistake of keeping a tight line on a jumping fish and pull the boat under the fish so the fish lands in the boat. Green or jumping fish should be kept well away from the boat when possible (move the boat if necessary), and all jumping fish should be given a slack line until in the water again. The slack-line technique (bowing to the fish) is standard with experienced tarpon fishermen, and should be practiced with any large jumping fish. Aside from minimizing the dangers of pulling a fish into the boat, it prevents the fish from exerting full pressure and weight on the line. In the water a fish weighs less than in the air, and its movements are slowed by the water resistance.

# 5
# Fish Handling for the Table or Trophy

If you are going to keep a fish for a mount or for the table, handling it properly will help get it on the wall or on the table in the best condition possible.

## TROPHY HANDLING

Fish for wall mounts should not be cleaned or filleted. The taxidermist will clean it by making a cut along the side of the fish that will be against the wall, and this is best left to him. Keep the fish on ice, preferably in a flat position. Avoid placing other fish on it that will squash the fish or damage its fins, gill covers, or tail. Keep the fish iced down and out of the sun at all times. As soon as possible, get the fish to a taxidermist or taxidermist's representative (they are available at almost all saltwater docks and many freshwater docks and marinas). If you don't have a cooler, cover the fish with a moistened rag to keep the skin and scales from drying out.

## HANDLING FISH FOR THE TABLE

The same basics that apply to keeping fish for a trophy mount also apply to keeping fish for the table. For freshwater fishing, you can keep fish alive on a stringer, in a mesh fish bag, or in a live well if your boat has one. Never keep any saltwater fish on a stringer or in a bag in the water, whether in a boat or wading, since this will attract sharks.

Saltwater fish should be iced down immediately. Tissues of saltwater fish seem to break down far quicker than those of freshwater fish, and while a short time laying on a deck might not adversely affect freshwater fish, it can ruin a saltwater catch for table use.

To keep fish properly, there is no substitute for a good ice chest. Some lightweight inexpensive foam chests are also good provided that they have thick enough walls. Many of them do not, and the ice melts too rapidly.

A bottom drain, standard on most good ice chests but only rarely found on the foam chests, is a must to allow for draining melted ice water. Ideally, fish should be on ice, but not in the melted water. One way to avoid this is to build a light wood rack for your ice chest that will hold the fish slightly above the bottom, and allow the water to flow out the bottom drain.

## FILLETING AND CLEANING KNIVES

A sharp knife of the right style is mandatory for proper filleting and cleaning. Cleaning knives are generally stiff bladed and relatively short, while filleting knives are long and flexible to enable you to work around bones. While filleting knives are different lengths, they should be long enough to reach from the back to the belly of any fish that you want to fillet.

Recently, G-96 introduced a series of fillet knives in which the blades extend not from the center of the handle, but from the side, making it possible to keep the blade parallel to the cleaning table, even on flat fish such as flounder.

Regardless of how sharp knives are when you start filleting fish, if you have a lot of cutting to do they will quickly become dull. We like to carry several knives on those occasional trips when we want to stock a freezer and have a lot of filleting to do. It is far easier to sharpen them at a home workbench than on a cleaning table with fish sitting in the sun.

Fish cleaning and filleting can be dangerous if you aren't careful. The fish are slippery, knife handles become slippery, and it is difficult to hold a fish steady while concentrating on cutting. The biggest dangers are getting your hand in front of the knife blade, even for an instant, or reaching inside of a fish to guide the knife in cutting where you can't see. Always keep your free hand in back of the knife blade.

## CLEANING AND FILLETING

The best method to preserve maximum flavor of any fish is to clean or fillet it at once. If you are on a rocking boat this might prove impossible, but where you can do it, it will improve the flavor of the fish. Cleaning is ideal for smaller fish, while filleting is better for larger fish. Also, filleting won't leave you with scales all over everything and with bones to pick out at mealtime.

**Cleaning.** Begin by killing the fish immediately, scale completely then cut off the head, remove the gills, and remove all fins using serrated kitchen shears. (Nonserrated shears will slide on the spine in the fins.) Allow the blood to drain. Blood will break down quicker than any other part of the fish, so draining it will keep the fish tasting fresh longer. One way to drain it with a minimum of mess is to use a bucket with an elevated wire-mesh bottom that will allow the blood to drain through, while keeping the fish clean.

After you remove all the scales, scrape the fish with a sharp knife to remove any remaining slime, which helps prevent too strong of a fishy taste. Use a sharp knife to open the body cavity, beginning the cut at the anus and extending up to the gills.

Remove the entrails, being careful not to open them. Remove the dark "blood line" (actually the kidney) that runs along the backbone of the fish. With many freshwater fish, you can do this with your thumbnail, but with larger fish, including most saltwater fish, use the handle of a spoon, a grapefruit coring knife, or a similar instrument with a round end.

You can wash the fish at this point, but some authorities feel that washing only destroys some of the fresh flavor. As an alternative they suggest wiping with towels moistened with a salty solution. Use or freeze as soon as possible.

**Filleting.** Filleting is an ideal way to prepare fish, but improperly done it will waste a lot of fish. Filleting on smaller fish is often too much effort for the size of the fillets that result.

For most fish, begin to fillet by laying the fish on a cleaning table and making a dorsal-ventral cut through the side of the fish, just behind the gills, but only cut as deep as the backbone. Then, turn the blade to continue the cut along the length of the fish, taking the long fillet knife along as close to the backbone as possible and cutting the ribs from the backbone. If done right, you should be able to feel the knife blade as it goes over each vertebra of the fish's backbone.

Continue to the tail, but do not cut the skin free of the fish at this point. Flip the fillet over, leaving the skin still attached as a "hold-down" point for removing the skin. Run

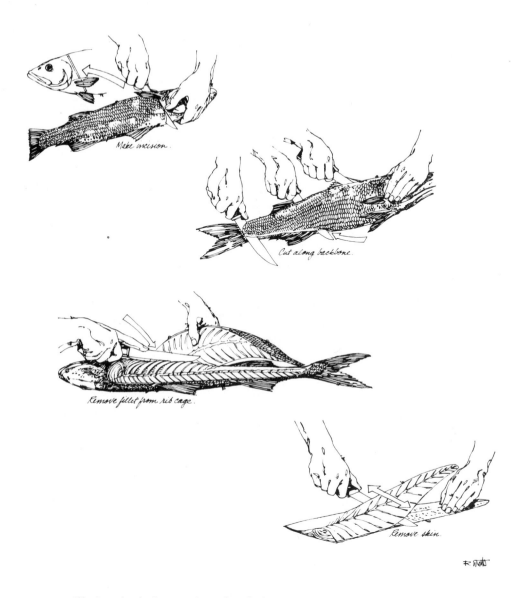

*Proper filleting includes cutting the flesh of your fish off down to the backbone and removing the skin.*

your blade into the flesh at the tail, and down to the undersurface of the skin. Hold the knife steady and work it in a sawing pattern as you pull the skin of the fillet against the knife. If you wish, however, you can leave the skin on the fillet for some fishes.

Once the fillet is removed from the skin, take the fillet knife and carefully cut out the ribs that were cut through as the knife cut close to the backbone.

Repeat this same procedure on the other side of the fish. Wrap and freeze your fillets as soon as possible.

If you don't like the idea of cutting through the rib cage and later removing the ribs, it is possible to use your knife in such a way that you work around the ribs when making the cut along the fish's side. It takes a little longer and is a little more difficult, but it will keep your blade sharp longer, since you aren't cutting through bones on each fillet.

## FISH BUTCHERING AND STEAKING

The same techniques apply to butchering or steaking a fish as to filleting or cleaning, only you will be working with bigger fish. Steaking is cutting off the head and fins, removing entrails, and then cutting through the fish's body to make steaks. To get sizable steaks, you need a fair-size fish to start with.

Butchering is a less well defined term. It involves the same techniques as steaking, but often involves cutting large fish into large pieces to be used as steaks, in chowders, and so on.

## FREEZING

To preserve the fresh taste of fish, freeze as soon as possible after cleaning or filleting. If you have a lot of fish to freeze, set the freezer on a higher setting for the first 24 hours, use the quick-freeze section of the box, and  keep as much air space as possible around unfrozen pieces until they are frozen.

If you are going to use the fish fairly soon, frozen-food paper will suffice as a wrap. If you plan to keep some of the fish longer, it pays to take more time to prepare it. One way to keep the fresh taste is to freeze the fish first, then place it frozen into a cardboard milk carton saved for the purpose. Fill the carton completely with water to cover the fish, and freeze again. The "shield" of ice around the fish will prevent freezer burn. Another way to reduce oxidation is to coat the fish with a cooking oil, wrap, and freeze. Wipe the oil off after thawing the fish and before cooking.

## QUESTIONABLE AND INEDIBLE SPECIES

While almost all gamefish can be eaten, some are in the questionable category, and some should definitely not be eaten. Most freshwater species are widely known to be edible and fit into certain categories, such as the bass, perch, trout, catfish, carp, pike, and sunfish families.

Saltwater species are another matter. Florida alone boasts over 600 species of saltwater gamefish. Although many of these would be in the little-known or rare-catch categories, the point is that there are more fish out there than any angler can hope to be familiar with all of the time, and some doubt might exist as to their edibility. In some fish, such as the puffer, or blowfish, the dorsal strip of flesh can be eaten, while the rest of the fish is highly poisonous. Others such as the barracuda of Florida, the Caribbean, and the Atlantic coast of Central America, are often poisonous in larger sizes.

## CIGUATERA POISONING

The cause of this poison has yet to be exactly defined, but it is responsible for the toxicity in barracuda. The generally accepted theory is that tropical species eat smaller fish that eat small reef organisms that are poisonous to man. As a result, the poison builds up in the flesh of the predator fish, which is the gamefish sought by sportsmen.

While this theory is oversimplified, it does present the angler with the problem of deciding which fish to eat. Ciguatera poisoning has been identified in over 300 species of fish, and in semitropical and tropical waters of the Western Hemisphere it is most prevalent in the barracuda, the yellowfin grouper, and the amberjack. The theory that it comes up the food chain from the reefs is widely accepted, since the Pacific Coast barracuda is perfectly safe to eat and there are no similar reefs and reef organisms there. (Ciguatera poisoning is also found in the reefs of the South Pacific and around Australia.) Unfortunately, the poison may occur in an area previously known to be safe or may occur in a species previously known to be safe.

The methods of telling whether or not a fish is safe to eat are only old wive's tales; there is no layman's method of telling whether or not a fish has ciguatera poisoning.

Symptoms of ciguatera poisoning are a slight tingling of the lips, tongue, and mouth, numbness, nausea, cramps, vomiting, diarrhea, weakness, muscular pain, blurred vision, partial blindness, sensitivity to light, skin blisters, or a rash and accompanying itching. Mortality rate is less than 10 percent, but recovery is slow and sometimes takes months.

Thus, if there is any question about ciguatera poisoning in any fish you catch in tropical waters, release it. We can only recommend two broad guidelines here: first, relatively small fish are usually safer to eat; second, when fishing in heavily reefed areas, obtain information from local health authorities.

## POLLUTION POISONING

Unfortunately, in today's world fish are sometimes unsafe to eat because of the environment they live in. One recent example was the Kepone poisoning that occurred as a result of leakage of the chemical from a plant into the James River in Virginia. The Kepone subsequently reached the Chesapeake Bay. While the Chesapeake Bay fish weren't affected, some areas of the James River were closed to fishing and anglers were advised not to eat fish caught in these and adjoining areas.

The scare of mercury in tuna and swordfish a few years ago is another example.

Similar situations have existed and will continue to exist in other areas of both fresh and salt water. If there is ever a question, don't eat the fish, and watch for news reports of possible contamination of areas that would affect your fishing. Look for verification that the situation has been cleared up from authoritative sources before using the fish from these areas as table fare again, or check with your local health department.

# PART TWO

# 6
# Safe Wading

Wading is an inexact science. Variables include the angler's agility, weight, and size; current or tide; bottom characteristics; and wading equipment used by the angler. In terms of safety and comfort, wading equipment is very important. Wading generally falls into three categories: wet wading, wading with hip boots, and wading with chest-high waders.

## WET WADING

This offers the easiest fishing for most of us—just step into the water and walk out to the fishing. You can wet wade in sneakers and swim trunks or long pants. Unlike wading with hip boots or chest-high waders, there are no limits (beyond common sense) as to how deep you can wade. You also don't have the heat, weight, and expense of waders or hip boots.

Whether you should wet wade or not depends upon the temperature of both the water and air. In most areas, wet wading is comfortable all summer and into early fall. In the South, it is possible almost all year. In northern areas, in extremely cold mountain streams and creeks, or in cool mountain lakes, it may not be comfortable any time of the year.

Relatively warm water temperature is important to prevent high heat loss, while air temperature and breeze or wind will determine how comfortable you will be when you leave the water or move from a deep hole to shallow water.

Wading barefoot is not recommended. Always wear some form of foot gear, even in sandy-bottom areas. There is often a possibility of broken bottles, rusty cans, snags, or rocks on the bottom on which you might injure your feet. Sneakers provide some protection against rough bottoms. Low sneakers can be pulled off in mud or muck, so many anglers use high-top sneakers or canvas-sided shoes available from sport and surplus stores. Tackle stores and mail-order tackle firms also sell canvas-sided shoes for use with stocking-foot waders. Wear heavy socks with any sneaker or wading shoe. Socks will provide some cushioning to your feet and also minimize any abrasion from the sand and grit that may get into your shoes.

Swim trunks or shorts are fine for summer wading in open water, but long khakis or blue jeans are better for wading in cooler water. In cool water you can also wear a pair of inexpensive plastic rain pants or overalls. They will allow some retention of body heat. Long pants are also good when fishing small streams, creeks, and rivers that are rock or snag filled. The long pants will protect your legs from cuts and scratches and fireweed irritation if you must walk through the woods at either end of the fishing trip. Long pants are also necessary for salt-water wading as protection from corals and sea fans.

In addition to being simpler and less expensive, wet wading has some tangible advantages in the water. Since you are not wearing boots or waders, there is less bulk and less water resistance, which is important in surf fishing and heavy-water river fishing where fast currents increase the effort needed to get around or to stand in one spot.

# WADING IN HIP BOOTS AND WADERS

**Soles.** Most canvas wading shoes come with soft-rubber or felt soles that will grip most bottom rocks and structures well. Some of the heavier canvas or leather wading shoes designed for stocking-foot waders can be used with sandals for felt soles or cleats, but most of these shoes are too light or not high enough for the strapping necessary to attach the sandals. Rubber soles will work well on all types of bottom except those with a heavy algae cover or saltwater jetties covered with mussels and weeds. For these areas you will need a special shoe or a sandal with a special sole of felt, metal cleats, or metal ribs to grip the rock.

Most hip boots and waders come with a very heavy, ridged boot sole, although many manufacturers make them available with an optional nylon or smooth felt sole. The heavy, rubber-ribbed soles are ideal for most purposes and the felt soles will hold on those slippery limestone and freestone streams where the rocks are covered with a thin layer of algae.

Some wading shoes or boot-foot soles on waders have hobnails permanently attached to them to bite through any weeds or algae to prevent slipping. Usually these have to be added at experienced tackle stores or by the factory, although some good shoe repairmen can do the job. Golf spikes may be used on some heavy-leather soled wading shoes such as those designed specifically for stocking-foot waders.

Boots or wading sandals that have smooth soles or on which the soles have worn smooth can be fixed with felt soles if desired. Some companies make resoling kits for this purpose. An alternative that works well in many wading areas is to use indoor-outdoor carpeting glued with waterproof cement to a smooth sole. Use the felt-type carpeting, not the newer "artificial-grass" type; the latter will not grip or wear as well.

Cleats and chains are available as strap-on sandals for wading in heavy, rough waters where it is necessary to bite through heavy algae, crustaceans, or weeds to grip the rocks or bottom. Usually these are made of chains or interlocking links of metal, which allows flexibility, reduces weight, and will allow the best possible purchase on any type of bottom.

Those of aluminum will wear out sooner, but this soft metal will grip securely on any rock. Those of stainless steel must have sharp edges to grip, since these are not soft enough to conform to the rock as does aluminum.

**Boot-foot versus stocking-foot waders.** Boot-foot waders (and hip boots) are heavier than stocking-foot waders, they take up more space in a suitcase, are more tiring to wear on long hikes, and are hotter on hot days or when fishing in warm climates.

Stocking-foot waders, even with the necessary wading shoes, generally occupy less space and weigh less than boot-foot waders. However, they are generally not as durable as the heavier-fabric boot-foot waders (a notable exception are the new, lightweight Royal Red Ball waders of a very thin but highly tear-resistant fabric). Stocking-foot waders are a little more of a nuisance to use, since heavy wool socks both under and over the waders are necessary to prevent the wader foot from wearing out. Also, good wading shoes are necessary.

**Hip boots versus chest-high waders.** Hip boots are lighter, less expensive, and easier to put on and wear than waders. The obvious disadvantage is that you can't wade in as deep water with them. They are ideal for most stream-wading conditions, working jetties where the surf isn't too high, or other fishing situations where the water will only come about halfway up your thigh. If you will be in water over that depth, use waders. Waders

(Upper left) *Waders should be fitted so that you can get out of a vehicle or step over logs without the knee or crotch binding.* (Lower left) *After they are put on, inflatable flyweight waders by Red Ball can be inflated easily with a small tube.*

vary also in their height, with some only about elbow high while others are armpit high. Everything else being equal, the armpit-high waders are best because you can wade deeper with them.

# WADING ACCESSORIES

**Suspenders.** Suspenders are necessary for chest-high waders and most wader manufacturers sell them to fit their product. Suspenders should be wide for maximum comfort and elastic to allow you to bend over and move easily. A type of suspender is also available for the lower hip boots and are much more comfortable to wear than the commonly used straps looped onto the belt.

**Wading belt.** Wading belts are designed to fit high around a pair of waders to prevent excessive amounts of water from shipping into the waders should you slip or wade too deep. Most commercial wading belts are made of canvas with a buckle. Unfortunately, many buckles are shiny, which can reflect light onto the water and frighten fish. Some have sharp edges that in time can wear through the wader fabric. You can make your own wader belt by purchasing about 1½- to 2-inch-wide canvas webbing and sewing two large D-rings onto one end. In use, the end of the webbing is threaded through both D-rings and then back through the inside ring to hold securely. The smooth D-rings won't wear out the wader fabric.

**Wading staffs.** You can pick up one along the stream for temporary use, make your own, or buy one.

Sometimes it becomes necessary to cross a fast, high, or dangerous piece of water. In most areas usually you can find a slender, strong piece of driftwood that will serve as a wading staff to help you in the crossing. Pick a piece of wood between four and six feet long, relatively light, and not waterlogged. Test before using to make sure that it isn't rotten or weak.

A ski pole with the ring and webbing removed or a piece of one-inch aluminum tubing (available from most hardware stores) fitted with a bicycle grip at the top and a crutch tip

*Equipment frequently worn by a wading angler includes a vest filled with fly boxes, leader materials, and tools. Note the double D-ring belt at the waist to prevent shipping of water in case of a fall-in. The D-ring buckle prevents chaffing of the waders.*

*Wading staffs are handy in any water and necessary in rough or deep water. Three types of wading staffs include* (top to bottom) *home-made wading staff of aluminum tube, bicycle grip, and crutch tip; modified aluminum ski pole; and commercialy available wood wading staff.*

at the bottom work well. Both can be fitted with a screw eye or an eyebolt at the top to which you can secure a lanyard. You can loop the lanyard over your shoulder or you can use a clip-on key chain, which you attach to the back of your belt or wader top to keep the wading staff out of the way when not in use.

A wide variety of commercial wading staffs are available, ranging from multipiece collapsible metal ones to wooden ones that are less noisy in the water. Before buying, test for stiffness; a tip appropriate for the bottom that you will wade, and one easy to use in the water. Broad rubber tips are best for sandy, muddy, and clean rock bottoms, while pointed metal tips are best for cutting through weeds or algae. Plastic-tipped staffs are multipurpose.

**Flotation vests.** Flotation vests of some type are a must when wading heavy or strong water. Many styles are available. Probably the best for anglers are those that combine a fishing vest for carrying fly and lure boxes with flotation compartments that can be instantly inflated with carbon-dioxide cartridges or by lung power through plastic tubing.

In addition, there are also instantly inflatable flotation devices that can be clipped to your waders to provide protection should you get into water that is too deep. These are for emergency use only and are *not* United States Coast Guard approved personal flotation devices.

## WADING TECHNIQUES

Techniques for wading will vary with the type of water, type of bottom, movement of water (current or tides), and type of wading gear. Wading in a quiet pond, slow river, or over a smooth, sandy bottom with no dropoffs or rocks presents few problems. But with a fast current, high water, and uneven bottom, wading requires the utmost care. Most wading situations fall between these two extremes, and the three factors to keep in mind are water depth, water speed, and bottom structure.

**Water depth.** The deeper the water that you wade into, the greater the tendency for your body to float and the less hold your feet will have on the bottom. How deep you can wade safely will depend upon the water movement and bottom structure. For example, if the water is not moving and the bottom is smooth, you can wade with security to chest-high depths. The fact that deeper wading gives you less hold on the bottom is particularly a problem in fast water; if it is fast enough and strong enough you can get to a point where your feet will no longer hold the bottom against the force of the water and the current will push you downstream. A slippery bottom adds to the difficulty of getting and keeping a good foothold on the bottom structure.

**Water speed.** In some fast streams the current can be so great as to prevent any wading over about knee depth. The water striking your body tends to push you off your feet. The deeper you wade, the more surface area for the water to push against and the less hold you

*Wire fences can puncture and waders or hip boots. Cross fences on stiles and use extreme care.*

have on the bottom. This is particularly a problem in high-surf conditions, since waves are harder to adjust to than the steady current of a river.

In both cases, the best way to cope with any strong force of water is to face sideways to the current or waves, since this presents the least surface area to the force of the water. In rivers, this means wading directly across current or walking sideways when moving up or down the river. Surf anglers can often move directly into the surf, timing the waves to turn sideways when the full force of one hits.

**Bottom structure.** The easiest wading is on a sandy or gravel bottom. Wading becomes more difficult as the gravel turns to softball-size rocks then to small boulders, then to ridges, dropoffs and large boulders. The importance of caution and wading one step at a time in these latter conditions can't be overemphasized. Different types of bottoms present different problems.

A sand bottom is no problem in calm or quiet water, but in a fast current, surf, or ocean tide, the sand will be pulled out from under your feet. Repositioning the feet frequently might be necessary under these conditions.

You'll sink more into a mud bottom, and in a fast current it will be washed away as will a sand bottom. A mud bottom will tend to hold onto your boots or wading shoes more tenaciously. If you are wearing wading shoes while wading this type of bottom, be sure to tie the laces tight so the shoes aren't pulled off.

Gravel is a good wading bottom, although it can be washed from underfoot in a fast current. While usually not that slippery, if the gravel is round and marble-size or covered with slime, felts might help.

Small rocks are dangerous since they will roll with you and can cause a turned ankle. Either felts or cleats will help to hold on the rocks, but care must be taken to guard against rolling stones.

Large rocks are often interspersed with smaller rocks or with gravel or sand. They present a real danger in murky water since they can't be seen unless they are exposed or are close enough to the surface to create a ripple. In situations such as this, it is best to move slowly, testing each new step to be sure that you don't stumble over a rock.

*C.B.P. with the accoutrements of wading: chest-high waders, tight waist belt, and wading staff.*

*This posed picture shows the wrong way to wade. Water pressure increases tremendously when one faces into the current; wade sideways.*

Many rivers, particularly those on the East Coast, have ledges that run across the river. These underwater ledges contribute to good fishing, since they are ideal holding spots for fish, but they also present a dangerous situation for the wader. When they can't be seen because of murky water, it is easy to hit your shin on one of the high ledges, to catch your foot in a crevice between the ledges, or step off the crest of one ledge into the deep water between ledges.

We highly recommend the use of a wading staff on such rivers to feel where the next step can be made and to steady the transition between the abruptly different depths encountered when wading ledge or "shelf" water.

## USING A WADING STAFF

A wading staff used properly can be a tremendous aid in wading anywhere, and particularly in fast-moving streams and rivers. Anglers differ in their methods of using a staff, some using it on the upstream side, others on the downstram side, while moving sideways to the current.

There are pros and cons with each way. In water with light current, the best use of the staff is on your upstream side, moving the staff out ahead of you each time to test the bottom structure, depth, and current. This way, you will be leaning against the wading staff and into the water current, so that if the staff slips, you will fall against the pressure of the water, which will tend to help you regain balance.

In a heavy-water situation when you are in too deep and can't gain enough hold on the bottom to lean into the water, it is best to have the wading staff on the downstream side of the river so that you can lean your weight against the staff and stay upright against the current. The one danger of this is that if the staff does slip, or if the current sweeps it off

*This is the proper way to wade into a heavy current, with the wading staff upstream so that it can be leaned on.*

*An angler sideways to the current with the wading staff on the downstream side.*

*On rough and rocky rivers such as this one, improvised wading staffs made of a stick found along the bank can be used to help maintain balance.*

the bottom, you have nothing to keep you from going downstream, often into faster or deeper water. The main purpose of a wading staff in any situation is to give you a third leg for added support. It is also essential for wading strange, very slippery, or murky waters to feel ahead for faster current, deep holes, rocks, ledges, and so on.

Sometimes you might get into a situation where you are in danger of falling or slipping, yet you don't have a wading staff. Here, you can use your rod to help retain or regain your balance. Push your rod rapidly down on the surface of the water in the direction in which you are falling. The pressure of the rod against the surface of the water may provide enough momentary resistance to help you regain your balance. Do *not* push the rod under the surface against the bottom or try to use it as a wading staff unless you are in a serious situation.

## WADING DANGERS

**Tides.** The rise and fall of tides can be slight (generally in southern waters in the United States) or great (generally in northern waters in the United States). The danger with tide is that you may be fishing a point, jetty, or spit of land on a low tide and get cut off by a rising tide. Similarly, it is possible to wade through a low-tide surf to reach a sandbar and then get stranded when rising water gets too deep in the slough to wade back to shore.

There is no way to guess how far a tide will rise in relation to how deep a slough will get, or if a spit of land will become a temporary island. Such situations can be embarrassing at best, and extremely dangerous at worst. The only way to prevent them is to check with local anglers about dangerous situations and if at all unsure of a given tidal situation, don't take a chance.

**Rising waters.** Rising waters resulting from heavy rains upstream on a river or flood

*A posed shot of an angler in serious trouble while wading deep water. The wading staff on the downstream side helps to hold him in position while trying to regain footing.*

gates being opened on a dammed river can also create a situation in which you could become trapped on a rock or point of land.

Most dams have signaling devices to warn downriver anglers of the release of water and allow them time to leave the river or take to high ground. Usually this consists of flashing red lights or sirens that precede the release of water by 15 minutes or more.

Be aware of any such signals and take heed *immediately*. Get out of the river when you hear or see the first warning signal.

## STRINGERS AND FLY LINES

Wading anglers have a potential problem with these items. Both can become tangled with your feet or with each other, making fishing difficult and wading dangerous. Fly rodders, for example, usually strip line in and let it lie on the water's surface until they complete a retrieve and are ready to cast again. However, fast currents will cause the line to swirl around and under the surface or lines can become waterlogged and sink. If a sinking fly line is used it will go straight to the bottom in the first place. There are several solutions to this problem.

In fast current, strip the line away from you so that it will drift off downstream away from your feet. This does create the difficulty of shooting the line on a cast, since the water drag will make it difficult to get the line off the water.

A second solution is to use a stripping basket. Often used by West Coast deep-water steelhead fishermen, the stripping basket is a half-moon-shaped basket strapped around the waist to hold the line and keep it off the water. It does require a very short strip of line on the retrieve to keep the line coiled in the basket.

*This posed shot of Lefty Kreh shows the problem of wading with fly-rod outfits. Fly lines swirl around your legs and get caught around your feet. Note the wet wading gear of sturdy tennis shoes and lightweight long pants.*

*One way to prevent fly-fishing tangles is to strip in coils of fly line and hold them in your mouth while making the next cast.*

Another solution is to hold the line in coils as you retrieve it to keep it off the water. This also helps when you are making another cast or shooting the line. Keep the coils as neat as possible to prevent them from tangling.

You can also hold the line in your mouth (held only by the lips pressed together) as you retrieve it or switch it to your mouth as you double haul to make another cast. This will allow you to hold several coils to shoot as you use your line arm to double haul for maximum distance.

Stringers can tangle with your feet or tangle with a fly line, if this is the tackle in use. The best approach, assuming you want to keep fish, is to keep the stringer very short and attached to the back of your fishing vest or belt. This way, it will be out of the way of the fly-line coils and in back of you while you wade instead of in front of you. In any case, it will keep the fish away from you and the stringer should drift with the current as you wade sideways to the current. *Do not* use a stringer while wading or surf fishing in salt water since it will attract sharks.

Another problem that can be dangerous as well as expensive is when a fish hooked with a treble hook gets the hooks caught in your waders as you try to land it. To prevent this, use plugs with single hooks where possible and tire each fish before attempting to land it. If at all possible, use a net; hand-landed fish can often slip as you pick them up.

If a fish wraps line around your waders and drives the hooks into your waders, wade to shore or shallower water if possible and unhook the fish. Unhook the fish carefully, since it will be dangerous on such a short tether. Then you can work the hooks out of your waders, make emergency repairs with tape or another method. You can make proper repairs once you get home.

## NIGHT WADING

Provided that common sense is used, night fishing presents no more danger when fishing from shore than daylight fishing does. Since you can't see as well, it is imperative to watch your casting at all times for nearby anglers and to have your tackle arranged so that someone won't step on a rod or trip over an open tackle box. Many anglers use a camping lantern on their night-fishing trips to prevent such accidents.

Wading at night is another story. The rivers and surf that look so easy to wade during daylight hours become difficult if not impossible to wade at night. This is especially true of river fishing. At night, it is impossible to see the bottom in many cases, even with a flashlight. Lights are essential to get out of the river. A headlight is best, since it leaves your hands free to hold your tackle and a wading staff.

However, a headlight gives a bright beam of light that can adversely affect your fishing success if you flash it on the water while changing lures or flies: the small clip-on flashlights especially designed for fly fishermen or a small one-cell AA flashlight, which can be taped on to an arm of your eyeglasses or to the side of the brim of a fishing cap, are best. These lights have a low level of illumination, making it possible to change flies and lures with minimal effect to your night vision.

The same type of light is fine for boat fishing, or use a larger lantern in which the beam is filtered by tissue paper or colored gels to reduce the light intensity and to reduce the effect on night vision as well as the possible effect on the fish.

## UNDERTOW

Undertow is a strong outward current from the beach, usually at an angle, that can take swimmer and surf-fishing angler alike out to sea. Undertows can be slight or so strong that you can hardly stand up in them when knee deep in water. If caught in an undertow, the advice of experts is to not fight it, but instead to swim parallel to the beach in the direction of the undertow. Since the undertow is strongest close to the bottom, the waves should bring you back to the beach or make it easy to angle your swimming slightly to reach the beach.

## FLORA AND FAUNA DANGEROUS TO WADERS

Aside from barked shins from ledges and rocks and perhaps an occasionally dampened pride and body from slipping, the main dangers to wading anglers exist in salt water. These include sharks, barracuda, stingrays, jellyfish, and sea urchins.

Small and large sharks can be found all along our coastline, but the incidence of shark attacks is minimal compared with the numbers of swimmers in the surf each summer and the anglers fishing the surf year-round. While nothing can be done to prevent casual sharks along the beaches, fishermen in particular should be careful about their catches, bait, or any food discarded into the water that could attract them. Most surf anglers on the Atlantic and Pacific coasts keep their catches out of the water, but some wading surf anglers in the Gulf are known to wade far out in the shallow waters and to tow a stringer behind them. This is dangerous since the fish on the stringer attract sharks. Avoid it at all costs, even if you have to stick close to the shore. Release the fish you catch, or use a nearby boat to hold fish.

Stingrays are also found all along the beaches, while sea urchins are common only in southern and tropical waters. Fortunately, the sea urchins are generally visible if you are looking for them. The problem comes when you are wading barefoot and not watching where you are stepping. The best solution is to wear an old pair of sneakers for wading shoes and to shuffle your feet along rather than raising them on each step as you do on land. The same shuffling motion will also tend to move stingrays and skates out in front of you.

Jellyfish are annoying, and in the case of the Portuguese man-of-war, they can be dangerous. Jellyfish along the coasts are often prevalent both in the ocean and in bays and estuaries. If you are shore fishing, jellyfish can still be washed up along the beach and can sting you if you walk barefoot, even if they are dead. If they are prevalent in the

*When fishing and wading southern or tropical waters, wear tennis shoes to avoid injury from sea urchins.*

*A good reason to avoid wading in shark- or barracuda-infested flats. This bone fish was slashed once by a small shark.*

water, your line will pick up strands of jellyfish and you can get stung while removing them or from just handling the line.

An easy way to rid your line of jellyfish is to pull the taut line like a bowstring to flick off as many of the strands as possible before they get to your reel or other tackle. If you get jellyfish caught on a lure, slap the lure on the water with the rod which will knock off much of the slime. This same technique can be used to rid lures of other unwanted debris (algae, seaweed, small sticks), but take care to keep the rod from hitting the water, the boat gunnel, or other equipment, since the force used could break the rod.

If you wade and fish where jellyfish are prevalent, the best way to protect your legs and feet is to wear long pants or khakis and wading shoes. Even then, they might get up under the pants, so that high-top sneakers, long socks, and pants held down with bicycle clips or rubber bands are necessary.

The man-of-war is very dangerous. Almost everyone is familiar with, through photographs and news reports if not actual sightings, the puffy, purplish-blue sail beneath which hang long strands of the stinging tentacles of the man-of-war. Typically found in tropical and temperate waters, it does occasionally drift into colder coastal zones. Avoid it at all costs. While we have seen Belizian guides pick up a Portuguese man-of-war by the sail (only the tentacles are poisonous), such a practice is hazardous, since when found in shallow water the tentacles could hang over the sail and sting on contact. The poison is a neurotoxin that is not considered fatal, although extensive contact coupled with other illnesses could result in death. The Portuguese man-of-war is particularly dangerous in shallow water to wading anglers because only the sail portion is visible above the water and the long tentacles might trail off 30 feet or more to the side.

*Portugese Man O' War jelly fish are extremely dangerous. Their tentacles can extend thirty feet from the sail (shown here) and endanger wading anglers.*

*Long-spined sea urchins can cause serious injury to barefoot anglers. Wear wading shoes at all times.*

# 7
# Surf Fishing

Surf fishing is in certain respects a very specialized type of fishing. It requires special knowledge in such areas as beach vehicles (called beach buggies) and equipment in order for you to get the most out of the sport safely.

## BEACH BUGGIES

Beach buggies are specialized vehicles designed to take the surf angler onto the beach and carry everything needed for surf fishing and overnight camping. If you spend a day on any heavily fished beach you will see a variety of vehicles, including the typical four-wheel-drive vehicles along with a smattering of vans and modified trucks and automobiles. Strongly recommended as equipment and features for beach buggies are the following items.

**Four-wheel drive.** Four-wheel drive is a must for vehicles to gain the maximum traction on soft sand and to get out of places that would have a regular vehicle spinning its wheels and dropping the chassis down to the axle in sand.

**Proper tires and tubes.** Best tires for beach buggies are oversize to fit the standard wheel or oversize wheels fitted with oversize tires for extra width and traction. Best ones are almost bald tires that will not dig into the sand. Because very low tire pressures are used on the beach (15 to 20 pounds of pressure), tubes should be used to keep the tires from breaking away from the seal at the wheel rim and deflating. North Carolina surf guide Ken Lauer recommends radial tires if you plan to switch frequently from the highway to the beach and back, since they will stand the abuse that will ruin other tires.

Lauer says that two spare tires are necessary, since most beaches have a lot of tire hazards such as broken glass, nail-filled boards, or scrap metal from ships. Fit the spare tires with tubes for beach travel, but keep both at highway inflation because they can always be deflated for beach use.

Lauer, who drives about 25,000 miles a year mostly on the beach near his Buxton, North Carolina base, also recommends a six-cylinder engine rather than an eight cylinder; the larger engine will have more power, which can cause you to dig into the sand rather than to ride over it. He also likes power steering because turning on the sand is difficult. He always uses a four-wheel-drive vehicle and recommends an oversize radiator because you will be driving under stress conditions that can otherwise cause the beach buggy to overheat. He doesn't like tackle boxes or ice chests mounted on the front bumper since this will impede air flow to the radiator.

Spare hoses should be carried since radiator hoses can break on the beach. Carry the necessary tools for minor repairs and to remove hose clamps for hose repairs. For both human and radiator use, extra water is needed. Carry a two- to five-gallon can of fresh, potable water and replace it frequently so that it is drinkable in an emergency as well as suitable for the radiator.

**Jack.** There are times in spite of all precautions that you will hit a patch of soft sand or turn the wrong way and get stuck. A good jack is sometimes the only way to get the vehicle out of the sand. Most anglers prefer the bumper jack because it is easier to operate in emergency situations than an axle hydraulic jack, which must be placed under the car in the sand.

You will need some support for the jack in the sand, so bring along, also, two or more long, wide boards. The best sizes are two-by-six or two-by-eight boards about four feet long. You will need to carry at least two so you can place one under the jack and the other under the tire for traction.

**Air pump.** In the past few years, dozens of air pumps have appeared on the market. Some are excellent, some are fair, and some are poor. Some in the past worked by hooking up to a spark-plug thread in the engine block and letting the air pressure of the

*Twelve-volt operated pumps as this Coleman Inflate-All 150 make it possible to pump tires up from the battery. Some surf anglers carry both pumps and air tanks.*

pistons pump air into the tires through a long tube. Most today are electric pumps, working off the 12-volt cigarette-lighter hook-up to power small motors that work a compresser that pumps air into the tire. There are also a few foot-operated pumps available in which constant pumping works a compressor to pump the air. The electric types that come in a complete kit and carrying case are best.

**Air tanks.** Many surf anglers, who are on and off the beach a lot don't like to bother with air pumps and instead use surplus or stock air tanks, which are designed and built to take a lot of pressure. With a hose fitting, it is easy to run the hose from the tank to the tires and pump them as required for road travel. Then at the next gas station you stop at you can pump up the air tank to its recommended load to be ready for the next beach trip.

The advantage of this over the pump is that it is easier and quicker to work. The disadvantage is that if you forget to fill it at the gas station regularly, you can run out of air on the beach. Some anglers favor either pump or tank, while many carry both in their vehicles, using the tank most of the time, but keeping the pump for emergency use.

**Rope or winch.** A rope will help in case you or a comrade get stuck in the sand and need the extra pull of a beach buggy. A rope or cable will allow you to hook up to any vehicle, while a winch on the front end will allow you to pull yourself out if required. However, pulling yourself out with a winch is not an easy task, since there are no trees on the beach to tie up to. It involves a long, laborious process of finding a large piece of driftwood, levering it into the right position, and digging a deep trench to bury the driftwood to give leverage. Unless you plan to visit those areas as yet unvisited by surf fishermen, you may not require a winch.

**Shovel.** This is necessary for digging out and planting boards for traction.

**Tire gauge.** Use frequently to check your tires when deflating them for beach travel and when inflating them again for highway travel. Get a good one and use it regularly.

**Fire extinguisher.** This is necessary for those emergencies when no other help is available.

**Spare spark plugs.** These are important because the low-speed driving on the beach will often cause plugs to foul. Be sure to include a spark-plug wrench with the spare plugs.

**Self-contained toilet.** Federal and state officials are taking an increasingly closer look at beach use all along the coasts, and two things in general disturb them. One is driving on the dunes, which destroys the dune line to weaken the natural defense against the sea. The other is camping at any spot along the beach and using the beach as a primitive latrine. Most areas prohibit camping for this reason except in designated areas with appropriate facilities. Fishermen are allowed on the beach at night provided that they are fishing. But nature does call on such fishing trips, and a portable toilet is the way to keep the beach clean.

Optional accessories usually added to beach buggies for increased convenience in fishing include the following items.

**Front-bumper rod racks.** Many surf rods are too long to fit into a vehicle and it takes too much time when the fish are breaking to untie rods from roof-top racks. Surf anglers should have a front-bumper rack to carry spinning and/or conventional surf rods. Front-bumper racks are nothing more than vertical pieces of tubing to hold rods so that they are secure while traveling on the beach or highway.

Commercial racks are available, but racks can also be made easily with PVC, ABS, or similar plastic pipe. Two-inch-diameter pipe is usually best to hold the larger handles and swelled butt caps found on some surf rods. The pipe should be long enough (usually 24 inches) so that it will hold an entire rear grip of a rod, and it should be mounted so that the bottom of the rack is level with the bottom of the vehicle bumper and no lower. Low-mounted racks could hit on driftwood and curbs, while short pieces of pipe could cause the same problem even if the rack is mounted properly, because rod handles would extend too far below the bumper.

*This surf rod rack bolts easily to the car bumper, and the plastic tubes are long enough to prevent the rod handles from coming through the bottom where they could be damaged. The V-shaped groove in the top of each tube holds the stem of the reel foot, preventing it from swinging while the vehicle is in motion.*

To make such a rack, get enough of the pipe to make each length 24 to 30 inches and enough for about 10 to 12 rods. Plan on mounting the pipes about 8 to 10 inches apart to keep reels and reel handles from knocking together. If in doubt, measure the width of the widest reel, add two inches for clearance, and position the tubes accordingly. Use two U bolts to secure each tube to a 2-by-10- or 2-by-12-inch board, which in turn is bolted to the vehicle bumper. If possible and if your budget allows, use stainless steel or brass to avoid rust. Drill the board and bolt the tubing in place.

Since spinning gear is used in most surf fishing today, cut a notch two inches long beginning it about one inch wide and tapering the notch to a v shape in the top of each tube to hold the leg of the spinning reel, which prevents it from swinging around. These notches should face forward to keep all the reels facing forward; however, the tubes on each end can have the notches placed at a 45-degree angle outward to insure further against reel contact. Another way that you can lessen the possibility of damage is to use the notches and alternate long and short tubing so that a reel will not be adjacent to another reel at the same height.

The entire rod rack can be mounted on the bumper by bolting through the bumper or with J-shaped bolts or open-eye bolts bolted to the upper and lower lips, which allows removal of the rack if desired.

**Car-top rod racks and storage box.** These racks hold the rods horizontally on the top of the vehicle, usually by means of v grooves cut in a board at each end of the vehicle with the rods held down by shock cord. Some anglers use these holders on the top of large wooden boxes on car roofs. The boxes are designed to hold spare tires, spare tubes, extra equipment, emergency equipment, air tanks, and other such items; it gives added room for more rods, which is especially good when several anglers are fishing from the same vehicle. The boxes can be open or with lids. Most are homemade of a sturdy plywood base and shelving-board sides placed on a rectangular car-top boat rack. Such boxes are great for extra equipment, especially equipment not used regularly but needed in an emergency or unusual situation.

Such a box can be made easily from 5/8- to 3/4-inch plywood for the base, 3/8-inch plywood for the top (if a lid is desired), and 1-by-6- to 1-by-10-inch shelving for the sides. Secure it to the top of the beach buggy with car-top racks or you may wish to bolt it directly to the top, using silicone rubber as a seal against any air or rain leaks into the car. Before you mount the box, drill some drain holes in the bottom (if using car-top racks that will keep the box elevated) or side drain holes where it meets the bottom (if you are bolting the bottom directly to the car) to allow for rain drainage out of the box.

**Front-mount ice chest.** Many surf anglers like to eat their catch and so include a large ice chest (80-quart or more capacity) on the front bumper. Usually, welded brackets are made up and attached to the front bumper to serve as a frame for holding the ice chest. When this is done, the vertical rod racks are mounted on the front of the ice-chest frame. A variation of this is a large open box to hold equipment, with the rod racks on the front.

**Car-top racks for boats.** Some surf anglers also carry small, deep-v, aluminum boats (often called tin boats in the New England area where they are most often used) for launching in the surf to reach fish beyond casting range. In these cases car-top racks are a must to hold the boat. Usually the car-top rod racks and car-top boxes previously mentioned are incompatable with boat racks.

**Outboard-engine racks.** For anglers fishing from the small boats, power is needed. To preserve space inside the vehicle, many anglers rig racks to hold the outboard on the front bumper, rear bumper, or on the back door, with the latter using the same technique often used to hold spare tires on vans. If using a clamp-on rack such as this, be sure to include a lock to lock the engine to the car should you have to leave the vehicle.

**Lure racks.** Since saltwater fish can be extremely fickle in their choice of lures, and since many anglers today fish right out of the back of their beach buggies, many anglers use racks to hold popular lures. Racks are often attached to the inside rear-door window or the rear side window. Rack arrangements include hardware cloth (wire mesh) to hold plugs by the hooks; horizontal strips of plastic foam to hold plugs; bins specially made for plugs, hooks, and sinkers; and rows of short lengths of golf tubes into which plugs can be dropped and kept separate from other lures.

**Inside rod racks.** Rod racks inside the beach buggy make it possible to keep spare, rigged rods out of the way, or to keep lightweight rods for specialized fishing (light spinning rod, popping rod, or fly rod) ready for use should your fishing take you off the beach in a small boat or otherwise allow use of the specialized equipment. There are two basic ways to make rod racks: overhead (running as close to the roof as possible to allow maximum head room) and along the sides. The latter is only possible on vehicles such as vans that have sufficient room, and overhead racks are generally preferable.

Some overhead racks consist of only two bars placed near the roof line and spaced far enough apart to support and balance the rods. Others consist of plastic, metal, or wood boat-rod holders adapted to horizontal use. Often the racks used for storing big-game trolling rods in the cabins of sport-fishing boats are ideal for this use and will hold rods without any modification. One way to make racks is to use the rear section of a boat-rod rack and two-inch PVC or similar plastic pipe as a sheath for the forward part of the rod and guides. Two-inch pipe is generally sufficient, but you might use larger or smaller pipe to accomodate rod guides.

**Camping fittings.** For many surf anglers, fishing is a family affair and thus many beach buggies are rigged for camping. Insides of large vans and bakery-type trucks sometimes include small propane stoves, refrigerators, permanent or fold-down bunks, and other equipment for camping.

**CB radio.** A CB might be considered necessary equipment or an added fishing accessory. It is useful for both purposes and should be considered essential by serious surf anglers. A CB is often needed to obtain help in a hurry, but it also serves as an informal network about fishing conditions along a section of beach. The cost of a CB can be justified by the decreased gas use and vehicle wear that it makes possible. Each section of beach or each fishing club will use different frequencies, so learn which one is in use in the area you wish to fish.

Be sure to make the obvious provisions for equipment and accessories on your beach buggy if you plan to travel long distances to and from fishing spots. For example, if you have horizontal rod racks on top of the buggy in addition to front-mount rod racks, you can store rods safely on top of the car for long-distance travel. For security, you can obtain

*The forward rack consists of ski racks modified to hold surf rods and provides enough clearance for the reels to be left attached. The rear lidded box holds other surf gear and accessory equipment.*

ski racks, which you can lock. These racks are readily available and cushioned so they won't damage the rods.

Summer highway driving can be demanding upon a vehicle's cooling system, so be sure to remove equipment boxes and ice chests from front-bumper racks and store them in the vehicle for long-distance traveling.

## DRIVING ON THE SAND

The best way to approach driving on the beach is to use the same cautious techniques that you use when driving in deep snow. But there are different types of sand; some types are better to drive on than others while some should be avoided at all costs. A very fine, powdery sand, sometimes called sugar sand, often will quickly work out from under the wheels when any power is applied. Sugar sand blows around a lot, is frequently found on the dunes (which should not be driven on at all), and can get a car buried up to the axle in a hurry.

Wet sand, located in small, shallow pools along the surf edge or where the surf keeps it constantly saturated, should also be avoided, since it acts like quicksand. The high water content gives very poor traction to a tire and it sinks quickly. Gravely sand, made up of small rocks, bits of shells, and coarse sand should also be avoided at all costs since it will not form a firm base for driving.

*This camper-type beach buggy has a front-mounted ice chest and side-mounted rod racks so that the ice chest can be reached without removing the rods.*

The two best types of sand for beach driving are dry or moist regular sand. Regular sand is coarser than sugar sand, will not blow around as readily, and is the type found on most beaches. It forms a firm base and is easy to drive on. Even better is the same type of sand that has become wet but is no longer saturated. This type is often encountered along the edge of the beach in a receding tide, and it forms a very firm base for driving.

When entering a beach area, stop and deflate the tires to about 18 pounds of pressure. Fifteen to twenty pounds is a good range, and the best tire pressure will depend upon the type and size of tire, vehicle weight, and sand conditions. Experiment until you find the right pressure for your vehicle. Cross only at designated beach-crossing areas. Don't drive on the dunes; it is illegal in most areas because the dunes protect the mainland from the surf. Once the dunes and their protective grasses go, the beach will go also.

Once you are on the beach, travel in the tracks made by other vehicles, if possible. These tracks will already have the sand packed down. Driving in these tracks will be

*Moist regular sand provides a hard, packed surface upon which to drive.*

easier on the car engine, the tires, and the driver. Use a light touch on the wheel, allow the vehicle to follow the tracks, and don't oversteer. You should travel slowly, usually not more than about 10 miles per hour. Make turns slowly, as you would in snow, to allow the car to make a new track without digging into the sand. Constantly watch ahead to avoid poor sand conditions and make any changes in direction slowly and begin them well in advance.

When you stop, make sure that it is on a firm base. Surf guide Ken Lauer also recommends backing up about four to six feet before starting again so that you have a firm track on which to gain momentum before encountering the fresh sand. Failure to do this can result in your digging your tires in where you sit. Also be sure to start with your tires straight ahead and turn only after you have gained momentum.

If you get stuck, see if you can back up to gain a new starting position, or lightly and gently rock the car loose. Don't do this if there is any tendency to spin the tires. Often, you can get out by deflating the tires further (to about 10 pounds of pressure) to give added traction on the sand. If this fails and you are down on the frame, jack up the car from the bumper enough to get the pressure off the tire, place a board underneath and drive slowly out in second gear.

Start all driving in second gear, because it keeps the torque to a minimum and decreases the possibility of digging into the sand. Accelerate slowly and smoothly to prevent digging in, and drive in the highest possible gear that you can for any given speed, taking into consideration sand conditions, vehicle control, traffic, and safety.

After each trip to the beach, check your air filter. The fine sugar sand described earlier may quickly clog air filters and decrease engine performance.

## NIGHT DRIVING ON THE SAND

Often the best surf fishing can be found after dark. Some species such as drum, channel bass, and striped bass will hit as well as or better at night than in daytime fishing. As a result, beach buggies are just as common on the beach at night as they are at high noon.

Since most fish are particularly susceptible to bright lights flashed on the water, most

*Ken Lauer purposely showing the effects of wet sand—his tires are rapidly sinking.*

driving is done with parking lights only, with the main headlights turned off when entering the beach area. Even low beams can shine on the water from far away, so avoid disturbing other anglers and use only parking lights. Give your eyes a few minutes to become accustomed to the night driving before traveling down the beach with parking lights only. Follow the tracks of other vehicles. Take particular care to travel slowly enough to avoid any dangerous conditions, such as surf-invaded pockets on the beach, wet sand, driftwood and other beach debris, and shelving of the beach (which occurs under strong tide conditions).

Shelving (a high shelf along the edge of the beach with soft sand on top of the shelf and wet sand or surf below) is particularly dangerous. For example, if you are driving toward the water, you might drive off a shelf into the surf or onto wet sand before you realize it. Similarly, driving parallel to the beach, a wheel too close to the shelf could cause the shelf to cave in, pitching the vehicle at a steep angle or even rolling it onto its side.

As you approach the fishing area, watch for other beach buggies and such angling gear as sand spikes and beach chairs. Find a spot and park your vehicle so it does not block others or infringe upon the fishing activities of other fishermen.

After stopping a beach buggy, always back up and get a running start. Note the notched rod holders on the front bumper of this vehicle.

Ken Lauer making a sharp turn in soft sand. Note the almost bald radial tires, which are best for beach travel.

*When traveling the beach, it is always easier to follow in the tracks of another vehicle, especially in soft, powdery sand.*

## SURF BELTS

Surf belts provide an easy way to hold the gear—gaffs, knives, fishing pliers, sand spikes, and so on—that you will need while fishing. They also provide an additional safety factor; a tight surf belt around a pair of waders will reduce the amount of water taken on should a high breaker roll over you or should you slip and go in over your wader tops. The best surf belts are of canvas since they won't harden as will leather after use. Army-surplus belts designed to hold such gear as canteens are ideal because they are adjustable to size and are ringed with grommets to hold just about anything that you want. The ones with brass fittings to prevent corrosion are best. The one disadvantage of these belts is that they are very wide and thus you might have to make special sheaths or holders to slip on the belt. An alternative is to rivet or sew sheaths or holders for the items that you will always use to the belt. Some items that you should consider always having with you on your surf belt include the following.

**Fishing pliers.** These should be of the Sportmate or G-96 type that have parallel-acting jaws with side wire-cutters to clip wire or heavy monofilament shock leaders. If you plan to be in the high surf frequently, use a sheath that has a snap to keep the pliers from getting washed out. Since bare metal is slippery, use pliers that have plastic grips or add grips with dip-in vinyl coating for tool handles or the slip-on grips for tools that are available at most hardware stores.

**Fishing knife.** Carry a fishing and bait-cutting knife in a sheath. Best are the short fillet knives that have a very sharp but flexible blade that will enable you to cut chunks or strips of bait.

*Extra-long sand spikes such as this PVC pipe strapped to a long length of aluminum angle make it possible to keep rods high over the surf.*

**Surf gaffs.** All gaffs pose some storage problems to protect both the points and the users from the points. Surf gaffs have an additional problem in that they are carried on a surf belt and must be sheathed in some way to protect waders and the angler from injury. Some gaffs are made specifically for surf anglers and come with belt sheaths of leather, or better, of salt-and-sun-impervious plastic. If your favorite gaff does not come with a sheath, you can make one, using bolted or riveted plastic, leather, or heavy canvas. Plastic is best since the point will slide along it and not dig in and catch, as it might on leather or canvas. The best sheaths hold the gaff securely with two flat sheets to protect the full-point of the gaff. Those that have snaps, ties, or buttons are a problem from the standpoint of getting the gaff out easily and, in time, from the standpoint of maintenance and corrosion.

To keep from losing the gaff, attach it to your surf belt with a cord that will allow you to reach far enough to stick a fish. The best way to accomplish this is to use a coiled telephone cord or coiled electric cord that will retract to stay out of the way yet stretch out when needed. If you use any sort of cord to attach the gaff to your belt, be sure to have a weak link in the system so that if necessary, the cord will break. The last thing that you want is a cord that won't break if a large fish tries to take advantage of the undertow and pull you to sea by a gaff that won't come free or break loose.

# CROWDED BEACHES

A crowded beach with elbow-to-elbow fishing is becoming more the rule than the exception, especially when the fish are in. To cast and fish on the beach under such conditions requires courtesy and common sense.

Make sure that you move into a spot on the beach only when there is room for you. If a spot becomes vacant on the beach because an angler is landing a catch, it is common courtesy to leave that spot for him when he returns from parking the fish in the ice chest of his beach buggie. When a spot does become free, move in carefully, and make only overhead casts. A sidearm cast in a situation such as this is impossible, even if it is only at a slight angle. Since other anglers are likely to be moving around and landing fish, take

*Surf fisherman can avoid being swamped by waves by jumping at each wave, by wading out, and by turning sideways to reduce water pressure.*

care to check behind you on each cast to make sure there is enough room.

Wade out to where the line of anglers is in the surf, no farther and no closer. If you don't wade out that far, you will risk casting over someone or they might not realize that you are there when they make a cast. If you move out farther than other anglers you will risk having casts made over your shoulders as well as risk being too far out.

Wait to see where anglers are casting and make your casts parallel to theirs. If the bottom is good, and if there is no undertow or current, this will most likely be directly in front. If there is a current or tide carrying sinkers or lures in one direction, most anglers will cast upcurrent to allow the lure to drift back or the bait to roll along the bottom.

If all anglers do this, then all the lines will clear even though you will be casting over one or two lines each time you make a cast. It is important to make your casts the same distance as other anglers. Too long a cast might mean that your line will be caught by other anglers when they cast over you, while too short a cast will hook other lines before your lure gets a chance to drift with the current. If other anglers aren't doing this, you might suggest this method to those around you.

The reason this works is that any cast will swing in an arc in a current (assuming that you aren't free-spooling line or retrieving line). As a result, any lines that have drifted through the surf will be close to the beach and will not hook a line cast over them. Also, when you and an adjacent angler are casting, wait a few minutes between casts so that the lines will have a chance to sink and drift.

Fighting fish is equally important under crowded conditions to prevent losing the fish and losing surf-fishing friends by tangling up their lines. When a fish hits, warn other anglers nearby so that they will have a chance to move out of the way and bring in their lines if necessary to give you room. If the fish stays in the surf at relatively the same position to the beach, there will be little chance of tangling lines on either side of you. However, most larger fish, over which you will not have immediate control, will run up or down the beach.

In this case, it is important to run with the fish, warning anglers of your intentions as you move along the beach. Depending upon when the fish hits in relation to your retrieve and how far out other anglers are casting, the fish may be either inside or outside of other lines. In most cases, it will be beyond other lines. Thus, as you approach each angler, quickly determine by raising or lowering your rod tip the relative positions of the two crossing lines. If you are on top, pass in back of the other angler; if underneath, drop your rod and duck under the other line before continuing along the beach.

If you work rapidly, you should be able to keep the fish at a position almost at right angles to your spot on the beach and work the fish into the beach without tangling other lines. Utilize proper drag on the reel so you can pump the fish into the surf without losing line while cranking (which will cause line twist with spinning tackle).

Use the surf to pull the fish into you. Pump strongly on the rod when a breaker pushes the fish toward shore, and slack off but try to hold the fish when the undertow pulls the fish back out to sea. Time your retrieves so that you can tire the fish and use the breakers to push the fish into the beach shallows where it can be gaffed and dragged up onto dry land. Once the fish is landed, it is common courtesy to thank those anglers along the beach who helped you when you crossed their paths.

# 8
# Ice Fishing

Ice fishing is growing in popularity throughout the northern part of the United States. However, it presents circumstances that anglers new to ice fishing must consider before going out and that experienced ice fishermen must constantly reevaluate for their own safety and the safety of their companions.

## SAFE ICE THICKNESSES

The Virginia Department of Game and Inland Fisheries recently published the following chart suggesting safe thicknesses of ice for ice fishermen.

| | |
|---|---|
| One ice fisherman on foot: | 2 inches of ice |
| Group of ice fishermen in single file: | 3 inches of ice |
| Automobile up to 2 tons gross weight: | 7½ inches of ice |

Note that the figures in this chart are based on safe, solid ice. A number of factors will affect these figures. For example, the figures in this chart are based on ice at an air temperature of 30 degrees Fahrenheit or less. These figures should be doubled at air temperatures of 30 to 40 degrees, and tripled at air temperatures of 40 to 50 degrees.

## OTHER FACTORS AFFECTING SAFETY ON ICE

Here are some factors about ice that the ice fishermen should know in order to fish safely.
- Ice freezes faster when the humidity is low.
- Ice melts slower when the humidity is high.
- Ice melts first around the edges of a lake or pond.
- Wind, current, temperature, and other factors will affect the safety and thickness of ice, and these factors may vary from day to day.
- Ice may not freeze thickly around docks, boats, piers, springs, runoff drains, moving water, or tributaries to a lake or river.
- Ice formed by melting snow is generally "rotten." It thaws quickly and presents extreme danger.
- Lakes and ponds do not freeze uniformly.
- When the ice gets wet on top, as it does late in the season or in southern parts of the ice-fishing range, it is time to get off. Ice will weaken rapidly at this point and will be extremely dangerous.

*Rubber boots and heavily insulated pants and jackets are necessary for ice fishing. Note the short rod used for fishing in the hole.*

- Snow hides weak spots in the ice, or holes made by ice fishermen on previous trips. Avoid it.
- Dark spots frequently indicate weak, thin ice.

## RULES FOR SAFETY ON THE ICE

- Use the buddy system. Never fish alone.
- If fishing in a group, avoid gathering together unless absolutely sure the ice is sufficiently thick to support the group's weight.
- Always allow sufficient distance between fishing holes; this depends upon the thickness of the ice—check with local ice fishermen and use common sense.
- Always use an ice auger or ice spud to cut holes in the ice. An axe or hatchet will

*A full-knit face mask will give you protection from the wind while you ice fish.*

*A special ice-fishing spud makes it easy to cut round holes safely in the ice. A lanyard attached to the ice spud and the angler's wrist will prevent loss if the spud slips through the hole.*

make an unnecessarily large, ragged hole, and may glance off the ice to hit you or a companion.
- Always warn other ice fishermen of the presence of your ice-fishing holes and of any other danger that you may have detected.
- Never build a fire on the ice. It will weaken the ice in the area around the fire—the area where fishermen will want to gather in groups.

## RESCUE ON THE ICE

Just as a first-aid kit should be kept in every home for emergencies and carried in every boat and tackle box, ice fishermen must be prepared for the possibility of someone going through the ice. We feel that every ice fisherman should carry a set of spikes. A set of two spikes are often available commercially in ice-fishing areas, or they can be made easily. Sixty-penny nails work well if sharpened and fitted with a slip-over handle. Large-handled, short-bladed screwdrivers with the end sharpened to a point also work. Howard Eberly, a custom rod builder of Pasadena, Maryland, uses short, inexpensive screwdrivers, sharpened to a point with the handle covered by hypalon material such as that used for handles on fishing rods. He heats the end of the points to drive the spikes together so that they fit as a set (the points into the bottoms of the handles). In that way, they won't tear clothing and can be kept ready for instant use.

If you do fall in, use the ice spikes as follows: take a spike in each hand and get as close to the edge of the ice as possible. Stab the ice with the spikes to drive them as far as possible into the good ice. Then swing one leg up onto the ice with the leverage provided by the ice spikes.

Once one leg is up, reposition the ice spikes if possible (one at a time), and bring the other leg up. At all times, lay on the ice to distribute your weight over the weakened ice as much as possible. Once you are completely out of the water, use the spikes to pull your body toward good ice, or roll toward good ice. Seek help from others as quickly as possible.

Groups of anglers who ice fish regularly should have at hand some form of rescue equipment. Basically, this equipment can be anything that will allow you to reach the person in the water. It can be a rope, ladder, long board, long tree limb, sturdy coat, spare tire, ice-fishing sled, or another such item. Obviously, some are better than others. If using something short, such as a coat or spare tire, stretch out on the ice and extend the rescue equipment to the angler. Once he grasps it, inch backward until he is out of the water and on safe ice. If the ice is thin, use several anglers in a human chain (each holding the ankles of the person in front of him) to distribute weight evenly on the ice. This same technique can be used if there is no rescue equipment available. During rescue, don't stand near a hole since the ice may give way under you. If rescue equipment is not available, don't take the time to look for some—the angler in the water could die in the meantime. An accompanying chart published by the United States Coast Guard shows times of survival at different water temperatures.

| Water Temperature | Time to Exhaustion or Unconsciousness | Expected Time of Survival |
|---|---|---|
| 32.5 °F | 5-15 minutes | 15-45 minutes |
| 32.5-40 °F | 15-30 minutes | 30-90 minutes |
| 40-50 °F | 30-60 minutes | 1-3 hours |

## ICE-FISHING SHELTERS

Ice fishing varies from one region of the country to the next in terms of the temperatures experienced and the degree of shelter needed. We both live in Maryland, a borderline state for ice fishing. However, there is some ice fishing in late January or early February on the lakes in the northern half of Maryland, although temperatures and wind-chill factors aren't severe. Most of the fishing requires nothing more than grabbing the minimum of equipment under your arm, walking out on the ice, and fishing. However, anglers aren't usually so spartan, and a typical "shelter" would consist of a large children's sled fitted with a large wooden box to hold the equipment (and hopefully the fish on the return trip), which also serves as a seat to make the wait for a strike a little more relaxing. If there is any degree of comfort added, it is usually by those anglers who add a propane or gas lantern or catalytic heater to the box to keep the seat warm while they wait.

As you go farther north, the necessity of some sort of shelter to break the wind becomes greater as the temperatures drop and the winds rise.

There are too many combinations to list all of them and too many individual ideas on what makes a good shelter, but there are some basic requirements to be met. First, a shelter must be portable so that you can take it out and back on the ice easily on some sort of sled or towing apparatus. Second, it must be easy to erect and take down without

*A lantern or catalytic heater in a box on an ice-fishing sled can be used as a hot seat while ice fishing.*

jamming or freezing up, especially in snow, rain, hail, and sleet. Third, it must provide the maximum protection possible for the design from the elements. Fourth, it must be lightweight for easy handling. And fifth, it must be sturdy so that it won't blow down or blow over. Designs for shelter include the following:

**The bifold frame.** For want of another term we'll call this the bifold, since it resembles a short, wide, bifold door—the kind used for many closets. Usually these are only about four feet high, since you will be using them sitting down on a seat or sled, and about two feet wide per panel. They are hinged, and fold flat to carry and set up easily.

Some are made of light, one-quarter-inch plywood while others are made of a wooden frame over which is stretched a canvas or nylon wind-proof covering. The fabric is lighter, the wood is sturdier. Sitting free, these won't resist a high wind, so most anglers use them with a floor either hinged to the panels or attached with rods, hitch pins, hooks, or a similar set up. Your weight when you sit on the box or sled on the floor guards against the wind blowing it over.

**The trifold frame.** This utilizes the same type of construction, materials, and dimensions as the bifold frame, except that a third panel is added so that the frame can be set up in the shape of a u, or three-sided structure, to provide more protection from the elements. Some also have a hinged roof that folds over the top to give protection on all but the side you need to watch the hole.

**Metal-frame shelters.** Some anglers like a metal frame from plumber's pipe and fittings mounted on a wooden base, which is towed to the ice-fishing spot and covered with a canvas windbreaker. It is lightweight for the shelter that it gives, but it must be mounted on a secure wood base, to keep it from acting like a sail.

One way to make a lightweight, easily-taken-down, metal-frame windbreaker is to use short, six-inch lengths of pipe attached to pipe flanges on the base, and insert an aluminum fold-up frame into the pipes. The frame is held in place with cotter pins in holes drilled through the frame and pipe lengths.

**Self-erecting tents.** Tents with self-erecting frames and no center poles are ideal shelters for ice fishermen. They come in several sizes, have wide doors that zipper shut in bad weather, and nylon fasteners that make them easy to set up and take down. Some arrangement has to be made to hold the tent down in high winds, and a wood floor or another method to anchor the corners to the ice will be needed.

This type of shelter is great if you want shelter to watch tip ups that are strung out along the ice. There is a disadvantage if you want to be completely in the tent watching an ice-fishing hole, since most tents have sewn-in floors that would have to be cut to get to the ice hole. Of course, you can set up the tent just to one side of the ice fishing hole and sit in the entrance. You'll still get the shelter of the tent and can fish right in the hole.

# PART THREE

# 9
# Types of Boats for Fishing

Boats for fishermen come in a number of different types. The proper choice of boat depends on individual needs and preferences of anglers, waters to be fished, type of fish sought, and the number of anglers that are going to fish from the boat. The different types of fishing boats include the following.

## JOHN BOAT (OR PRAM OR JON BOAT)

These are flat-bottomed, snub-nosed craft that are ideal for inland fishing on protected waters. They come in wood or aluminum, with the latter being the most popular. Most are 10 to 16 feet long, and the smaller ones are usually best only for careful, farm-pond fishing. The larger 16-and even 18-foot craft are designed mainly for commercial fishermen working southern waters with trot lines, seines, and other such tackle than for sport fishing.

John boats are also ideal for float fishing down rivers. They provide good stability, lots of room, and enough seaworthiness to make them safe for most rivers. It's usually best to use two cars, leaving one at the launching spot and one where you plan to take out. The john boat is launched upstream then fished downstream, usually three to ten miles, depending upon the water and the quality of the fishing available. For best results, use a drag anchor to keep the prow of the john boat pointed upstream and on course, which makes casting from either side of the boat both easy and safe.

For the sport angler the 12- and 14-foot craft are ideal. While length is an important consideration, beam also must be carefully checked. For example, while our 14-foot john boat has a 55-inch beam at the gunwale and thus is about as stable as you can find in a john boat of this length, john boats of the same length are also available with a 44- or 48-inch beam, which makes them a bit more tippy, and they require a bit more care and more deliberate movements while fishing. They are easier to move and thus are often used by anglers poling, rowing, paddling, or using small engines to fish swamps, rivers, sloughs, and so on, where a narrow boat is easier to control.

John boats have the distinct advantage of offering a lot of interior space for the length and cost. The square bow offers a lot of room for the angler at that end to move about when fishing and to avoid cramps. The distinct disadvantage coupled with this blunt prow is that the boat is not designed for and will not take any type of rough water. For rough water you need a sharp prow that will cut into the waves and lift the boat up and over the heaviest ones. Using the john boat in saltwater, larger bodies of fresh water, or any water during a storm can result in it being swamped or at least shipping a lot of water over the bow. Provided you realize their limitations, john boats are inexpensive, comfortable, and great fishing craft. We wouldn't be without one.

## V-BOTTOM ROW BOATS

We'll use this term to describe the small 12- to 16-foot, pointed-bow, open boats that are designed for two anglers, for fishing small and protected waters, and to give lots of room for comfortable fishing. While the small seat in the pointed bow might cramp one angler a little, most of these craft have a center seat as well. But be careful when casting from the center seat, since this places anglers close together.

Often these boats require a little more draft than the flat-bottomed john boats, but because of the pointed bow they take rough water better since the bow will cut into waves and ride up over them. As a result, they are a better choice for bigger and rougher water, although they are still open boats that should be used cautiously when the weather turns nasty.

## STEELHEAD RIVER DRIFT BOATS

Steelhead river drift boats have sharply tapered sides and pointed bows and sterns. They are specialized crafts for fishing the rough, turbulent West Coast steelhead rivers. The pointed bow makes it possible for them to slide through rapids easily without

*Typical fresh-water fishing craft.* Mercury Marine

This Grumman Sportsman is a good example of a small and efficient fishing boat that allows room for running and tackle storage.

A typical pointed-bow open fishing craft.

shipping water. The pointed, or almost pointed, stern prevents water from coming over the transom as would occur with low-transom, square-stern boats.

There are two basic types of boats. The Mackenzie River boat, named for the river where it originated, takes a guide and usually one angler and is fished with the stern downstream, the guide maintaining the position in the river with oars. The wider Rogue River boat is fished with the bow downstream, the guide facing downstream and rowing backward, and one or two anglers in the bow fishing the water ahead of the boat. The design of these boats, while unusual, makes them ideal for their purpose of fishing the rapids, pools, and around boulders of rough-water rivers.

## CANOES

Canoes vary in size from the little 11-footers to 18-footers to larger freight canoes. Today, canoes are made of canvas (wood with a tight canvas shell), wood, aluminum, fiberglass, and various plastic and plastic-fiberglass combinations. Each type of material has specific advantages and disadvantages, based on the type of fishing to be done. While the smallest canoes are ideal for a single fisherman, usually a 15-footer is considered the smallest practical canoe for two anglers. While canoes all have the same basic shape, there are differences in configuration that should be considered in light of where and how they are to be used. For example, there are very slim canoes, usually 16 to 18 feet long, that are ideal for paddling long distances over large lakes when you want to keep a straight course as easily as possible. For these cases, the regular deep keel (or T-type keel) holds the craft on course best, while the slim shape makes paddling easy. For fishing rivers where you might want to paddle sidewise and change direction frequently, the best choice is a 15-foot canoe with a shallow shoe keel that makes change of direction easy. All fishing canoes should have a low profile at each end, unlike the traditional raised curved prow of the Indian canoe. The result is less wind resistance and easier paddling in a crosswind.

Fishing canoes are best when they have a relatively flat bottom. While the result might be a craft that is a little slower than one with a different bottom, it will result in a more stable platform for casting and fighting and landing fish.

There are also specialized craft similar to canoes that are used in certain parts of the country for fishing, including the pirogue of the Gulf states (particularly Louisiana) and

*A boat designed for use by one angler. Note the extension handle on the outboard control and the gas tank in the forward part of the boat, which helps maintain proper trim and balance.*

*Trolling, such as these two anglers are doing, is easy when a side bracket motor is mounted on a canoe.* Johnson Outboards

*Square stern canoes allow you to mount small outboards for easier fishing.* Evinrude

the kayak, which is popular everywhere. While some anglers do fish from these craft, they are highly specialized craft that require keeping the center of gravity as low as possible, and they are very tippy. As a result, they are best left to those specialists who find a need for them in terms of weight (they are very light and easy to handle) or their shallow draft (which allows them to float easily in very shallow water).

Canoes are also available in square-stern models to accommodate small outboards, although special side-mount brackets are available for outboards on regular canoes.

# RUNABOUT

This catchall term refers to boats of about 15 to 19 feet, usually with a lengthy, covered forward deck, steering console just aft of the deck, and several stern seats. Power is usually outboard, although some inboard-outboards can be found. As fast, comfortable, small boats to run around a lake, water-ski behind, and have family outings with, they are great, but they lack a lot for fishing.

*Note the padded gunnel on this fishing craft to make it easier for standing anglers to brace themselves when fighting fish in rough weather.* Evinrude

First, while the hull design and shape is fine for fishing, the closed forward deck cuts off a lot of fishing room, even if it does provide storage beneath. Second, the seats, which are designed to make the craft comfortable, are constantly in the way for serious fishing of any type. Third, they usually lack rod racks, deck space for tackle boxes, room for ice chests, space for landing nets to be kept at the ready. For an occasional trip they are better than nothing, but should not be considered by the serious fisherman. For serious fishing, a similar hull shape and length, either in a open boat, center console, bow rider or open cuddy-cabin craft would be a wiser choice.

## BOW RIDER

These boats are similar to the runabout, except that they have a wide bow utilizing the cathedral or trihull design, and the bow area is open. Usually the center of the windshield at the console swings out like a door for passage between the stern of the boat and the bow. Since the bow of any boat is rocky at best when running, the open bow portion is best reserved for use after the engine is shut down. Bow riders offer more room than runabouts for fishing, and the open space can provide room for tackle and ice chests while separating two anglers to markedly reduce the possibility of casting accidents.

Unfortunately, most of the bow riders are designed strictly for family fun, boating, exploring, waterskiing, and so on. As a result, extensive seats and plush upholstery in the bow along with bow rails, cleats, lights, and anchor-storage space make these areas less than conducive to serious fishing.

*This larger 20-foot fiberglass Mako with twin outboards, center console, and bow rail is a popular inshore saltwater boat.* Johnson Outboards

*A high-sided outboard makes fishing in rough water pleasant and safe.* Johnson Outboards

## CUDDY-CABIN BOATS

We'll list these boats as those with a small, almost tiny, forward cabin at the bow for storage and sometimes a head. The console is thus much farther forward in the boat than on a runabout, while the rear of the boat is open, uncluttered, and ideal for fishing. A friend of ours has such a boat in a 21-foot model that provides almost unlimited space for two or three anglers, ample storage space for emergency equipment, boating and fishing equipment, and ample room on the sides for rod racks, gaffs, nets, and so on. The hull design is a deep v for good planing, good handling in rough water, and a smooth, comfortable ride in all but the worst weather.

Many boat companies specializing in large craft make such boats, and most models are designed for multipurpose use, including fishing, exploring, scuba diving, swimming, camping, and waterskiing. How they are used is often determined by the purchaser, who can lay out the deck area for his particular sport. The distinct advantage is that such a boat allows fighting fish from almost any angle around the boat's perimeter without crawling over seats, engines, or out on forward decks, while tackle boxes, ice chests, and other necessary equipment can be placed at the stern, under the forward pedestal seats, along the gunwale, or in deck compartments. These craft are ideal for light-tackle fishing, rigging with downriggers, or fitting with outriggers.

*A large sportfisherman with flying bridge and cuddy cabin; the open cockpit permits easy fishing.* Johnson Outboards

*A short tuna tower on a small boat will make it possible to spot top-water feeding activity in this small offshore sportfisherman.* Johnson Outboards

# CENTER-CONSOLE BOATS

These boats have a full walk-around deck, forward and rear casting platforms, and a center console from which the boat is run. They were designed in Florida for light-tackle and flats fishing, where a semi-v hull was required with shallow draft to run the flats and to allow anglers to cast to sighted fish and to fight the fish effectively once hooked.

Most are of fiberglass, although occasionally you find one of wood or aluminum. In size they range from 16 to 23 feet with a wide beam for stability. Some, for example, have wide, walk-around gunwales.

Since many of these boats are designed for a high percentage of time spent fly-fishing, extra care is often taken to make sure that there are ample flush-deck or casting-platform storage compartments and a clean, uncluttered deck and fishing area that will not catch fly lines when coiled on the deck.

## BASS BOATS

These boats evolved from the emphasis on bass fishing by the Bass Anglers Sportsman Society and the tournament fishing that resulted from increased interest in the freshwater bass as a prime gamefish.

Most bass boats have a trihedral or cathedral hull, are 15 to 19 feet long (most are 16 to 17 feet), of fiberglass construction, and fitted with high-horsepower outboards. The purpose of these boats is to provide the maximum in efficiency and comfort for the serious bass angler. As a result, they are fitted with a small side console for running the boat, comfortable fore and aft pedestal seats mounted on high platforms that double for storage or to hold fuel. Often special compartments are built into the sides of the boat to hold completely assembled casting and spinning outfits up to seven feet long.

*A weed guard placed over an electric motor propellor makes fishing in weedy waters possible.*

The wide bow allowed by the hull design gives extra stability when fishing from the bow along with an easy way to mount a foot-operated electric motor for fishing a shoreline or maintaining position against wind or current. Usually the decks are covered with indoor-outdoor carpeting or an artificial turf. Other features include aerated live-bait wells, aerated fish wells, provision for two boat batteries (one to start the engine, the second for the multitude of electronics and other 12-volt accessories often favored by bass fishermen).

The advantage of these boats for those who are serious about the single sport of lake and reservoir bass fishing is that they include everything that might possibly be needed

*Good interior layout is shown in this Grumman 15' 1" bass boat with recessed gear compartments under the fishing platform.*

by the large-water bass angler. However, they always impress us as being like the socket-wrench sets that come in a case, the inside of which is custom molded for the sockets, handles, and other accessories sold in the kit—try to add a socket handle or screwdriver not included in the set but necessary when you work on special projects, and it won't fit. With bass boats, particularly the large deluxe models, you sometimes barely have room to walk around the narrow deck portion left between the rear and forward seat platforms, much less be able to find a spot for a tackle box. Carefully consider your needs and fishing interests before buying a boat such as this that might be complete but also somewhat restrictive as to the type of fishing that you can do from it.

Bass boats are ideal for fishing large water for bass and other inland species, covering lots of water in a hurry to hit the hot spots of the lake, but they aren't good for shallow rivers or fishing large, open waters where more than a slight chop might occur. Some writers have suggested these boats for saltwater fishing provided that they are fished with care and modified for saltwater needs, but it is unusual to see these boats put to this use.

## LARGE OPEN BOATS

These are like the small, v-bottomed aluminum craft discussed previously, except they are larger, from 16 to 25 feet in length. Most companies make them in fiberglass, aluminum, or wood. Usually they are completely open, but often have the option of seats (bench or pedestal) and a small forward storage locker. They are fitted with a side or forward console and have provision for live-fish wells, outriggers, downriggers, rod racks along the spacious sides, and a Bimini or other top or protection from the sun and weather.

*A typical bass boat with high-performance hull, high-horsepower outboard, bow-mount electric motor and pedestal seats.* Johnson Outboards

Most are run with high-horsepower outboards. Some are inboard-outboard models or have inboard engines, particularly in the larger sizes. The advantage of this type of boat is that they often have high sides, and thus can take heavy water easily while giving the angler something to support his thighs against while fighting a fish during a boat-rocking chop. Depending upon how they are fitted, they can allow many different types of angling—from heavy freshwater fishing to trolling deep for Great Lakes salmon to inlet fishing in salt water to long-distance offshore fishing for big-game species on light tackle.

## HULL TYPES

Fishermen may choose boats with various hull types depending upon their angling requirements. Basically, hulls can be broken down into two types: displacement and planing. Displacement hulls are those in which the hull displaces that weight of water equal to the weight of the boat and its contents. Under the power normally used with the boat, the boat will continue to displace water even when moving. Examples of craft with displacement hulls would be the canoe and the row boat. Planing hulls are those designed to lift a boat quickly so that under power it rides on the top of the water, or planes, rather than pushing the water aside to make progress as does a displacement hull.

Planing hulls at rest displace water in the same way that displacement hulls do. The difference is that the planing hull usually has a deep-v or semi-v or one of the trihedral or cathedral hulls ending in a flat bottom toward the stern to jump the boat up on plane with minimum power. Boats vary in their capacity to jump on plane, but with the high-horsepower engines available today (along with the well-designed hulls), planing is easily accomplished. Virtually any fishing craft can be a planing hull with the application of enough power, and a john boat or pram can be placed on plane with enough horsepower behind it.

Planing is desirable in the larger boats, since it takes far less effort from the engine (and less fuel consumption) to move a boat over the top of the water than it does to move the boat through the water. As a result, planing allows the angler to get to a favorite fishing spot quicker, with less effort, and on less gas than the slower displacement method.

Boat hulls also fit into more specific types, each with its advantages and disadvantages.

**Flat.** This is the type found in prams or small wooden rowboats. It has the advantages

*Aluminum side storage compartments for rods and side console make this pointed bow fishing craft easy to use and safe in heavy water.* Johnson Outboards

of fair stability in protected water, low cost, and maximum space in the boat for the length of the craft. Usually, flat-bottomed boats are made of aluminum, such as the ubiquitous john boat, although some wooden craft are both homemade and commercially offered. Since fiberglass lends itself best to complex molding, it is rarely used for these simple craft.

**Round bottom.** This type of bottom with a pointed prow can be found in a number of small aluminum, fiberglass, and molded-plywood runabouts and in all open boats. It is more seaworthy and stable in rough water and costs more to make than flat-bottomed hulls, but it offers almost the same space as the john boat, with the exception of the lost space in the bow.

**Deep v.** These craft are designed for heavy, rough water. The sharply cleaving bow makes easy progress through rough water and high seas while providing the maximum comfort to the passengers. Often these boats are combined with a flat, planing, stern section of hull and they plane easily. At rest, they often rock far more than a semi-v or round-bottomed craft.

**Semi-v.** These boats have less of a v to the hull than the deep-v hulls, yet they provide much of the same comfort and advantages of the deep v while making it even easier to get up on plane in flat- and shallow-water situations. Florida-originated flats boats, some runabouts, and utility craft are often made with this hull design. Also, they will rock less at rest for more comfortable fishing.

**Trihedral hull.** This hull design originated from the idea of using three hulls joined together to allow a more comfortable ride and to markedly increase the space in the bow of the boat. From the front, one of these hulls looks like two arches. The theory is that the v of each of the three "bows" breaks up the water as it cleves through it, and the hull rides for the most part on the spray caught between the outside and center-hull v's, dampening any shock. They have their enthusiastic supporters and also some detractors. Those who like them find them comfortable, with maximum space, and ideally suited for a number of craft, including runabouts, bow riders, flats boats, and some center consoles. We've found them to be hard riding with more spray due to the hull design and low bow than from a deep-v hull of same length.

**Cathedral.** This hull type is essentially the same as the trihedral, except that it has only two v's rather than three, yet still has the same spacious bow and, in our opinion, the same disadvantages of spray and hard riding as the trihedral hull has.

## BOAT MATERIALS

Boat hulls are made of a variety of materials, each with advantages and disadvantages for the fisherman.

**Wood.** Inexpensive and easy to work with or modify for the home craftsman, wood lends itself readily to straight-sided construction of boats such as john boats. Wood does require maintenance on a regular basis and can leak at the seams if not carefully caulked. Lap-strake boats, traditionally of wood (although this design in the hull is now also made with fiberglass molds), has the advantage in the water of helping to correct side-to-side rocking while the strips of wood also help throw the spray down when running in heavy seas.

**Aluminum.** Aluminum varies widely in type and in the various alloys that make it such a useful product for manufacturing. For most boats, hard-tempered marine aluminum is used in thicknesses ranging from .039 up through .050 and .064 inches for john boats and runabouts to .072 and .080 inches for large craft (up to about 25 feet). Larger sport-fishing offshore hulls use aluminum in thicker sheets.

Aluminum must be reinforced with ribs and stringers, usually made of the same aluminum folded in u-channel strips to add strength to the hull structure and allow it to flex but resist serious bending or denting.

The advantages of aluminum are that it is lightweight, easy to handle when out of the water, and it can be painted any color desired. It also requires no maintenance when unpainted, and takes the rocks and slight dents of fishing rocky areas and rivers that would seriously mar fiberglass or wood. The only disadvantage is that the aluminum tends to "grab" rocks whereas fiberglass or some of the plastics will slide off rocks.

**Fiberglass.** Fiberglass boats begin with a carefully designed mold in which a gel coat and the color of the craft is sprayed, and then alternative layers of fiberglass cloth and resin are built up in predetermined fashion for the maximum strength and rigidity required for the boat, its expected use, and the hull design. Because of the way in which the soft cloth can be cut and placed in the mold, fiberglass is often used for boats with complex hull designs such as the trihedral, cathedral, deep v, and semi-v. The cloth does not provide complete strength, and boat designers still use stringers of fiberglass-coated wood for reinforcing the longitudinal stability of the boat, and ribs or cross pieces of wood to strengthen the sides and to resist twisting or bending.

The best boats will be those in which the fiberglass cloth is carefully layed up by hand and with no use or minimal use of chopped fiberglass blown from a gun. The latter is used only as a filler on the best boats, but is used extensively on some low-cost fiberglass boats. Because the fiberglass is chopped into relatively short lengths in this process, it cannot be as strong as the warp and weave of fiberglass cloth laid intact into a boat hull. You can't usually see the inside of a hull to check for this, or when chopped fiberglass is a filler, to check how much was used. The best check is to rely on a good name of a manufacturer or to check the descriptive literature carefully when buying a boat.

The quality, beauty, and color of the gel coat of the fiberglass boat is far superior in the opinion of most anglers to that of wooden, aluminum, or plastic craft. However, while you can repaint a wooden craft or bang out a dent in aluminum, once you damage the gel coat of the fiberglass, it is difficult if not impossible for the angler to repair. It can be done, but should be done by a qualified repairman in a marina or boat-repair facility.

A disadvantage in use is that the fiberglass hulls scar easily if used on a rocky river. Any touch of a rock or pebble while floating downstream is sure to leave a long, deep scratch in the hull that can't be easily removed. The fiberglass hulls are excellent for deep water where there are no obstructions, but avoid them for rocky or stump-filled waters unless you are willing to suffer the consequences.

**Plastic hulls.** Many boats and canoes today are made with plastics such as ABS or with laminates of plastic and fiberglass. Most of these plastics have good impact resistance in comparison to aluminum (which will dent) or fiberglass (which will shatter or crack from a hard blow). Some of the laminates have fiberglass or other shiny plastics on the outer surface, which have poor abrasion resistance, while other laminates have good resistance to scratches and scrapes.

# 10
# Installing and Using Boat Instruments and Accessories

All the boat instruments available make it easier to operate boats safely and surely. Many of the instruments contribute to your fishing success. However, it is important to install them correctly so they do the job they are designed to do.

Before installing any instrument, read the instructions carefully. Most of them you can install yourself, but some you might want to leave for your marine dealer to install. You can also check with your dealer for tips and suggestions on proper installation and operation. The old carpenter's adage, "measure twice and saw once," is applicable here—check to make sure that you understand what has to be done before picking up the first tool. If instructions aren't carefully followed, your instrument can give incorrect readings.

Before mounting, lay out your instrument dials for the best arrangement if you are planning to add more than one. Check under the dash for clearance when you drill. If there are a lot of wires from other installed instruments, use a blocking sheet of thin plywood to prevent the drill from chewing up wires when you drill through. Or, where possible, remove the dashboard completely so that you can work on the installation holes in your workshop. Most holes can be completed with a hole saw, or in the case of very large instrument dials, with a sabre saw following an outline after drilling a starting hole for the saw.

Compasses are sensitive to steel and should be mounted as far as possible from any large steel fittings. Since most modern boats are manufactured of fiberglass, wood, or aluminum, this is usually no problem. However, check your boat's steering wheel, since the plastic-rim wheels are often molded over a steel core, which would radically affect readings of a compass mounted near the wheel.

The pickup tubes of speedometers are very sensitive and can be affected by variations in water pressure or flow along the bottom of the boat. Strips molded into boat bottoms and propellers can affect speedometer readings.

Also, the principle of capillary attraction can affect electrical wiring, and the small strands in each insulation covering can act as a candle wick. If one is placed in water or where it will receive constant spray, it can draw water slowly up into the wiring until it reaches the instrument to which it is connected.

There are a number of small additions that any angler can make to improve his boat for fishing. Boating and angling magazines frequently carry a number of tips and hints that should be considered for application to your boat and fishing. Boats vary so much in

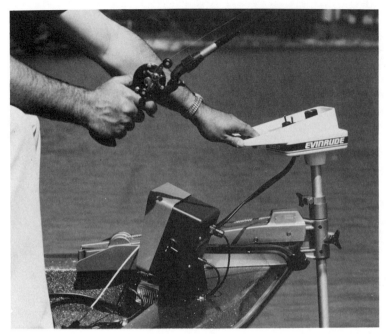

*Accessories included on most modern bass boats are electric motors, depth finders mounted on the bow, and recessed deck lights (located in photo beneath depth finder).* Evinrude

*Electric motors like this one can be raised when running, and easily dropped back into place. A foot control leaves the angler's hands free for fishing.* Johnson Outboards

Charts are an important and inexpensive investment for any serious boat fisherman. This chart of the Louisiana coastline shows compass readings and distances to various reefs, wrecks, and oil rigs, where fishing is excellent.

Two views of a well-organized offshore sport-fishing boat complete with spare (trolling) engine, Bimini top, out-riggers, depth finder, radios, adequate compass, and other boating requirements.

construction and interior layout that detailing specifics here is impossible, but some of the following tips might help.

## NOISE ABATEMENT

In the past, anglers used to speak only in whispers while fishing, thinking that the fish can hear. They can, but you can yell your head off above water and they won't hear a thing. However, scrape a tackle box along an aluminum bottom, knock a gunwale with an oar, or drop an anchor into a locker, and nearby fish will hear it. Noise is particularly a problem while fishing shallow water where the fish are already skittish or for those species that are known to be normally wary. Some suggestions for curing the noise problem are:

- Indoor-outdoor carpeting on the deck and casting platform of your boat. Instead of this, you might obtain small squares of sample carpeting used by rug stores and salesmen; every time that they change a brand or style, all the samples are of no value to them, but the samples are seamed and bound and just the right size to place under tackle boxes, ice chests, in anchor storage areas, or to serve as knee pads for canoe angling.
- Use a rubber mat under your six-gallon gasoline can to avoid noise and also to prevent the hard, steel gas can from damaging fiberglass or aluminum hulls.

    The heavy rubber mats sold in most hardware and variety stores that are designed for use on stand-up jobs are best, although you can get regular mats designed for this purpose from marine stores. Also, soft rubber lips that fit directly onto the edge of the gas can are available, along with permanent clips that hold the can in place by means of brackets and a strap.
- Fasten split-rubber or plastic tubing over the gunwales where you will paddle to prevent noise from knocks against the gunwale by the paddle. You'll need three-foot-long tubing on each gunwale, both fore and aft (four pieces in all). The slip-on tubing can be easily taken off if you use your canoe for other water activities. Regular molded rub rails are also available from some manufacturers and are designed to fit the configuration of their canoe gunwales.

## SAFETY ACCESSORIES

Safety is paramount in a boat. Slipping and falling is frequently the cause of accidents in a boat (as opposed to a boating accident caused by rough seas or poor boating procedure). Boats are usually wet, and sometimes slimy from fish. One way to avoid slipping is to keep boat decks as dry as possible as well as insisting that fellow anglers wear the right type of deck shoe for your fishing. For summer, deck shoes are best, while for winter and cold weather similar soft, gripping-sole boots are best.

To otherwise reduce slipping onboard you can add lightweight plywood floors to the forward part of v-bottomed boats to allow for more comfortable and safer walking. Most v-bottoms have sharply sloping sides that can be very unsafe when wet or when wearing leather-soled shoes. Use a cardboard template to measure the size for the plywood, and reinforce underneath if necessary with one-by-one- or one-by-two-inch stringers. If possible, make the plywood a size and shape that will fit between the bow and seats or other rib supports so that it easily stays in place without extra fasteners and can be removed for storage or cleaning.

Also, you can add self-adhesive safety strips for better footing wherever necessary. The safety strips, similar to the nonskid strips made for bathtubs and showers, are sold in packets or by the foot in several widths. Place it on deck areas where you will walk or stand while fishing, such as the forward part of a john boat with a sloping, square bow, the bottom of canoes, the wide gunwales where you step into larger boats from a dock, or

*Non-skid strips can prevent nasty spills.*

the forward deck of any decked boat for better footing while lowering or raising an anchor. There is also a spray-on nonskid coating that accomplishes the same thing.

In larger boats, grab rails can be added to the console, gunwale, around the windshield, or any spot where a fisherman will reach or want to reach when a boat hits some rough water. Grab rails accomplish two things: they prevent injury to passengers by providing a firm support when needed, and they prevent damage to boat fittings by passengers grabbing instruments, windshields, and other fittings in an emergency.

## KEEPING THE BOAT DRY

Keeping your boat dry can be easily accomplished by a number of methods. First, all boats, with the exception of small boats and canoes, have drain plugs. Usually drain plugs are designed so that they can be removed while running to drain the boat of excess water. To prevent the possibility, however slim that it might be, of losing the drain plug overboard, use a short length of nylon cord to tie the plug to a rib, transom support, or other part of the boat structure.

Larger, double-hulled fiberglass boats often have a self-draining hull in which a drain hole or holes are above the water line but below the deck level. Thus, any water coming aboard in the form of spray, rain, or so on will flow out of the drain holes either while running or at rest. However, some of these boats do not have adequate one-way exterior flaps on them to prevent the water from sloshing in through the drain holes when at rest, in heavy seas, or when backing down. The result can be a lot of water on the deck, which results in sloppy and unsafe fishing. One solution is to get an exterior drain plug made in the form of a soft rubber ball strung on a chain. In use, the chain is attached to the two sides of the drain hole, with some slack in the chain, so that the ball will float out of the way when water is draining from the boat, but will plug the drain hole from external water pressure.

Use bailers such as a regular commercial bailer, a capped one-gallon plastic bleach bottle, milk carton with the end cut off, or a sponge. Use the bailer for large amounts of water and the sponge to clean up afterwards, to get the last drop of spillage, or to clean up after landing fish.

## CUDDY-LOCKER CONSTRUCTION

One way to provide for additional storage on an open, small to medium-size boat is to build a cuddy locker in the open bow. While some boats come with a cuddy locker, most do not. Simplest construction is with marine plywood, using three-eighths-inch for the top bulkhead and a doubled layer of the same for the floor if you plan to build a floor in.

When building a cuddy locker, be sure to allow for ample space for knee room forward of the front seat. Where possible, use cardboard templates to lay out the parts for the locker.

Be sure to plan for ventilation louvers in the cuddy to prevent fungus or rot, and to plan for a spray rail directly above the door in the bulkhead that opens into the cuddy locker. Before beginning, consider clearance for the door and whether it should hinge from the right, left, top, or bottom. Generally, side or bottom hinging is best. Be sure to use marine caulking around all edges of the locker as you proceed with the construction.

Use stainless steel or brass fasteners and hinging throughout to avoid rust or corrosion. When complete, sand and paint with marine paint.

Such a locker will not detract from the usable space in the boat. It will provide up to several cubic feet of dry storage space for seldom-used but important items, such as flares, emergency flag, flashlight, first-aid kit, life jackets. It also provides space for those items that you want to keep handy at all times, such as foul-weather gear, anchor, rope, and dock lines.

## OTHER STORAGE TIPS

Other ways to increase additional storage space on small boats is to make wooden boxes that will fit along the gunwale between seats, on top of, in front of, or behind a seat. Boxes are easy to make with light one-quarter- to three-eighths-inch plywood, provided

*A cuddy locker built into a bow of an open fishing boat.*

that corner braces are used to strengthen the box or dovetail construction is used with waterproof glues. If you do plan to make your own boxes, measure the space to be used carefully, and be sure that you will still have enough room to move around after the boxes are in place. It is best to think of additional storage boxes in the bow, stern, or along the sides of the boat to allow for walking and fishing room amidships.

When you plan the boxes, be sure to plan for hinged, overhanging lids to protect the contents from water damage. Also, since some water will probably seep in anyway, drill small drain holes in the bottom of each storage box to allow any water to run out. Where possible, use all aluminum or stainless steel for hardware (the latter is best for saltwater use).

Such boxes can be permanently bolted into place, or they can be arranged for easy removal with shock cord, cleats, and latches to hold them in place against the side of a hull. You can also use a hole-and-doweling system to allow removal when desired.

Storage racks and bins sold in houseware departments and designed for kitchen storage often can be easily adapted to boat use. Racks to fit on the cabinet doors to hold cleaners, paper bags, cleaning utensils, and so on can be used for holding such items as maps, charts, and binoculars. These racks can be fitted to consoles, under dashboards, in cabins, in cuddy cabins, or under deck compartments. Golf tubes or PVC pipe can be mounted in out-of-the-way places to store rolled-up charts. Pull-out plastic drawers can also be mounted in boats, but should be fixed with a stop to prevent the drawer from sliding out when in rough water.

## BOAT COVERS

Covers offer many advantages to boat owners. First, they hide from view any loose possessions that you carry in your boat. While a boat cover obviously is not theft proof and won't take the place of locks or other protective measures, it does keep your possessions out of sight. Second, a boat cover used on a trailed boat will keep hard rain off the boat interior and protect the boat from any flying debris or other highway hazards. Some anglers use their boat covers when trailing boats. This is fine, and will help to cut wind resistance and reduce fuel consumption provided that the boat cover fits tightly and

*Chuck Edghill demonstrates the plywood locker built into C.B.P.'s john boat. The recessed area forward of the locker is left to store the anchor line.*

*A lidded trash can pro-vides waterproof storage for fishing accessories.*

does not flap in the wind. Lacking this, you are better off using your boat cover only for boat storage, removing it before traveling. Third, a boat cover when your trailed or moored boat is stored will protect the contents from the sun and prevent or reduce fading, cracking, and crazing of boat parts and materials.

The best covers are those that will fit the boat and engine exactly and go on easily and come off easily. Covers come in a wide variety of styles, colors, and materials, but the best are probably those of water-repellent cotton. They will shed rain yet still breathe so that water won't condense on the underside and cause more trouble than would be caused by a hard rain on an uncovered boat.

## ANCHORS

Anchors vary widely in type and size and must be chosen for the size of the boat, the type of boat, and most importantly, the type of water and bottom over which you will be fishing. For fishing from boats of 14 feet or smaller, almost any type of anchor will often work well in the smallest size available. For larger boats check the owner's manual or an anchor-manufacturer's chart for the proper size and type of anchor suitable for the bottom frequented. Types of anchors are described below.

**Mushroom.** This type of anchor resembles a small mushroom inverted with the eye at the bottom of the mushroom stem. They come in several sizes, but most are small for small inland boats anchoring over a sand, mud, or gravel bottom. While they can be used with a chain, most are tied directly to the anchor line and are designed to dig into the bottom as the line is pulled when the boat comes to rest against the anchor line. Mushroom anchors are not recommended for larger boats or for hard marl bottoms. The rounded lip of the mushroom won't dig into the marl or a hard rock or slate bottom. They are great for small boats with light loads fishing rivers, farm ponds, reservoirs, and inlets.

**Yachtsman.** This is the type of anchor that most people think of as a typical anchor, with the rounded flukes and straight stock at right angles to the flukes to drive them into the bottom. They are sometimes used on larger craft, chocked on the bow ready for use, but because of the space that they require either above or below deck, they are not often used on smaller fishing craft. They do work well on sand, mud, and gravel bottoms, and the 90-degree angle between the flukes and stock helps to turn the anchor so that the flukes immediately begin to dig into the bottom. It should be used with a length of chain to hold the anchor on the bottom and cause the flukes to dig in under stress.

**Danforth.** This type of anchor depends for its holding power upon the broad, flat flukes that begin to dig in once the anchor is lying on the bottom and is pulled by the boat. As a result of aluminum construction, broad flukes, and lack of crosspiece (the broad flukes and a stock extending from them cause it to lie flat on the bottom) it takes little space, is as light an anchor as can be found for its holding power, is easy to handle by any crewman, and is easy to store either in chocks on the deck of a large craft or in an anchor locker of a small craft. Many sizes and several similar styles are available.

**Navy.** This type of anchor combines the lack of stock of the Danforth with weight and relatively wide flukes on a pivotal shaft that allow them to dig in easily on most types of bottom. These anchors are avilable in many sizes and are ideal for small boats. They will hold well on most types of bottoms, including rock when the flukes can catch a crack or crevice. They can also dig into a hard gravel bottom.

**Drag anchor.** One of the best ways of fishing a river or large stream is to drift downstream at a rate that will allow you to cast to all the likely spots within range of the boat. One way to slow your rate of travel and also keep your boat or canoe in a straight line for easier and safer drifting and casting is to use a drag anchor from the bow that is designed to slip along the bottom and allow the boat to drift stern-first with the current or tide.

There are several ways to accomplish this. The easiest is to use a three-to four-foot length of chain with links of an appropriate size to slow the boat yet light enough to keep it from stopping and anchoring completely. Boat types, boat loads, and river currents vary widely, so you will have to use a trial-and-error method to find the right combination for your fishing.

We have used chain-drag anchors for years on our boats and as a rough rule, find that one-quarter- to three-eighths-inch links on a chain of about three feet long works best. If you are concerned about the noise that this might make in some fishing situations as it slinks along a rocky bottom, you can cover the chain with a piece of thin-walled, large-diameter rubber or plastic tubing, punching a hole in the tubing at one end so that the line can be tied to the last link and the tubing at the same time. The result will be relatively quiet both on the bottom and when you store the anchor in the boat. Use a bowline or spliced-loop to attach a nylon or polypropylene rope to the drag chain so that it can be dropped to the right depth and payed out the right distance to slow the boat to the right speed. Depending upon the current, wind, and the water depth, you may need a little rope or a lot. You might find that an anchor-line release catch attached to the bow makes it possible to change the length of rope as needed to adjust for different depths or different current rates that you might encounter in a day's fishing. We fish a lot of very shallow rivers and often find that a short, constant length of rope works fine.

For this, we use a trick to prevent the line from getting tangled with the engine or prop when moving upriver or across river to try another drift. And, while this might seem careless on our part, it becomes easy during a day's fishing to forget that you have an anchor line out the bow and start the engine and cause damage before you realize it. The solution to this on shallow rivers is to use a combination of chain and rope that when tied to the bow eye or bow handle will not allow the end of the chain to reach the engine. That way, if you use a rope of this length, you can still shorten it as required, but not worry about it as you alternately drift and motor to new spots.

While chain-drag anchors are used primarily for inland fishing on rivers, the same technique can be used in saltwater fishing to slow a boat in a tide, for example, while fishing sloughs for flounder, or to drift over an oyster bar for white perch. Obviously, with larger boats and deeper water, heavier and longer lengths of chain will be required along with longer line to create enough drag for the conditions.

**Mule.** The mule is a new design of anchor for small boats, consisting of a lead doorstop-shaped anchor (about eight inches long by three inches wide and two inches high) with an eye bolt at the narrow side of the stop. In use, the anchor, which weighs about 10 pounds, works like a sled or plow to dig into the bottom when it is pulled. It is good as a first anchor for small boats and a second, lightweight, accessory anchor for larger boats for temporary anchoring.

**Homemade anchors.** Many small-boat fishermen fishing protected waters in canoes and 10- to 14-foot boats use small anchors made from a coffee can filled with concrete and fitted with an eye bolt before the concrete hardens. Depending upon the size of the can and the amount of concrete used, such anchors can weigh from several pounds up to 15 pounds or more. In terms of effectiveness, they are very poor in comparison with scientifically designed anchors. In terms of practicality, for small boats and canoes they are very good, but rely solely on the weight of the anchor to hold the bottom. Because of their design, they will usually roll on a gravel bottom and slip on a rock or slate bottom, and thus are poor choices for these conditions regardless of the size of the boat or the weight of the anchor.

Other homemade anchors include sash weights, short lengths (4 inches to 10 inches) of railroad rails, and grapples welded of reinforcing bar.

*Small-boat fishing anchors include* (left to right): *chain drag anchor, rubber-covered chain drag anchor, two types of homemade lead anchors, small navy anchor, mule-type door-stop anchor, and mushroom anchor.*

**Sea anchor.** Unlike other anchors, a sea anchor is used not to hold the bottom and keep the boat in one spot but to hold the bow of the boat into the wind or current and thus reduce the possibility of broaching under high seas. In this sense it is an emergency piece of equipment. It also can be used to slow a drifting boat, or to reduce the amount of movement under sharp, choppy waters, and thus serve as an aid to fishing. Technically, sea anchors are constructed of canvas and wire, funnel shaped with a large opening at one end and a very small opening at the other. A heavy wire lip on the large end holds the sea anchor open, while three or four lines placed evenly around the edge of the lip rim hold the lip toward the seas. A long line running from the bow to the sea anchor absorbs shock and also allows the sea anchor to sink, where it will be most effective. The water pouring into the large opening and out through the small tail of the funnel serves as an effective drag to slow the boat and keep the bow into the seas.

**Emergency sea anchors.** While the above system is best, in an emergency when the sole goal is to keep a dead boat (boat without power or engine) into the seas to keep it from broaching or capsizing, almost anything can be used as a sea anchor. Acceptable substitutes are buckets, tackle boxes, bundles of clothing (don't use clothing that you will need to keep warm until rescued), weighted ice chests, weighted seat cushions (provided that you still have, as required by law, one PFD for each person on board), or anything that will sink and create a drag in the water to slow the boat and head the bow into the sea.

**Chain.** For optimal anchoring and digging in of your anchor, you should have a length of chain shackled between the anchor and the nylon line. Three to six feet is usually ideal, and many marine stores carry ready-made chain lengths sized for the type and size of anchor and length of boat. The chain helps to hold the anchor on the bottom and helps to cause the flukes to start to dig into the bottom as you turn the line around a cleat to pull up the boat.

**Line.** Line, or anchor rope, of nylon, manila, or polypropylene are all used with most anglers preferring nylon. Nylon does not rot or mildew, is easy to handle, is readily available, and has some stretch to it as a shock absorber once the hook is on the bottom. For small boats, use three-eighths-inch line. For large boats, use one-half-inch line or consult your marine dealer.

Most boat manuals and dealers will recommend 100 feet as standard for any anchor line. This is correct, but can be modified for small-boat fishing in shallow and protected waters where much less line will be required. Also, if you fish many different types of water, you might want anchor lines of different lengths. It is not necessary to carry 100 feet of line when you have a small boat and will be anchoring in water no more than five or six feet deep. For our fishing, we use one line of 25 feet for shallow-water rivers, ponds, sloughs, and streams while keeping a coil of 100 feet for those times when fishing deep reservoirs, salt or brackish water, quarries, and so on.

**Chaffing gear.** Chocks for anchor lines are present on most boats larger than about 16 feet. They are designed as guides for anchor line running from the bow cleat. To prevent damage to other parts and fittings of the boat, it is important to use the bow cleat and anchor chocks, which are designed to take the strain of anchoring. However, chocks do cause wear on the anchor line when the boat constantly strains against the anchor. To prevent this wear and early replacement of the line, use some sort of chaffing gear to keep the line from rubbing directly against the chock. Rags, canvas, or any covering can be used, but for continued anchoring, an ideal choice is to keep on board several pieces of old garden hose, car radiator hose, rubber tubing, or flexible polyethylene tubing. Make each piece about 18 inches long and split it lengthwise to fit over the anchor line at the chock. If the chocks are set well back from the gunwale, make chaffing gear long enough to protect the line and boat finish at these points, also.

**Scope.** Scope is the ratio between the length of rope used to the depth of water in which you will be anchoring. Thus, if you are anchoring in 10-foot-deep water and using 50 feet of anchor rope, the scope will be 5:1. This ratio is important for proper holding power of the anchor and most experts recommend a scope of between 5:1 and 8:1. Obviously, conditions will vary, which will require increasing this ratio or allow decreasing it.

Conditions that may allow decreasing the scope include:

- Length of chain between the anchor and the line that will help to hold the anchor down and increase holding power.
- Anchoring in gravel, which once hooked, will hold securely.
- Anchoring on a calm day when the boat will not rock or pitch against the anchor.

Conditions that may require increasing the scope include:

- Anchoring without a chain between the line and anchor, which will reduce the holding power of the anchor.
- Anchoring in a loose bottom of mud, sand, or rotten soil, which will prevent good holding of the anchor.
- Anchoring on a rough day, which will cause the boat to pitch and rock, tending to pull the anchor free.

## ANCHORING TECHNIQUES

On boats up to 14 feet, anchoring can be looked at as a simple operation of positioning upcurrent or upwind of the spot you wish to fish, lowering the anchor hand over hand until it touches bottom, and then paying out a little line to give the rope a slight scope. While boating experts might not like us saying so, practical fishermen know that with a small boat on protected water with a firm (but not rock) bottom, you can get by with a scope ratio of as little as 1½:1 or 2:1.

For larger boats that will require more scope and that are more difficult to maneuver, anchoring is a little more complicated. First, consider the depth that you will be anchoring in by checking your depth finder. Multiply by five for a scope of 5:1 to find out the length of line that you will need (under average conditions) and move the boat slowly uptide, upcurrent, or upwind to a position where you want the anchor to catch. If you err, try to err on the side of going too far, since you can always adjust position by lengthening the anchor rope, provided that it doesn't slip. Also, you need several feet for the anchor to catch.

Next, come to a complete stop and lower the anchor over the side of the boat until it touches bottom. As the anchor touches bottom, begin backing down the boat while you pay out line so that the anchor and chain are positioned properly to take hold. When about half of the line is out, snub the line briefly around a cleat to cause the anchor to rest properly on the bottom. Once you feel the anchor biting the bottom, let out the rest of the line. Tie off the anchor at the bow cleat, place chaffing gear around the line, and position it in a chock.

To raise an anchor, regardless of the size and type of boat, move the boat over the anchor while taking in line and then lift the anchor carefully. Take care when the chain and anchor come out of the water to keep both clear of the side of the boat to prevent damage to the boat finish. Once the anchor is on board, coil the line carefully and store the anchor properly in chocks or an anchor locker to keep the anchor and line ready for use at the next fishing spot.

It is important to anchor safely, out of the way of other boats, not crowded in with other boats (wind and tide shifts will cause boats to swing on anchor, causing problems when two or more boats are anchored in close proximity), and out of the way of shipping routes, channels, busy harbors, and so on.

**Cross-current anchoring.** Sometimes two anchors are necessary or desirable to hold a boat in a certain position for the most effective casting or fishing or, in the case of river

*This cam-type release mounted on the bow gives the angler control of the anchor from any spot in the boat.*

*A deliberately posed photograph of how not to release an anchor. An anchor should be dropped carefully over the side.*

fishing with two or three anglers in a boat, to hold the boat at right angles to the current for downstream fishing for bass, catfish, carp, and other such species.

Cross-current anchoring requires the use of two similar anchors, both capable of holding bottom, and sufficient line to give enough scope to hold the boat in a current. Heavier anchors will often be needed than those needed for regular river anchoring, since the force against a boat crosswise to the current is much greater than against a boat with its bow facing into the current.

It is extremely important in this type of fishing that you use a wide, stable boat capable of holding the anglers and equipment and with a high freeboard as protection against any tipping and shipping water that is pushed up against the hull when anchoring in this manner.

When anchoring, take care that you move carefully in the boat to prevent the gunwale from dipping below the water's surface and capsizing the boat. In all cases, be extremely careful with this type of anchoring, and be ready at any time to slip one of the anchors should conditions dictate. This is particularly important when fishing on rivers below a dam where opening a floodgate will markedly increase the water flow.

Reservoir anglers can use the same double-anchor technique, without the dangers mentioned above, and with lighter anchors, to hold a position against the wind.

## ANCHORING ACCESSORIES

In addition to the chocks that hold anchors at the ready on the forward decks of large sport-fishing boats, there are also useful devices that can be made or purchased to help drop an anchor in a hurry when you are suddenly on good fishing  For example, on the Potomac River near where we live, many anglers fish for smallmouths from 15-foot aluminum canoes. The canoes are ideal because they provide enough interior room for rods, tackle, and a light lunch, they are maneuverable in the quiet pools and fast riffles of the river, and they will slide over the rocks or can be dragged up along the shore without damage to the hull.

Most fishermen along this shallow river use small, lead-filled tin cans for anchors, fitted with a u-bolt at the top to tie in the anchor line. To drop this anchor easily over the side when they have both hands full of a rod connected to a smallmouth, they use a 12-inch length of aluminum strap, half of which is bolted to the stern deck of the canoe, the other half projecting as a hanger for the anchor eye bolt. The anchor is hung over the outside of the craft, and it is easy to knock the anchor over the side with an elbow or hand. This works best for light craft, and can be used for john boats and prams as well as canoes.

Anchor line releases attached to the bow of the boat can allow a one-handed anchor

*A posed picture showing the dangers of cross-current anchoring in fast water. The boat is very close to capsizing due to current pressure.*

line operation, using the same technique of leaving the anchor outside the craft while fishing. We use this technique on our john boats, tying the anchor line directly to the mushroom anchor so that it can be snubbed up close to the bow. Use of chain would prevent this and the anchor would hang down in the water. On larger craft, it might hang free, but then you would risk hitting the hull with the anchor and scratching the finish. The anchor release used in this system is bolted to the bow of the boat so that the forward part of it extends over the water.

In use, the line runs through an eye and under a cam that jams the line. Pulling the line pulls the line from under the cam, slowly releasing it allows the line to go out through the hole. A quick release of the line jams the line under the cam to hold it.

Using this method, you can run with the anchor snubbed to the bow, release it along with any amount of line necessary to hold bottom and then snub the line to hold fast. You can also retrieve the anchor the same way, pulling the anchor up to the bow and out of the water while you move to another fishing spot. We recommend placing the anchor inside the craft for long runs or runs in very choppy water at high speed where the anchor might knock against the boat or create undue strain on the release fastenings.

The Worth Company makes an Anchormate anchor control that consists of a bow mount to hold the anchor on small boats and a reel that can mount to any part of the boat. The reel holds up to 100 feet of three-sixteenths-inch nylon anchor line. By means of a button, the anchor can be released and stopped at any point, while a handle makes it easy to crank up the anchor. Swivel pulleys and line guides (not included in the kit because of the requirements of different boats) allow release or cranking of the anchor from any spot in the boat. A heavy-duty Anchormate II is for larger anchors on larger boats, has capacity for 150 feet of three-sixteenths-inch line, and the bow mount has a pivotal arm that holds the anchor more securely in a horizontal position. Both Anchormates are designed for mushroom anchors.

Similar anchor releases and hoists that are electrically operated are also available, and sometimes are provided as a standard item or as an option for some deluxe bass boats. They have the advantage of not requiring any elbow grease and the push of the appropriate button will put your anchor down or pull it up. Most of these are also designed for the larger mushroom anchors.

# ANCHORLESS ANCHORING METHODS

**Staking out.** Staking out on the flats to fish for bonefish or watch a tarpon channel is an established method of fishing in Florida and involves fishing from a tethered boat, although not anchored with the traditional anchor, chain, and line method. Staking out is possible only in those waters shallow enough for a pole to be stuck into a sandy marsh or mud bottom. It is not possible in rocks or gravel. The best method of getting the pole secured is to stab the bottom with the pointed end and then work it back and forth to force the point into the bottom enough to hold. Once the pole is in the bottom, it is easy to loop the painter or anchor line around the pole and hold it with an overhand knot. This will hold securely for as long as you want to stake out, and yet can be rapidly untied if you hook a tarpon that threatens to run for the horizon and must be chased with the boat.

**Brush anchors.** These are nothing more than spring-loaded clamps designed to clip onto brush along a lake, pond, or river to anchor the boat. Brush anchors are sold by tackle stores and mail-order houses catering to bass fishermen, but you can make your own by attaching spring-loaded woodworker's clamps or spring-loaded lamp clamps to a short line.

**Bridge Anchors.** Anglers fishing under bridges often use an adaptation of the brush anchors to hold their boats to bridge supports, pilings, or ironwork on the underside of a bridge. Some are nothing more than brush anchors, while others are long, thin aluminum tube arms fitted with hooks on the end. Some are attached directly to the boat cleats while others are attached to the boat with short lines. All are homemade and adapted to specific fishing locations.

## BOAT POLES

Boat poles allow easy boat propulsion when the water is shallow enough for their use. Generally, these are waters anywhere from just deep enough to float the craft to perhaps a maximum of 8 to 10 feet. If you are fishing shallow water from a canoe or small pram, you might not need a pole longer than about 6 or 7 feet—just long enough to touch bottom and allow you to lean on it to give the boat a good push. In contrast, some Florida fishermen might use a pole as long as 18 feet to push their heavy, 17- to 21-foot flats boats. In any case, don't get a pole that is longer than your boat, since it will cause storage problems.

The advantages of a boat pole are many. It is easier to grab one pole than two oars to move the boat a short distance. They are usually quieter than oars and make much less water disturbance. It is easy for one angler to handle while the other fishes. They can be easily mounted on the outside of the boat to keep them out of the way and so are far less of a nuisance than paddles or oars and since they are out of the boat, they don't drip water into the boat. Finally, they can be used to stake out a boat.

You can buy a boat pole or make your own. Options include fiberglass poles (which are usually pole-vault poles) that are sold alone or with pole-end attachments. The attachments include a pointed aluminum end for staking out on a flat or next to a channel, and a y-shaped end for pushing along the bottom to move the boat. Both ends are cemented into the hollow pole with epoxy. Some anglers don't like the aluminum fittings, and instead plug one end with a dowel or wood for staking out, and use a cypress

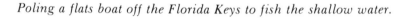

*Poling a flats boat off the Florida Keys to fish the shallow water.*

knee for the y at the other end. Cypress will not rot or decay in water and has adequate strength for this application. Make sure that the pole is dark colored and that any shiny finish is removed to prevent scaring fish.

Large-diameter bamboo with the ends cut at the nodes (the solid separations between the hollow sections), wrapped with cord or fiberglass tape, and epoxied also make good, durable poles. In time they might split, which means that they both sink in the water because they fill with water and that they will pinch your hand while poling. But the price is right if you can find wild bamboo where you live or have a friend in a rug company (rugs are often wrapped on bamboo poles for storage).

Aluminum poles of 1¼- to 1½-inch diameter are also favored by a few anglers, but they are difficult to obtain in lengths over eight feet unless you have access to an aluminum-supply distributor. Lengths up to eight feet are often available at hardware and lumber stores. Fittings can be attached as they are on fiberglass poles.

Straight-grained closet rods in about 1⅜-inch diameter are also ideal for boat poles, but will break down after a couple of seasons of use. Get the length that you need from your lumberyard and make a block-wood shoe for one end. You can paint the pole or liberally and regularly coat it with linseed oil to protect it.

*The circles show forward and rear boat pole brackets on a small john boat.*

*Pop rivets hold this U-shaped aluminum boat pole bracket on C.B.P.'s boat.*

**Boat-pole storage.** Florida anglers and guides use special boat-pole holders to keep the pole ready for instant use by placing it on the outside of the boat, or on the top outside of the gunwale. Either way works well, and both are far superior to letting a loose pole roll around on the inside of the boat—a noisy, dangerous, and inconvenient practice.

Boat-pole holders are readily available, or you can make your own from two short lengths of two-inch diameter PVC, ABS or similar plastic pipe. For the stake end, use a section about 12 inches long and flare it by heating over an open flame (be careful not to set it on fire) and pressing the end over the neck of a soft-drink bottle to widen it.

Use a three- to six-inch length for the other end, cutting a piece off one side so that the pole will snap in place. Fasten the stake end fitting to one end of the boat hull, high up near the gunwale or on a wide gunwale. Place the other fitting with the open side vertical to the poling end of the boat. You can slip the pointed end of the pole into the flared opening of the plastic sleeve and snap the other end into the open side of the pipe. If you have the holders against the side of the boat, the curve of the boat will bend the pole slightly and help to hold it in place.

# 11
# Safe Boating

There are certain conditions and practices that all boating anglers must familiarize themselves with to insure safe boating.

## AVOID OVERLOADING

Many fatal accidents occur when boaters fail to realize the safe weight capacity of their craft and consequently fill the boat with weight that exceeds the safe limitations. All boats have a Boating Industry Association (BIA) plate that indicates the safe load for the boat. This is a maximum load for safe, proper boating on moderate seas. It might have to be adjusted downward as conditions dictate. The maximum load indictaed on the BIA plate includes anglers, equipment, and engine.

## AVOID IMPROPER LOADING

Too much weight on one side of the boat, in the stern, or in the bow can result in unsafe boating. The boat can capsize, be swamped by following seas, or, when bow heavy, plow into seas that will flood it. Proper loading of both equipment and anglers means spreading the weight throughout the boat so that it will rise to meet seas, will not list to one side, and will not be stern heavy. When loading equipment, also consider the weight and position of the engine and any gas tanks.

## RIGHT OF WAY

Many fishermen on open waters never come across other boats close enough or frequently enough to feel that they have to worry about right of way when boating, or about proper passing or meeting procedures. Accidents happen when skippers are suddenly faced with a situation and realize that they do not know the rules for safe operation. United States Coast Guard regulations list specific "rules of the road" for boaters.

Textbooks and handbooks on boating completely cover this subject and before going to sea any boater should consult these or take a course in boating. As a general rule, boats that are in the area from straight off your bow to slightly astern of your starboad side (10 points or 112½ degrees) have the right of way, just as a car on your right has the right of way at an unmarked intersection.

Boats meeting head on usually pass to the port side of each other, such passage marked by one short blast by each boat. Two short blasts mean passage to the starboard side, and must be acknowledged by each boat. Coming from behind and overtaking another boat is acknowledged by each boat with one short blast when passing is to the starboard, and two short blasts when passage is to port. The purpose of the horn blasts is to indicate direction by the passing boat and acknowledgment of the same by the other boat.

*How* not *to load a boat. This posed photograph shows an untied boat drifting away while the angler attempts to carry tackle aboard.*

*You need to know the rules of the road in order to avoid accidents.*

## PFDS

Personal Flotation Devices, as life jackets are now called, are required for each person on board any boat. On small boats, under 16 feet, United States Coast Guard approved boat cushions are allowed for this purpose. On boats between 16 and 26 feet (the maximum size boat covered in this book), one approved vest type is required for each person along with one throwable device, which can be a boat cushion, ring, or similar item.

Some efforts have been made to have boaters wear PFDs at all times, or at least while the boat is moving. Ray Scott, President of the Bass Anglers Sportsman Society (BASS), requires all contestant anglers and press anglers fishing in his BASS-sponsored tournaments to wear a properly secured PFD whenever the boat is in motion. While this may be a long time in becoming law, it is an excellent idea for all anglers, and should be required for children. Small children should be required to wear PFD's at all times. Make sure the PFD is suited to the child's size and age.

The best PFDs to wear over other clothes that allow ample arm room for casting and landing fish are the complete vest type with the zip front, such as those manufactured by Stearns. The yoke- or horseshoe-type are good in that they will hold your head out of the water if knocked unconscious, but they are far more bulky and cumbersome for continued wear.

Make sure that PFDs on your boat are accessible and that all passengers are told of the location. Tragically, most boating fatalities, according to the United States Coast Guard, involve boats carrying PFDs that, if they had been worn or available at the time of the emergency, would have prevented loss of life.

## BOW RIDING

Riding on the bow is one of the most dangerous acts connected with boating, especially when the rider's feet hang over the gunwale. *Never do this or allow it.* It is easy for such a passenger to get knocked from this precarious perch and be seriously maimed or killed by the propeller. It is impossible to stop or turn quickly enough to avoid someone who has fallen from the bow.

## BOARDING BOATS

To avoid injury or serious damage to equipment when boarding a boat, make sure that the boat is docked properly with both bow and stern lines and if necessary a fender to protect the finish of the boat. Never carry equipment with you when you board a boat. Place someone on board the boat so that a person on the dock can pass equipment to the boat.

## STANDING IN A BOAT OR CANOE

Some excellent canoeing manuels show techniques of poling a river while standing in a canoe. For those experienced with canoes, rivers, and poling techniques this is fine, but it is best for anglers to stay seated in canoes and small boats, which keeps the center of gravity as low as possible and maintains a stable fishing platform.

If you wish to stand in a small boat or canoe, first make sure that your partner knows of your intentions. Second, place your feet far enough apart so that you will have good balance when you stand. When you stand up, keep your body in the center of the boat. Do not try to move your feet once standing, especially in a canoe, since it can start the canoe rocking and capsize it as you try to regain a stable position.

## BARE FEET

While bare feet seem synonymous with summer boating, anglers should always wear some kind of footwear to protect against a plug that might fall on the deck, loose hooks, or spines and teeth of fish just landed. In our opinion, you should never fish barefooted.

## ROUGH WATER

Do not boat when the water is too rough for your boat, your load, or for your fishing. You alone will have to decide what is too rough for your boat. A slight riffle or chop would be too rough for a canoe, while a 25-foot, high-freeboard boat might be able to handle five-foot seas with ease. Usually anglers are particularly aware of these conditions, since if it is too rough or windy to sit or stand comfortably, it is too rough to fish effectively. Establish your own limits based on experience and stick to them.

Blowers that work properly are a must for any inboard craft to prevent explosion from gas fumes in the bilge area. A compass should be the best that you can afford if you will be on large lakes, or along the coast and out of sight of land. A compass should have features designed for accurate navigation.

Buy, know how to read, and use charts on all large waters and waters with which you might be unfamiliar. Charts show the bottom depth and contours along with buoys, restricted areas, hazards, wrecks, docking areas, and other such features in much the same way that a good topographical map shows land features for hikers and inland stream and pond anglers. More and more maps or charts of inland lakes and reservoirs are becoming available. Both use standard symbols for various structures, which are always noted in a small key on the map or chart. Use your charts carefully with a compass to be sure of where you wish to go, how to get there, and how to get back to the dock.

## EQUIPMENT REQUIRED BY THE COAST GUARD

*(Note: local and state agencies also have regulations. Be sure to check with all agencies before venturing on the water.)*

| EQUIPMENT | CLASS A BOATS *(less than 16')* | CLASS I BOATS *(from 16' to 26')* |
|---|---|---|
| life-saving devices (PFDs) | one for each person on board | one for each person on board, plus one throwable type |
| sound signaling device | none | one hand, mouth, or power operated, audible for one-half mile |
| fire extinguisher | at least one Coast Guard approved fire extinguisher of two pounds dry chemical, four pounds carbon dioxide or one and one-fourth gallons foam extinguisher | |
| navigation lights | suitable Coast Guard approved navigation lights including one white light visible 360° for two mile and one red port light visible 112.5° and one green starboard light visible 112.5° from dead ahead | |
| visual distress signals | 3 parachute flares OR one electronic distress signal required if on the water between sunset and sunrise only | one orange flag OR three smoke flares required for day use PLUS three parachute flares OR one electronic distress signal required for use between sunset and sunrise OR, IN LIEU OF ABOVE three Mark 13 flares with alternate ends for day and night use |

(Check Coast Guard and state regulations for details on approved devices.)

## WATERSPOUTS

Waterspouts are tornadoes over the water that pick up a funnel of water and often move rapidly over the water before dissipating. As with tornadoes on land, they will destroy anything in their path. The best advice for boaters is to stay away from waterspouts and watch for them constantly during conditions or in areas that produce them. If you see one and it comes toward you, run your boat at right angles to the expected path of the waterspout. Do not try to outrun the waterspout, since you probably can't.

## PROPER POWER

Mississippi boating-accident statistics indicate that most boating fatalities occur with boats under 16 feet long and with more than 75-horsepower engines on the stern. Overpowering can be a major cause of boating accidents since it can lead to too much weight on the stern and the temptation to run full throttle, regardless of the water roughness or how well suited the boat is for the engine or water conditions.

Follow the BIA plate recommendations for the power for your boat and do not exceed it. These recommendations have been determined by the boating industry as the maximum for each boat, based on a number of factors including boat construction and expected usage.

On larger boats there is a case for installing a high-horsepower engine within the range of that recommended for the boat. Tests have shown that often a high-horsepower engine will plane a boat quicker, easier, and allow the boat to carry more equipment and anglers. At the same time, it will often allow running at a lower throttle setting so that fuel consumption is reduced and engine wear lessened compared to a lower-horsepower engine running at a higher throttle setting. Against these plusses you must consider the

*Spare shear and cotter pins can be kept mounted on or next to the engine block, or taped securely to the outboard motor handle.*

extra initial expense of the larger engine and the ability of your boat to carry it safely. Check with your dealer or the manufacturer for their information on this when considering engine size for your fishing boat.

## TWIN ENGINES VERSUS SINGLE ENGINES

One engine is standard for most boating situations, and one engine works well for inshore coastal and freshwater fishing on small lakes. For larger waters, two identical engines have an added measure of safety. Although they will add to the initial cost and the drag of the second propeller and skeg will cut some speed and increase gas consumption, if one engine breaks down you still have the second to allow you to continue fishing, trolling, and ultimately to get home.

Similarly, some anglers use a single large engine, center mounted, for running to the fishing grounds, with a second smaller engine mounted on the side of the transom that is better suited for trolling speeds and will still serve as an emergency engine should the main source of power breakdown. Some outboard-boat manufacturers offer a choice of a narrow- or wide-cut-out transom for the engine based on whether you will use a single engine or twin engines.

## KILL SWITCHES

Ray Scott, president and founder of the Bass Anglers Sportsman Society (BASS), has constantly stressed fishing safety in BASS-sponsored fishing tournaments and among the 400,000 members of this ten-year-old organization. One of the devices that he insists on for all tournament boats is a kill switch that stops the outboard engine should the operator be thrown overboard or thrown away from the controls while running the boat. The kill switch, offered as an option on many boat controls or available separately from a number of boating-supply companies, consists of a pull-out switch that disconnects the electrical circuitry of the engine to stop it. The pull-out switch is connected to a lanyard that is attached to the operator's clothing or wrist while running the boat.

Several efforts have been made to have them introduced as a required item on boats under United States Coast Guard or state regulations, but so far these have failed. They are a good, inexpensive safety device for any angler to install, especially when running in rough or stump-strewn waters or when fishing with children who may not be able to handle a boat in such an emergency.

## REFUELING

Both the conservation of increasingly expensive fuel and the safety mandated when handling gasoline make refueling extremely important on all boats.

First, don't smoke or allow anyone near the refueling operation who is smoking. If your boat is outboard powered and has portable fuel tanks, remove the tanks from the boat and fill them on the dock or ground. This way, if there is any vapor or spillage, it can't get into the boat's bilge area.

Once you refuel the tanks, wipe them clean of any spillage, cap them securely, and wait a few minutes for any vapor to dissipate. Then replace the tanks in the boat and secure them against shifting around.

If you have built-in fuel tanks, follow the boat- or engine-manufacturer's instructions for refueling. This involves shutting down all engines, turning off all appliances, opening all doors and ports, turning on blowers, opening removable floor boards or storage tanks to prevent the build-up of fuel vapor.

Refueling for two-cycle outboards also involves proper mixing of the gas and oil. Agitation is a must to mix properly the oil and gas to prevent erratic running or the possibility of mechanical damage. Most experts recommend that you add oil while pumping gas or, as a second choice, add some gas to the tank, then add the oil necessary for a full tank, and top off the tank with gas. Small, portable, six-gallon tanks can be hand agitated in addition. Large or built-in tanks can't be hand agitated, but you can help by fueling your trailed boat immediately after removing it from the water and before heading home, or you can do the same near home at the beginning of the trip. The road shock and vibration will mix the fuel as you travel.

With portable tanks, make sure that you have enough slack in the fuel line for the motor to tilt and turn completely while running and make sure that the fuel-line connector is securely attached to the motor and/or tank connection.

Use only gasoline recommended by the manufacturer or dealer. The energy crisis has brought and will undoubtedly continue to bring about changes in various fuel formulas for both leaded and unleaded gas. Some additives can damage outboard engines.

## EXTRA FUEL

The six-gallon standard tank sold with most small outboards is generally sufficient to run most small boats all day, and then some. Boats requiring larger outboards generally have built-in tanks sufficient for the size and fishing capability of the hull and interior design. Occasionally, however, you might run into a situation in which you want the

*The dangers of fuel are amply illustrated in this boat burning beyond salvage.*

extra insurance of more fuel. Overnight trips, extra-long runs to the fishing grounds, prolonged trolling, extra-heavy seas that make for more running time, and loads of anglers or equipment heavier than you usually carry are all circumstances that might require carrying more fuel than normal.

The best and easiest way to cope with this is to carry along a spare six-gallon tank. If possible, lash it down so that it won't bounce around.

If you plan to use more fuel than normal for an extended period, you might want to consider an additional built-in tank. Built-in tank additions are easy to fit, provided that you carefully follow the manufacturer's instructions as to placement and installation. Also, be sure to get the type of tank that is best for your boat. A 20-gallon tank, for example, might come in several shapes, depending upon whether it is to be placed under a center console, under a seat, or alongside the hull and under an overhanging gunwale. If you have only occasional use of extra gas in a larger boat, consider the lash-down brackets and fittings that will allow you to secure properly a portable six-gallon tank when required and remove it when not needed.

For permanent built-in, lash-down, or even temporary placement, carefully consider tank position in the boat. Most experts suggest avoiding placement in the bow or forward part of the boat, since the pitching and pounding will strain both a full tank and its fastenings. Transom placement might make a boat aft heavy—which makes it difficult to get up on a plane or may make it ride at an uncomfortable bow-high attitude. Also, use of gasoline from a tank in either position will change the boat's weight and balance, requiring constant adjustment of the propeller angle, occupants' positions or trim-tab use to keep the boat running in the proper attitude. Amidships is about right for most tank placement to lessen the effect of weight changes as you use the gas, and to provide for the most protected spot on the boat for secure fastening of permanent tanks.

## WATER IN GAS TANKS

Water in permanent or portable gas tanks can be a problem at any time of the year, but particularly at the beginning of the season after the boat has been stored for a long time. Water can enter the gas tanks when you're filling the tanks during a rain; it can enter during periods when excessive spray is coming on board while running in rough seas; and it can result from condensation of water in empty or nearly empty tanks. This latter problem is particularly prevalent in warm and hot climates, and most experienced boaters will refuel at the end of each trip to prevent such condensation.

Water in tanks can cause engine troubles that can range from minor problems while running to a stopped engine, ruined trip, and visit to a repair shop. Water in a tank can also cause corrosion on the inside of the tank, leading to more problems and the possibility of leaking later on.

In addition to the condensation caused by empty or nearly empty tanks, gas in nearly empty tanks will vaporize and mix with the air in the tank to form a violently explosive mixture. A full tank will not explode. Even though the gas in the tank might burn in the event of a fire, it won't blow up from a minor spark or flame.

To avoid water in your tanks, check your fuel filter several times during the season, and especially at the end of the season. If water begins to get in the filter, indicating that there is a lot of water in the tank, remove the water. If you have portable tanks, remove them and drain out all the gas or position the tank to siphon or pump out the water (water is heavier than gas) at the lowest corner. If the tanks are built into the boat, try to position the boat at an angle (in the water or on a trailer on a slope or hill) to make the water collect at a low point in the tank. Then, manually pump or siphon the water out.

For any remaining water that might be in the tank or in the gas, it is usually all right to use one of the water-removing products sold in automotive stores for eliminating water from automobile gas tanks. These products sink to the bottom of a tank and mix with residual water, which in turn will mix with the gasoline and enable the water to be burned off harmlessly as you run the engine. If you have a continuing water problem, consider using such products several times during the season, since each can of the product will remove only a small amount of water. Also, if there is any question as to the affect of the product on your engine, check with your marine dealer, outboard-repair service, or with your owner's manual.

## TIPS FOR FUEL CONSERVATION WHILE BOATING

The National Marine Manufacturers Association has a series of tips to help boaters get the most from their fuel, regardless of the type of boat or the way in which it is used.

- Throttle back after reaching a plane with a planing hull. By cutting back speed by 25 percent, you can save as much as 50 percent of your fuel.
- Make sure that the boat's hull is kept free of marine growth to prevent drag. Algae, for example, on inland boats can reduce speed by as much as 25 percent and increase fuel consumption by 25 percent.
- Check the engine performance for correct idle and choke adjustments, clean spark plugs, and make sure the propeller is the proper pitch and size. Also check propellers for dents and nicks that will affect boat performance, engine wear, and safety.
- At sea, take advantage of the tides, currents, and winds to get the most out of your fuel and running time.

# 12
# Transporting Boats

There are two basic ways in which anglers can transport their fishing boats to the launching spot: car topping and trailing. With either method, there are some basic procedures to observe for safe and easy transport of fishing boats.

## CAR TOPPING

One of the easiest ways for anglers to transport a boat is to car top a light boat or canoe of up to about 150 pounds or whatever weight you can easily handle. There might be some further restrictions on length, width, or weight when carried on small cars. Check compatibility of vehicle and boat if you are buying or trading either.

Safe car topping begins with sturdy racks to hold the boat. Buy the best that you can get that will fit your car. Some are detachable, but the best racks are those that can be permanently placed on the car by means of brackets fastened to the rain gutter or roof line. Once on, they should not wobble or twist, and fastening should be such that they will hold both the rack and the boat to the car during high-speed driving and under crosswind conditions.

The standard procedure for holding boats on car-top racks is with two straps that secure the boat upside-down on the racks, along with a bow strap and two stern straps fastened to the car bumper. Some straps over the hull of the boat buckle into place, but the best straps are those that clamp the strap or rope securely by means of spring-loaded clamps or tension. Ropes from the bow eye to the front bumper and from the stern handles to the rear bumper are equally important in holding the boat. The bow rope will secure the boat and keep a gust from breaking it free of the racks or pulling the racks off the car. The stern ropes also help stabilize the boat and prevent it from sliding forward during sudden stops. We use this method for carrying our john boats and have never had any problem.

Proper tension on the straps is very important to hold the boat down. This can be accomplished by spring-loaded clamps or by using nylon rope with a simple tie-down method that works like a pulley system to create maximum tension with little effort. Nylon, preferably braided nylon rope, is the best to use since it will stretch to create initial and continued tension. Use an s-hook on one end of the nylon to attach it to the rack or to the eye or handle of the boat. Tie a loop knot in the rope where you can reach it and about one to two feet above the tie-down eye. Run the end of the rope through the bumper or rack eye, back through the loop tied in the rope and pull down. The loops work like a pulley so that you can exert extra pressure and still easily tie the end of the rope to the bumper eye or rack eye. Since you usually only car top your own boat, precut all your ropes and label them with a color-coded dye or paint so that you will know which rope goes where. To keep the nylon from fraying, burn each end to melt the nylon or whip the ends with heavy thread.

*Sturdy roof racks, special rope tie-downs, and front and rear straps are necessary for efficient car topping.*

In most cases, car topping requires two anglers to properly mount the inverted boat on top of the car, but there are systems that don't require two people. They include racks with a rear elevated post attached to the bumper or trailer hitch that elevates the stern until the bow can be lifted and swung around to the front rack.

Another system consists of a set of racks that has rollers on the rear rack for rolling the boat in place once the bow is lifted up onto the rear rack. A third type, usually homemade, consists of a pair of ramps of lightweight wood or aluminum that run from the car-top rack to the ground on one side of the car; by means of pegs in the ramps a single fisherman can lever alternate ends of the boat up the ramp until it is on the top.

## TRAILERING

Hitching a trailer to your car quadruples your chances of having an accident, according to a Purdue University study. Maneuvering a car with a trailer attached is very different from driving a car without a trailer. Hitch equipment also contributes to accidents if not chosen properly or designed for the boat, trailer, or load. For example, one out of five trailer-related accidents results from hitch failure. These accidents need never occur if hitches are chosen carefully and checked frequently.

Here are some tips to avoid mechanical problems while trailing your fishing boat.

- Choose a trailer that is the proper size for your boat. Too often anglers will spend extra money for a larger boat or additional accessories, and neglect the importance

*Another example of a properly mounted boat strapped tight to the roof rack.*

of the trailer to their total fishing safety and comfort. If there is any question about the size of a trailer, you should choose one slightly larger than required or consider beefing up the trailer with heavier tires, bearings, and equipment.

Also, when choosing a trailer, figure the total weight that you will be carrying on it—not just the weight of the bare hull of the boat. Outboard engines weigh up to 350 pounds. Add to this the weight of ice chests, added seats, fuel, anchor, anchor line, mooring lines, fishing rods, tackle boxes, added electronics and accessories, and so on to figure the total weight that the trailer will have to carry. Often this can be 500 or more pounds greater than the weight of the boat alone. Use this total figure when buying a trailer. Also consider the maximum or optimal number of supports on the trailer needed to support the hull without damaging the hull surface or the internal stringers.

● Choose the largest tires available for your trailer, if there is a choice. The eight-inch tires are fine for small boats up to 15 feet in length that are light and that will be trailed to waters close to home. But for long distances and for larger boats, pick a trailer with regular-size (minimum 13-inch) wheels or larger and highway automobile tires. The eight-inch wheels will turn at many more revolutions for the same speed than will larger wheels, and the potential for damage from heating up

*A well-designed trailer showing rollers and a walkway that allows access to the bow of the boat when retrieving.*

and wear on tires can be enormous. When choosing tires, check the load-carrying capacity and never exceed it, especially with small tires.

If possible, choose trailer tires that are the same size as the wheels and tires on your car. Then between the car spare and the boat-trailer spare, you will have two spares for emergencies, and the tires will fit on either the car or trailer. For short distances on good roads with light loads, you might even want to save money and only keep one spare, since a double failure would be unlikely.

Underinflated tires, especially in the smaller sizes, can lead to severe overheating and wear on the treads. This leads to tire failure and early replacement. Carry a tire gauge and use it before each trip to check your car and trailer tire pressures.

- A car trailing a boat has four times the wind resistance at 50 miles per hour than the same car-and-trailer combination has traveling at 25 miles per hour. Thus, if you can reduce the drag caused by the boat, you'll save fuel and reduce car and tire wear. Ways to reduce drag include using a properly fitting cockpit cover, removing the boat's front windshield for long trips, removing pedestal seats in bass boats, and similar attention to wind-resistant accessories and parts of the boat.
- While most people have their car wheels and tires balanced regularly, many people will often ignore this important aspect of maintenance on boat trailers. It is just as

*Joe Zimmer retrieving his Hewes after a fishing trip. Note the electric winch, the double cord to the pulley hook in the eye bolt, and the cord held in Joe's left hand to operate the winch.*

important on regular-size trailer tires as it is on your car. It is even more important on the small tires because of the high speeds at which they spin. While unbalanced tires and wheels on a trailer might not be felt in the car, they will increase fuel consumption, increase drag, increase tire wear, and possibly loosen fittings and bolts through the constant vibration.

- Because trailer wheel bearings are often in the water, check them frequently. The lubrication can be washed out or diluted by the water. While all launching instructions recommend keeping the trailer axle out of water, this is often ignored by boaters, and sometimes the angle of the launching ramp or other specific conditions will require that the trailer be placed in the water below the axle and wheel bearings while launching or winching a boat.

In some cases, the wheel bearings may be hot from high-speed travel, and any air or grease in them is expanded by the heat. When the bearings are placed in the water, they suddenly cool, causing a vacuum and drawing water in. Fresh water is bad, while salt water is particularly detrimental.

On many of the better trailers, a set of "Bearing Buddies" are designed to take grease under pressure through a Zerk fitting, filling up the bearing space with grease and pressing an outer metal plate against a spring to create constant pressure. The spring will keep pressure on the bearing grease regardless of whether the bearings are hot or cool. When the outer plate is depressed by the spring, the

*Joe Zimmer winching his boat in place. The wheels of the trailer are barely in the water, so the wheel bearings are not affected.*

fitting needs more grease to provide protection.

One way to monitor bearings for possible overheating is through a bearing monitor made by J and L Tool Company, in which sensors fit into the axle with wires leading to a dashboard monitor that will tell you when the bearings or wheels start to overheat. Lights indicate right or left wheel, while a test light allows you to check the system. The sensors are specifically designed to take normal highway heat build-up and to register when overheating is about to happen to protect the bearings and wheel system before damage occurs.

- You should be extra careful in choosing, installing, and using your trailer hitch. We recently saw a news report about a boat trailer that came loose from a car, hit two cars, injured three bystanders, and came to rest in a restaurant window.

The most common mistake is to use too light a hitch. Most hitch manufacturers and the dealers who mount hitches have charts indicating the proper hitch for your car and the load (size and weight) that you plan to tow. For lightweight boat-and-trailer combinations you can use a light hitch with a 1⅞-inch ball. For larger boats you will need a hitch fastened to the underside of the vehicle. For very large loads you will want a frame-type hitch in which the hitch attachment will be under the entire car and the tongue weight (weight resting on the hitch) of the trailer load will be shared evenly throughout the car. These latter hitches are expensive and required only for large boats with heavy loads where such safeguards as additional braking systems on the trailer might be needed to carry the load safely.

Hitch weight, or tongue weight, should be about 10 to 15 percent of the total weight of the trailer, boat, and engine. Thus, if you are towing a boat in which the combined weight of the above three units is 2,000 pounds, the tongue weight should be 200 to 300 pounds. You can check tongue weight with a bathroom scale for small boats; for larger boats have the tongue weight checked by a marine dealer.

- Some boat fishermen like to have an additional hitch mounted on the front of the car to make it easy to get the trailer in and out of tight spots. While seldom used and seldom seen, such a front hitch does have the advantages of keeping the car's rear wheels higher on the ramp for better traction in slippery areas (common when launching in tidal areas at low tide), providing light when launching in the dark, and complete vision of the boat and the ramp while launching.

- Most car dealers will have manufacturer's listings of the recommended tow loads for each model of car. If your car is borderline for towing the load of your boat trailer, you might want to consult with your dealer about the possible advantages of extra-heavy tires, heavier springs, heavy-duty shocks, or a larger-capacity radiator (especially when towing in mountainous areas or if you plan to use air-conditioning or other accessories while traveling and trailing your boat).

- Tie-downs to hold the boat on the trailer accomplish several important things. They prevent damage to the boat while the trailer is bouncing along the highway. Such damage often is not visible, but can severely impair hull strength. The tie-downs also serve to hold the boat down in case of a high wind, buffeting from

*A winch hook will not sufficiently hold a heavy boat while trailering: an additional chain tie-down will do the job.*

*A painter attached to the bow cleat helps control the boat when it is launched.*

*One person can align a boat being pulled on a trailer using a long rope or two shorter ones.*

normal highway air resistance, on a very rough road, or when hard or emergency braking is required.

There are stern and bow tie-downs. The stern tie-down is a strap or quick-acting toggle-and-chain tension device. The strap fits over the stern of the boat, just forward of the outboard engine or inboard-outboard engine cowling, and it usually attaches by snaps to eye bolts on either side of the trailer. Most tie-downs of this type have tension buckles that are easily tightened and quick-release straps that make it easy.

One problem with the stern tie-down straps is that they often flap in the wind at highway speeds, which is annoying, and can damage the boat finish on straight-sided boats. You can prevent this by twisting the strap on each side. The twisted strap doesn't flap.

A second type of tie-down consists of strong tension toggles and chains fitted from the rear of the trailer to the stern or transom of the boat by means of padded hooks that fit on the transom on both sides of the engine. They work like miniatures of the lever-acting chains used by truckers to hold down odd-shaped loads on flat-bed trucks.

If you use this latter type of clamping device, make sure that the chains do not come close to or in contact with the stern of the boat, since highway travel could cause the chains to damage the finish of the transom. You can move the winch stand of the trailer forward on the tongue to provide more clearance for the chains when the boat is in place on the trailer—provided it does not markedly increase tongue load. It is also a good idea to cover the chains with rubber or flexible plastic tubing to protect the finish in the case of an inadvertent jostling of the boat and trailer.

Bow tie-downs are equally important but don't take the place of the stern tie-downs. Bow tie-downs are usually some form of chain or chain-and-toggle tension device to hold the bow eye of the boat to an eye on the winch stand or trailer tongue.

The tie-down must be down and back to prevent the boat from surging forward up and over the winch stand in the case of emergency stopping with a heavy boat. While small boats can get by with only the stern tie-downs, larger boats (those 16 feet and over) or heavy boats should have both bow and stern tie-downs.

- Standard bumper jacks provided with cars won't work with your trailer. You must have a jack that will lift the trailer under the axle. A hydraulic or scissors jack will do this. Keep one and a few boards for added jacking height.

## TRAILERING TECHNIQUES

Before taking your first spin with a car-trailed boat, practice on a large, vacant parking lot. Conditions under which you will find towing different and where caution is mandatory for safe driving are described below.

**Braking.** Adding a boat and trailer adds a great deal of weight to your car. As a result, you have to stop much more weight on the road at any speed, and greater stopping distance is required. As a general rule, double the distance that you normally would require for safe stopping of your car. You want your stops to be even and planned, since boat trailers can jackknife when the brakes are applied suddenly. Take it easy and plan on slow, deliberate stopping.

When in heavy traffic, plan on traveling at a speed that will eliminate stops or reduce the number of times you have to stop for red lights. You can reduce your traffic and braking problems by traveling through usually heavy traffic areas during nonrush hours.

**Accelerating.** Since you will have a heavy weight behind you, take your time to accelerate to your cruising speed. Flooring the accelerator will only increase gas consumption without an equivalent increase in speed. It will also increase the possibility of an accident should you have to stop in a hurry.

**Passing.** With the addition of a trailer you have added one more car length and possibly more to your total length. As a result, you will have to allow for this in passing other cars. Use your side or rearview mirror to check clearance. Keep in mind that your acceleration and speed will be decreased by the addition of the trailer, so that you must allow for additional road space to pass safely when crossing center lines.

**Turning.** When you make a sharp turn with a trailer, your trailer wheels will track closer to the curb than will the car, and they will also begin to turn before reaching the point at which the car turned. As a result, if you turn normally around a city corner, the trailer wheels will probably jump the curb. When traveling along curbed streets this is no problem with a left turn, but it can be a problem with a right turn. Proper turning involves one or more of the following techniques.

- Travel farther away from the curb so that when you start your turn the trailer will have room to clear the curb as you round the corner.
- If you are traveling close to the curb, pull out away from the curb several car lengths ahead of the turn to give the trailer more clearance.
- Pull your car up farther into the intersection before turning the wheels to give the trailer more clearance as it turns the corner.

    To a lesser degree the same thing affects you on the highway. For example, if you are traveling on a narrow road and have a sharp turn to the left, try to keep your car as far to the right as possible since the trailer will track to the left as you make the turn and could otherwise cross the center line. On a similar bend to the right, try to keep your car close to the center line to keep the trailer from running too close to the side of the road.

**Backing up.** Backing up a trailer is easily learned, but often botched by anglers anxious to get their boat into the water. Here are some tips on backing up.

- Make sure that you have as clear a view of the boat and/or trailer as possible as you

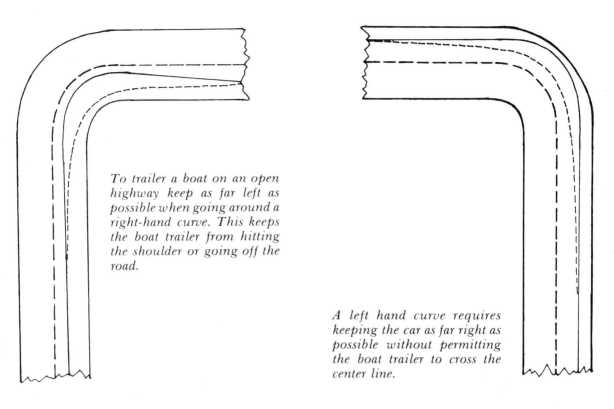

*To trailer a boat on an open highway keep as far left as possible when going around a right-hand curve. This keeps the boat trailer from hitting the shoulder or going off the road.*

*A left hand curve requires keeping the car as far right as possible without permitting the boat trailer to cross the center line.*

back up. The center rearview mirror is best, but if your boat blocks that, have adequate side mirrors on both sides of the car.

- Before attempting to back up, pull the car and trailer into a completely straight line with the boat ramp.
- Look over your shoulder at the boat trailer or use the mirrors to check the progress of the trailer as you back up.
- Use a system each time you back up so that you know just what to expect of your trailer when you turn the wheel. Turning the wheel clockwise turns the trailer to your left; turning the wheel counterclockwise turns it to your right. Some anglers like the system of placing the left hand on the top of the wheel and turning the wheel in an opposite direction from that which you wish the trailer to go. An easier method is to place your hand on the bottom of the steering wheel. This way, you turn your hand in the direction that you want the boat trailer to go.
- Back up slowly, since the slightest deviation in course will require correction.
- If the trailer gets too far off course, don't waste time trying to correct it. Pull up and start again.
- If you have a boat that you can't see through the mirror, have a passenger or a bystander guide you down the ramp. Backing up without being able to see the result is extremely difficult. A helper to check your progress is of great assistance even if you can see the boat.
- Practice your backing technique on an empty parking lot that has plenty of room until you are sure that you won't hold up other boaters when you make your first launch.

**Ramp safety and courtesy.** It's important to have a system when you reach the launching area so that you can prepare to drop your boat in the water as soon as a space becomes available. Some areas, such as the Delaware public ramps during the sea-trout run, become very crowded. Proper procedures can make it possible for everyone to

*The wrong method of turning a corner when trailering a boat. By handling a car as you would without a trailer, the trailer wheel may jump the curb.*

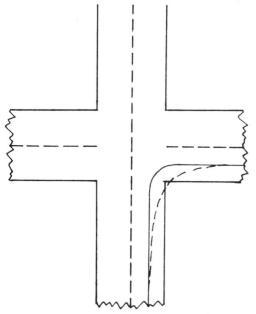

*One way to turn a corner safely while trailering a boat is to keep to the left side of your lane and make a wide turn for extra clearance allowing the trailer wheels to track close to the curb.*

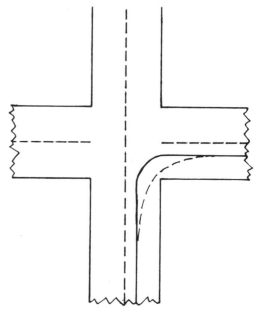

*A second technique is to move as far left as possible several car lengths prior to the corner and make a wide turn in which the boat trailer-wheels clear the curb. When you do this, pay particular attention to cars to the left rear of your vehicle and trailer.*

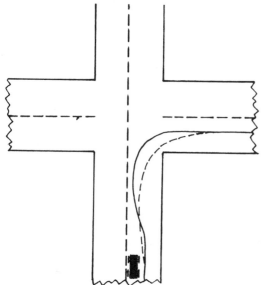

*Another technique is to make an extra-wide turn beyond the curb position, a technique similar to those used by tractor trailers. Remember to watch for cars in the street onto which you are turning.*

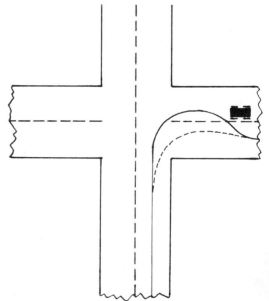

Drawings by Diana Volkert.

launch or pull out their boats with a minimum of time and trouble. Here are some tips on ramp safety, courtesy, and technique.

- When you get to a launching area don't back up to a launching ramp and block it while you load the boat, remove straps, and so on. Pull over to a side parking lot or another out-of-the-way place to do this.
- Remove the tie-down strap from the boat and store it in the car.
- Load the boat with the equipment that you are carrying in your car.
- Raise the engine so that the skeg won't hit on shallow ramp areas as you drop the boat into the water.
- Attach or pull out a painter tied to the bow of the boat for your partner to hold as the boat drops into the water.
- Ready chocks to place under the trailer wheels when you stop on the ramp to push the boat in.
- Disconnect the trailer light at the hitch to prevent possible shorts if the lights touch the water.

Once you are ready and it is your turn, have your helper get out of the car and help you back up carefully. Once your helper indicates that the boat trailer is far enough in the water for a safe launch, pull on the parking brake while your partner places chocks under the rear car tires. Stop the trailer so that the wheel bearings are out of the water. One tip here is to use chocks on a two- to three-foot-long nylon line with a dog-leash snap on the other end that can be snapped onto the trailer hitch. This way, you can drop the boat in

*Congested boat traffic makes carefully planned launching and retrieval a must.*

the water and pull away, pulling the chocks behind you to the parking area where they can be stored. It is the safest way, since you as driver shouldn't pull the chocks before getting in the car, and your partner will be busy holding the painter to dock the boat after launching and won't be able to leave it unattended to pick up the chocks. If your trailer has a breakaway feature in which the trailer bed hinges at the middle of the trailer chassis, release it so that the boat will drop into the water as smoothly as possible.

Have your partner grab the painter rope and release the winch rope to get enough slack to remove the snap from the bow eye, and push the boat into the water. If you have a ramp down the side of the trailer to walk on, it will make launching and pulling the boat out far easier than trying to balance on the cross members of the trailer as you push the boat out or attach the winch rope to the bow eye to pull the boat out. If a ramp is not standard on your trailer you can easily make one from a wide piece of cheap shelving; cover it with strips of nonskid tape or use paint sprinkled with sand while still wet to give the board a nonskid surface.

Once the boat is in the water and under control of your partner, lock the breakaway trailer in place and pull up into a parking space. Be careful to accelerate smoothly and lightly when leaving a launch ramp, since they are often slippery. A little sand carried in a bucket in the car trunk will help when these situations arise. Park and lock your winch handle in the car and the trailer to the hitch to prevent theft.

Pulling your boat out of the water is basically a reversal of the above. Maneuver your boat slowly into the ramp area, and if necessary, take your place in line with other boats waiting for ramp space. Stow all tackle and equipment so that you will be able to make a safe, sure docking at the ramp and quick retrieval of the boat. Have a painter attached to the bow of the boat to hold the boat in place while a driver goes for the car and trailer. Raise the engine if necessary.

When the driver backs the car and trailer into postion, maneuver the boat with the painter or by pushing the boat out into the ramp area if necessary, so that the driver can walk down the chassis of the trailer, pulling the winch rope or cable, and attach the hook to the bow eye of the boat. Often a helper can assist in lining up the boat by using a boat pole or boat hook to push the stern of the boat into position to line up the boat with the trailer. A helper can also use a painter rope attached to a stern cleat to pull or hold the stern of the boat in line if wind or tidal conditions require.

Once the boat is lined up, use the winch to pull the boat from the water. Throughout this process, check carefully to make sure that the boat is centered on the trailer and that all the rollers or skids come in contact with the proper part of the boat hull.

Once the boat is secure on the trailer, move to an unused spot on the parking lot where you can stow rods and equipment, remove drain plugs, lower the engine, and add the bow and stern tie-down straps and hooks. Check your brake lights and other lights on the car and trailer before leaving the parking area.

# 13
# Boat and Engine Maintenance

Proper maintenance of your boat and engine will insure their proper performance. Here are some factors to consider for maintenance of these items.

## ALGAE

The best boating and fishing is in warm weather and in the sunshine—factors that combine with water to produce a filamentous algae on boat bottoms.

The algae begins as a dark green scum at the water line and it eventually covers the entire boat bottom. Often it will hang in long strands like a shaggy rug. If not removed, the algae can increase fuel consumption by as much as 25 percent while at the same time reducing top speed by a similar percentage. One spring day of cleaning and waxing the hull will save you time and money in the ensuing fishing season.

Begin by pulling the boat from the water or working on your trailed boat in some spot where you can wash and wax easily. Wash the boat with mild soap and water. Remove any scum already on the boat with a soft brush and mild soapsuds. Avoid abrasive cleaners, particularly on the gel coats of fiberglass boats. If the hull has become pitted and the algal scum has hardened, remove it as best you can with mineral spirits or acetone. Afterward, wash the area with soap and water to remove the solvents completely. If the scum remains, sand the area with very fine, wet sandpaper, clean with mineral spirits or acetone, and finish with a sudsy wash.

Next, apply a heavy coat of marine wax to the entire hull. Double the wax coat at the waterline to make cleaning easier at this first point of attack by the algae.

During the summer, clean the waterline area each week by scrubbing with a soft brush. Monthly, you might have to pull the boat or go underwater to scrub the entire hull with the soft brush. If you use a trailer with your boat, wash the hull after you pull it from the water when necessary.

## ALUMINUM BOAT MAINTENANCE

One of the attributes of aluminum boats, aside from their light weight and relatively low cost, is that they require minimal care for seasonal maintenance. In fact, many owners of aluminum craft go for years without any maintenance except to wash the mud off the boat when pulling it up a ramp or when they turn it over in the backyard at the end of the season.

But there is some maintenance required, and here are some tips to make it a little easier.

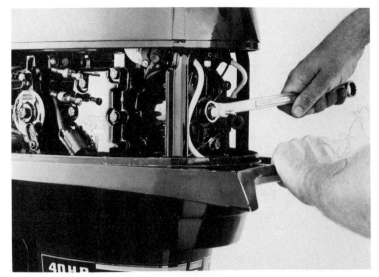

*A preventitive maintenance inspection of your outboard engine is necessary each spring; include a thorough examination of spark-plug leads and spark plugs, but be careful not to overtighten the plugs when you replace them.*
Mecury Marine

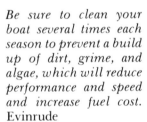

*Be sure to clean your boat several times each season to prevent a build up of dirt, grime, and algae, which will reduce performance and speed and increase fuel cost.*
Evinrude

Suggestions from David Bach, staff naval architect for the National Marine Manufacturers Association, include:

- Cleaning with a mild detergent followed with a clean-water rinse. This is ideal for natural aluminum surfaces and will keep them looking new longer.
- Clean painted aluminum boats with the same procedure, but then protect the paint with a liquid cleaner or wax. Stains or any light corrosion can be removed with a fine rubbing compound, by buffing, or with some of the many metal polishes on the market.
- If you have algae or other marine growth on the hull, remove it while it is still wet, or wet it before removal. If you plan to keep your boat in the water for a full season or for long periods of time, and if you have a marine-growth problem in your area, use an antifouling bottom paint, following the directions carefully. Never, however, use paints containing copper, mercury, or lead. When repainting an aluminum boat, prepare the surface carefully and follow the paint manufacturer's instructions.

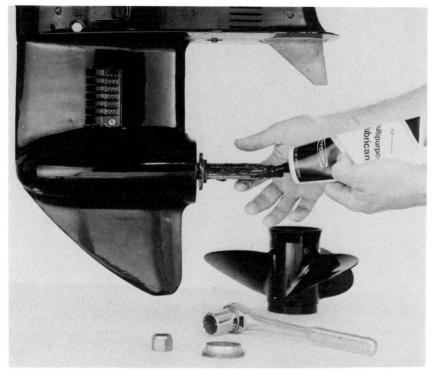

*Annually, remove the propellor from your outboard engine and inspect the hub for possible damage. Check the propellor blades for cracks or bends and trim or replace them if necessary. Before re-installing the propellor, coat the shaft splines with a waterproof lubricant.*

*Preventive maintenance of your engine should include periodic lubrication of the lower drive unit. Use a gear lubricant recommended by the manufacturer. Remove vent and filler hole screws and gaskets and add lubricant through the filler hole until it starts to come out the vent hole. Be sure gaskets are in place when you replace the screws.*

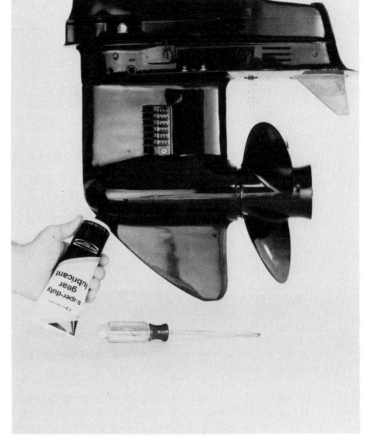

**Repairs.** A rubber mallet or automotive body tools will take care of any minor dents in aluminum craft. If you have more severe damage, such as a puncture, bent or broken rib, or loose rivets, seek help from a qualified repairman with the proper tools or take the boat to a shop specializing in such repairs.

David Bach also points out that modern marine aluminum alloys minimize corrosion problems, but that galvanic corrosion can still occur when dissimilar metals such as brass and aluminum become wet. If you plan to mount any nonaluminum hardware or fixtures to your boat, use a high-quality caulking compound as insulation between the two metals. For the same reason, aluminum boats should not be stored on the bare ground. Minerals in the soil and sometimes rain can cause the same problem. If you must store your boat outdoors, place the boat on saw horses or a couple of logs.

## PROTECTING GEL COATS ON FIBERGLASS BOATS

While many boat fishermen think that the fiberglass of their craft is completely impervious to air or water, the gel coat of the exterior is actually slightly porous. It won't leak, but it will let in enough air and sunlight to affect the resin on the surface of the craft. This oxidation causes the whitish chalking seen on the surface of so many older or poorly maintained boats. Over the years, this takes off the gel coat bit by bit.

To protect against this oxidation, wax the boat annually. The best time is often at the end of the season, the wax will protect the boat during storage. To wax the boat, begin by washing it and removing any chalking, scum, and loose pigment with a fiberglass cleaner-polish. Use a wax made specifically for fiberglass boats. The wax will also help to reduce algae and other marine growth.

## MILDEW REMOVAL

Mildew can be a problem on such items as boat covers, decks, plastic surfaces, hatches, and console covers. The best prevention is ventilation, careful drying, and cleaning of such surfaces and fabrics after each trip. To remove mildew, you can use one of numerous preparations found in hardware stores and marinas for this purpose.

## WINTER STORAGE OF OUTBOARD ENGINES

You can obtain winterizing service through your local marine dealer. Such service is particularly recommended for higher-horsepower engines that require a little more work and are heavier and more unwieldy to work with than the small, detachable models.

If you wish to do the job yourself, outboard-engine experts recommend the following procedures.

First, if you have any unused gasoline in your gas tanks, you can stabilize it for use next season by using one of the many gas stabilizers available. Most of these formulas absorb moisture in the gas as well as preventing gum and varnish build-up in the fuel system.

Next, leave your rig in the water or install a flush test device and warm up the engine. Remove the cowling, disconnect the fuel line, and while the engine is still idling, inject storage seal (available from outboard manufacturers) into the carburetor air intake. As the carburetor or carburetors (some high-horsepower models have more than one) start to run dry, apply an extra dose. This will distribute the protective compound throughout the crankcase and cylinder block to prevent internal corrosion and will at the same time use up any remaining fuel to prevent varnish and gum formation. If necessary, drain or service the water-separator filter to prevent damage during freezing weather.

If you have a small outboard, remove it from the transom of the boat, hold it upright on the skeg and allow the water to drain completely out of the gear housing. For large outboards, leave the engine on the boat transom and flush the cooling system with fresh water to clear out any silt, sand, saltwater residue, or chemical deposits. Make sure that all water-drain holes in the gear housing are open and freely draining and also make sure that the flushing plug (if the engine is so equipped) is removed so that all water will drain out. This is extremely important since if all the water is not out of the system it will freeze with winter temperatures and may crack the gear housing or water-pump housing.

Next, lubricate the swivel pin, steering tube, steering cable, throttle and shift linkage, thumbscrews, and all other points as directed by your owner's maintenance manual. Use an anticorrosion grease to coat all external bare metal parts.

Remove the air-vent screw and grease the filler plug along with the accompanying washers from the gear housing. Insert a tube of the proper lubricant (check with your dealer or owner's manual) into the grease-filler hole and inject new grease until the old gear grease starts to flow out of the air-vent hole, indicating that the housing is filled. If you have any water discharge, something is wrong and you should take the outboard to your dealer for service. Replace the filler screws, vent screws, and washers.

Wash or wipe down the entire engine. Spray all the parts under the cowling (the entire engine head) with a demoisturizing agent such as WD-40, CRC, PennsGuard, or LPS-1. Replace the cowling.

Remove the propeller and clean the shaft with steel wool, then apply a sealant or silicone grease and reinstall the propeller. Before reinstallation, check the propeller carefully for any signs of denting, twisting, nicking of the blade, and replace if required. If there is no major damage but some small nicking, dress the edge of each blade with a file to smooth out and remove the nicks, making sure that the metal removed is equal on each blade to prevent an unbalanced propeller, which could result in propeller-shaft and/or gear wear.

If you have an electric-start outboard, take the battery out of the boat and clean it thoroughly. Remove the battery leads and any accessory-equipment leads and tie them together into two bundles—one for positive and one for negative—so that you can easily and quickly replace the leads in the spring. Thoroughly clean the top of the battery, especially the terminals and terminal area, and apply demoisturizing agent or anticorrosion grease to the posts to protect the battery through the winter.

Check the electrolyte and add distilled water if necessary to bring the electrolyte to the correct level. Charge the battery until the specific gravity of the electrolyte reaches 1.260 or higher. To protect the battery, make sure that the recharge rate does not exceed six amperes. If you have a long slack season, check the battery every 30 to 45 days and take an electrolyte reading on the battery. Apply a booster charge when the hydrometer reading drops to 1.230 or lower. This is particularly important if the battery is stored in a cold location, since the battery might freeze if the specific gravity reading falls too low. Make sure that the battery is stored in a cool, dry place, up off of a concrete floor, and in an area where it will not be subject to wide temperature fluctuations.

Store the engine in a clean, dry location. It should be covered, but make sure that there is enough ventilation around the motor to prevent condensation.

## SPRING ENGINE TUNE-UP

Spring tune-ups begin in the winter with proper storage preparation. If this has been done, spring tune-up is a breeze.

First, reconnect the spark-plug leads after wiping them off with a demoisturizer to remove any corrosion or oxidation that might have built up on the plugs during the winter. Check the lower unit lubrication. If there are leaks, see your dealer and have him check the unit seals.

If you have an electric-start engine, check the battery water level, charge the battery if it needs it, and reconnect it. Check the main oil and grease points on the outboard to be sure that they are all smooth, work properly, and have enough lubrication to protect them during the fishing season.

## BOAT-TOOL AND EMERGENCY KIT

Everything made by man someday wears out or breaks. This applies to boats, and it sometimes seems that the severity of the breakdown is in direct proportion to the distance you are from the dock. The solution to this includes constant maintenance at home along with a boat/tool kit to repair or adjust any small problems while on the water. Be sure that your boat tool kit is on the boat at all times. Do not rely on raiding your workbench at the last minute before a trip to pick up enough of the right tools and parts to make needed repairs.

Keep your tools in an airtight box, such as one of the plastic freezer or Tupperware containers, or in a spare battery box that will protect the contents from rain and spray while allowing circulation of air to prevent rust. All of the following must be in the right sizes for your boat and engine requirements.

**Wrenches:** open-end or socket set along with an adjustable crescent wrench to fit odd-size nuts and bolts. Also include a spark-plug wrench.

**Screwdrivers:** both regular-head and Phillips-head and any other odd types that are currently coming into vogue. Carry a couple of short-handled models for tight spots.

**Extra spark plugs:** carry a couple.

**Spare propeller:** this is necessary, especially when fishing stump- or rock-strewn areas in fresh water and any inshore areas in salt water, where propeller damage most frequently occurs. Make sure you know how to remove and install the propeller.

**Flares:** for emergency use only, in case you need help from another boat or have to signal Mayday.

**Junk box:** this should include all the small parts you might need to make repairs on the water. Possible contents would include cotter pins, washers, nuts, bolts, lock washers, nails, screws, fuses for instruments, Boy Scout knife, pliers, tape, wire, cord, short lengths of rope, short lengths of tubing, and electric wire.

Add to this emergency kit any other items that are likely to break down on your boat or small, inexpensive repair parts that are easy to replace when required.

# 14
# Further Information on Boating

There are a number of places from which you can obtain further information on boating, boating procedure, and safe boating practices.

**United States Power Squadron Courses.** These are conducted by trained boatmen and cover boat handling under normal and adverse conditions, seamanship and common emergencies, rules of the road, aids to navigation, compass and chart familiarization, running lights and equipment, boat trailing, river boating, mariner's compass and piloting. For information, contact your state or local agencies governing boating in your area.

**American Red Cross courses.** This organization conducts courses on boating, rowing, canoeing, small-craft safety, first aid, and water safety. Local chapters schedule regular classes in a number of water-safety courses, covering the same basics as the United States Power Squadron courses. In addition, there are swimming courses for boaters. Most courses are conducted in the evening to make it possible for adults to attend. For information on courses available and scheduling times, contact your local Red Cross.

**United States Coast Guard Auxiliary.** Flotillas of the United States Coast Guard Auxiliary offer courses and boating-safety checks throughout the year. Courses are taught by experienced boatmen through slide shows, movies, classes, and demonstrations. Courses usually offered include a 13-lesson course in boating skills and seamanship, a 7-lesson course in principles of safe sailing, and special 1-lesson courses designed for children and youth groups.

They also often sponsor courtesy boating-safety checks for boaters interested in the quality and appropriateness of their boating-safety equipment and the condition of their boat. Such courtesy checks are not required in any state, are not a license to boat, and are not reported to anyone except the boat owner. They are a good idea for any boater, since they provide an unbiased check of a boat and its equipment and suggest any changes that may be needed.

There are often safe-boating checks, demonstrations, and boating events that you can learn from or participate in during Safe Boating Week, usually held the first or second week in June each year. For information on dates and events in your area, contact the United States Coast Guard Auxiliary District Office or state agencies involved with boating events and safety in your area.

There is a new safety and information guide produced under a grant from the United States Coast Guard that covers boating for the handicapped. The book discusses personal flotation devices, emergency equipment, procedures to follow with the physically handicapped, transferring disabled boaters to and from boats and dock areas, and special equipment for handicapped boaters. The book also includes a section on boating safety written in Braille, a bibliography of recommended reading, a list of recreational organizations for the handicapped, and a summary of current legislation affecting handicapped boaters. Copies of the book, *Boating for the Handicapped: Guidelines for the Physically Handicapped*, are available free while they last from the Human Resources Center, I.U.Willets Road, Albertson, New York 11507.

# PART FOUR

# 15
# Storing Tackle
# at Home

We have seen good fishing rods ruined by improper storage. The most flagrant example is when a rod—still rigged with reel, line, and lure—is leaned against a garage wall or suspended between two rafters. In both cases, the weight of the reel, combined with only two support points, one at each end of the rod, left the rod with a permanent set or bend that rendered it unusable. Storing tackle at home, whether it is rods, lines, or reels, requires some forethought and care.

## STORING RODS

Regardless of the method of storage used for rods, never store a wet or damp rod in a closed case. The high moisture content in the case will cause the finish on graphite and glass rods to blister, while split-bamboo rods can separate at the joints.

**Rod cases.** After a rod has been cleaned, dried, and wiped down following a fishing trip, place it back in its rod bag and rod case. If you don't have a rod bag and case for each rod, buy them for this ultimate protection. Be sure that the rod bag is long enough for the rod. The rod should slide in and out of the bag with ease. For best protection, each section of the rod should have a separate sleeve in the bag so that the sections don't touch and scratch each other while in the case. Cases of aluminum or plastic are readily available, and ideally should be about one inch longer than the rod sections (or one inch longer than the longest section if the rod is ferruled off center). Caps are usually chained to the case. If not, remove the rod from the case, drill a one-eighth-inch hole in the cap and top side of the case, and attach the cap to the case with a short length of cord, heavy monofilament, or old fly line. Even if you don't do this, you should drill a one-eighth-inch hole in the cap, if it doesn't already have one. This will allow dissipation of moisture in the case. The slightest bit of moisture in a case may damage a rod.

Rods in rod cases should be stored out of the way. Garages, sheds, out buildings, attics, and some basements are not good because of moisture along with a wide fluctuation in temperatures that might damage rods. Good places are in dens, heated and air-conditioned basements, recreation rooms, or a closet with the same controlled environment of your home.

Another advantage of a metal or plastic case is that it provides rod protection from the house to the fishing grounds. By far the vast majority of rods broken that we have seen or heard about, have occurred when an assembled rod gets caught in a house or car door.

**Rod bags.** Rod bags will provide soft protection for rods stored in a closet, game-room locker, or similar spot. The one advantage is that moisture can't build up in the bag, as it can sometimes in a closed case. The obvious disadvantage is that the soft cloth bags are no protection against physical abuse in the house, in the car, or elsewhere. Rods stored together in bags might also develop a set or permanent bend. If any number are stored in one spot take care to lay each rod bag flat (as on a closet shelf) or at least, lay them straight so that two rod sections don't cross.

Rods in bags can also be placed on horizontal racks. One of us used to store rods this way, using peg-board hooks to hold one or two rods horizontally. No damage seems to occur provided that the hooks are placed apart about one-half to two-thirds the length of the rod. Another good method is to hang the rods by the tie cord at the open end of the bag, so that they hang straight down. Rods stored on racks should have the reels removed to prevent strain and damage.

**Rod racks.** Some rod racks, both decorative and those strictly functional, are designed to be used with rod cases, rods in bags, or bare rods. One type has small cup hooks in a horizontal strip of wood to hold the rods by the tip-top. These are commercially made, but are simple to make for any number of rods. One outdoor writer that we know stores a majority of his rods this way and has never had any trouble with the method. However, we feel that this method should only be used with lightweight rods in order to avoid excessive strain on the tip-top guide where it is joined to the rod.

A similar type of rack uses a cam-action clamp so that the rods can be slipped into and out of the rack. The rod is removed by raising the rod straight up to reduce the holding action of the cam clamp. Any size or weight of rod can be held securely in these vertical clamps. Most of these rod racks are designed for display of the rods in a game room, tackle room, or den.

Another type of rod rack that is functional for out-of-the-way storage is the overhead rack. All types of fishing rods, uncased and assembled or in sections, are stored in overhead racks. It allows for immediate access to any rod, but is best for those anglers or fishing clubs with large numbers of rods to store. The racks themselves are placed on the joists of the basement, above head height. The rack consists of two strips of wood. On one strip, fasten large one-inch cup hooks every two inches. On the other, using a single piece of cord or nylon webbing, staple a loop every two inches. The loops should hang down three inches (six inches of cord or webbing is used for each loop). The handle of the rod is slipped into the loop and the upper rod section is slipped into the cup hook, somewhere above the ferrule. Light rods can be broken down and stored this way to reduce any strain on the rod sections. We do this with light spinning rods and all fly rods, with different racks used for different types of rods. Arrange spacing for the type of rod, so that there will be no strain on it, and thus no set developing in the rod. We have used this method for ten years with no damage to rods.

The obvious disadvantage of any bare-rod storage method is that since there is no protection from a hard case and since the rods are often assembled, extra care must be taken when handling them or when near them. Of course, the rods may be taken down from the rack and placed in individual cases or a large travel case for transportation.

Regardless of the type of storage used, it is important to remove reels to reduce weight and strain on the rod.

# STORING REELS

Reel storage is far simpler than rod storage due to the size and construction of reels. The problem is really no different than the storage problem of an electric drill, a bowling ball, or a set of Christmas-tree lights. Reels should be kept dust free, and provision should be allowed for possible leakage of oil or grease. Because they have line on them, they should be kept out of the light (ultraviolet rays can harm monofilament and other fishing lines) and out of the heat.

*C.B.P. shows one way to store many rods at home, using the loop-and-cup hook method described in the text. Bait-casting rods are shown but this method works well for all types of rods.*

**Case storage.** Most reels come with a cloth, leather, or plastic case. These cases are usually ideal for storing reels in the home as well as on a trip. The only disadvantage is that the finish on the imitation-leather or imitation-suede cases can in time crumble. This can lead to fine dust getting into the reel and ultimately damaging it. Otherwise, these cases are fine for home, travel, and field storage.

**Shelf storage.** Some anglers we know use closed or open bookcase shelves to store their reels. All the reels are on display. Spare reel spools and parts can be kept with the right reel. If closed, glass-front shelves are used, the reels can be displayed while still protected from dust. The greatest disadvantage of open-shelf storage is dust, but periodic cleaning will take care of that.

**Rack storage.** Storage on perforated-board racks is another method. Small, perforated-board hooks are used to hold the casting, surf, and saltwater reels by the pillar across the reel frame or by the reel foot. Medium-size hooks are used to hold the reel foot on spinning and spin-cast reels, and one medium to large hook serves to hold each fly reel by the cross pillar. The pegboard arrangement allows for easy changes or additions to the reel collection. Outdoor writer Lefty Kreh uses the same rack method for his reels, except he uses nails in a wood base for the rack and covers the front of the whole rack with a curtain of clear, flexible plastic to protect against dust. The plastic tarp keeps the dust off the reels; it is clear so reels can be easily selected; and it can be lifted up easily to gain access to any reel or spare spool.

## STORING LINES

Whenever possible, lines should be washed and dried prior to storage on reels. This used to be mandatory to prevent cracking of fly lines and rotting of linen saltwater line. Today's lines are far more durable, but they should still be washed if used in salt water or covered with dirt or algae. When possible, dry on a line dryer before spooling back on a reel. The line dryer can provide storage between trips.

Line should be stored in a cool, dark place. Additionally, fly lines should be stored away from any insect repellents, gasoline, or sun-tan lotions; all of these have solvents that can remove the plasticizers in modern fly lines. The plasticizers keep the fly line pliant and their removal by any solvent causes the line to become stiff and the finish to crack.

If you are serious about your fishing, it is best to purchase bulk one-quarter- or one-half-pound spools of line (other than fly line) and replace your lines at the end of each season. To store bulk spools, keep them in a cool, dark place. A drawer in your tackle bench or a shelf out of the sun is best.

## STORING LURES

Lures are best stored in tackle boxes or small lure boxes. If you do more than one type of fishing or fish more than one area or type of water where different lures are used, it's a good idea to have several tackle boxes, one for each type of fishing. A simple code or abbreviation on the outside of each box made with a permanent felt-tip marker makes it

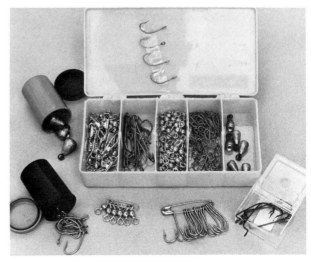

*Methods of storing small terminal tackle parts include the use of fishing-tackle lure boxes, small plastic boxes, safety pins, paper clips, 35-mm film canisters, and clear cellophane tape.*

easy to pick up the right box for the right fishing, even if the boxes are identical models.

Selection of the tackle box is important for it must suit the type of fishing, the type of lure, and the type of boat being used. For example, boxes for large lures—for saltwater fish, muskies, or cohoes—must have compartments large enough to accomodate these large lures. Spinner baits present a unique problem because of their shape. Many tackle-box manufacturers have special spinner-bait boxes or boxes that have a slotted vertical rack to hold the spinner bait by the bend in the wire. Otherwise, you need some large, almost square compartments in your tackle box to hold the spinner baits flat.

Tackle boxes must also be chosen with their ultimate use in mind. In a cramped boat, for example, a tackle box with slide-out trays would be a far better choice than one of the hip-roof types that must open on both sides for access to the complete lure selection. The advantages and disadvantages of different types of boxes are:

**Tool-box type.** This has a full lid that opens up to disclose two or more trays. Usually the trays open as the box is opened. The advantage is that the box is usually fully rain proof with the overlapping lip on the top of the box. The disadvantage is that they are usually smaller and hold fewer lures than other types. They also must be opened fully to get to all the lures, and this takes up space in a boat.

**Hip-roof type.** This is a bigger box and will hold more lures than the tool-box type. Usually they are best for small lures, since there are sets of trays on each side of the box that open out once the lid is opened. The seam of the lid on top of the box usually renders this type less than completely waterproof in a hard rain. Since the lid opens out from the center, it takes more space in a boat to open than the tool-box type. The advantage is that once opened with lure compartments exposed, all lures are visible to make selection easy.

**Sliding-tray type.** Some have a full deck of sliding trays while others have two to three trays over a bottom compartment reached by opening up the top, as with a tool-box or hip-roof tackle box. Both types are waterproof in a hard rain, and both have the advantage of taking up the least amount of room in a boat than any other type. They are

*Too many lures placed in one tray of a tackle box can result in a tangle. Organize trays for minimal lure contact and buy a tackle box large enough to carry the quantity of lures you'll need.*

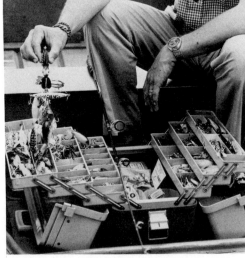

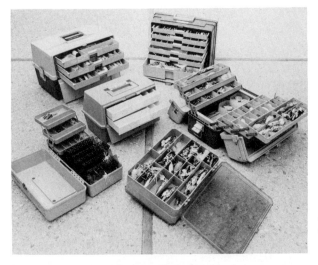

*Typical tackle boxes include hip roof, sachel, spinner bait, and pull-drawer types.*

particularly suitable in crowded bass boats. Some models even will fit under the pedestal seats of bass boats and low models will sometimes fit under bench seats in john boats and rowboats. A slight disadvantage is that only one tray can be seen at a time, and thus the full range of lures can't be viewed at once as they can in the hip-roof box.

**Suitcase-type box.** This comes in one- and two-sided models, both of which are like a suitcase in the way that they open. The compartments are often visible through clear or translucent covers and are often adjustable for size. They will hold a lot of lures for the space and it is easy to see the entire contents. The one disadvantage in two-sided models is that unless the lid is locked automatically when the handles are grabbed (some are made this way) the contents of one side can spill out when the box is turned over if you forget to latch it.

# STORING FLIES

Flies for trout fishing, bass fishing, shad fishing, and saltwater fly-fishing are kept much the same way as lures, using standard fly boxes to separate the flies as to type, size, species use, geographical area, and so on. Streamers and saltwater flies can be kept in felt or lamb's wool fly books, while bass bugs, panfish bugs, dry flies, and nymphs are best kept in lightweight, compartmentalized boxes designed for field use.

# STORING NETS

Landing nets should be washed out thoroughly, hung up to dry, and stored in an out-of-the-way place away from heat and light, which might break down the net mesh. Storage in closets, in overhead racks similar to those used for rods, or on pegs on the wall are all good methods.

# STORING BOOTS

Rubber ankle boots, hip boots, and waders will break down quickly, cracking, and/or rotting if not given the proper care. Today, boots are too expensive to let this happen. The enemies of rubber boots are oxidation caused by sunlight, air, and heat, and improper storage, which can lead to cracking at the folds and creases. Keep the boots away from heat, furnaces, hot-air ducts, vents, and direct sunlight. To keep air from breaking down the rubber, some manufacturers recommend coating the exterior of all rubber boots with a glycerine or dilute glycol solution, which will keep the air from attacking the rubber. Unfortuntaely, this is messy. It is also possible to seal the boots in a large plastic bag such as those used by commercial cleaners to cover a dress or overcoat. The boots can be left hanging without folds and the sealed bag will reduce to some degree the air contact. This can be aided by evacuating air from the bag with a vacuum cleaner, and tying it off to prevent air intrusion.

Proper hanging will do a lot to prolong boot life. The best hangers are those metal supports that hold the boot by the foot so that the rest of the boot hangs straight down. This minimizes creases and folds and keeps the boots open so that the interiors can dry properly. Similar racks can be made from wood.

An additional problem with rubber boots, according to John White, protective-footwear product manager for Royal Red Ball, is the damage from oil that can quickly cause the rubber in boots to revert to the natural chewing-gum consistency of raw rubber. Oil, gasoline, and many other solvents can cause this. The solution is to wash your rubber boots with soap and water after each use if you suspect any such contact.

One easy way to dry boots after a dunking or to remove perspiration that builds up in them in hot weather (in both rubber and leather boots) is to use a hand-held hair dryer. For best results, tape or fasten a length of flexible plastic tubing to the nozzle of the hair dryer that will reach to the boot bottom. This way, you can leave the dryer on to dry the boots while you go on to other jobs.

# 16
# Storing Tackle on Boats

Large boats generally do not present a problem for tackle storage. They usually have adequate rod racks and sufficient space in the deck, under seat compartments, and in consoles or cabins for storing rods, tackle boxes, and accessory gear. Small boats present a problem because space is at a premium for the proper storage and handling of all the equipment that anglers carry. The best place for tackle boxes is under a seat where they are readily available yet out of the way. For this, the sliding-tray type of tackle box is best. If no such space is available, the next best space is usually alongside the gunwale. This way the tackle box and lures can be easily reached yet there is still plenty of walk-around room in the center of the boat.

## STORING RODS ON BOATS

While rod cases are ideal to protect rods from home to the dock, they get in the way in any boat. Leave them in the car, unless you are taking along an expensive rod that you might use but don't want knocked around during the day's normal fishing activity. The major reason for rod breakage in boats is a lack of organized rod-storing space. This means that rod racks are needed on *all* boats, even the smallest. Some boats come equipped with rod racks. Others can be fitted with several commercial types, or you can make your own.

On our small boats, we use lengths of plastic PVC or ABS pipe fastened to the inside of the boat below the gunwale (to hold the tip section of the rod) while using a wood or plastic rack with J-shaped cuts or slots to support the rod handles. To keep the rods from jumping around while moving, use shock-cord loops over the rod handles. The loops should fasten onto the rack. Hold-down straps can also be made of Velcro on these racks to make it easy to secure such light rods as fly, spinning, spin-cast, casting, popping, and light saltwater boat rods.

## STORING LURES ON BOATS

Lures should be stored in tackle boxes, but you'll usually want a few out for quick changes. Some bass boats have dish-shaped depressions in the wide gunwales for this. There are other ways to store lures. The Bass Pro Shop sells a plastic lure holder that can be glued, screwed, or pop-riveted onto any vertical surface, and it holds a dozen lures. A similar lure rack can be made from a strip of wood with small screw eyes placed every

A well organized light-tackle in-shore saltwater boat with wide deck, central fish locker, adequate rod storage beneath the gunnels, and padded gunnels for support in rough seas.

C.B.P. (left) and Walker Zimmerman in a posed example of a completely disorganized fishing craft. Rods are scattered throughout the boat, tackle boxes are open, seat cushions, ice chest, and minnow bucket block movement, and an anchor line, anchor, pliers, knife, sheath and fish dehooker also clutter up the boat.

*Proper storage and organization on a boat can include notched rod holders. The notches hold the legs of the spinning reels preventing them from knocking together.*

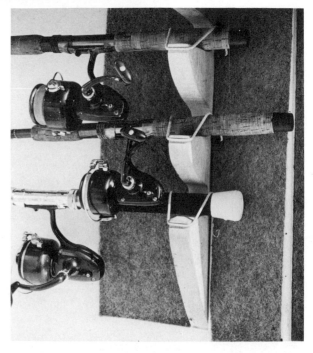

*Rod holders under the gunwale of a small sportfishing boat include shelves with bungee cord. Indoor-outdoor carpeting is glued in place to protect the reels if they knock against the side of the boat.*

*Golf tubes (shown) PVC, or ABS plastic pipe serves to hold the tip end of rods in small boats.*

*Commercially available plug holders mount to the sides of small boats to hold plugs for instant usage.*

inch to hold the hooks, or from closed-cell plastic foam glued to the boat to stick hooks and lures in. Don't leave lures lying on the deck since they can cause a fall, be broken underfoot, or slide into inaccessible areas of the boat. And don't leave lures on a seat because someone might sit on them. For center-console or windshield boats, an acrylic-plastic slotted rack designed to fit over the windshield will hold lures out of the way and ready for use.

## STORING ACCESSORIES ON BOATS

Nets are a problem on any small boat. If they are large enough to land the fish, they are too large to stow easily. The best solution that we have come up with is to stow the net alongside the gunwale and near the stern where it will be out of the way. Take care to keep it out of the way of oarlocks, stringers, tackle boxes, and other rods.

Any fisherman or boater ends up taking aboard a lot of miscellaneous equipment, such as raingear, sweaters, vacuum bottles, cameras, lunch, fish-cleaning knives, and so

*A small block of plastic foam glued to a boat can also serve as a plug holder.*

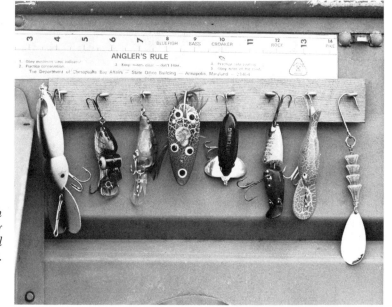

*A wood strip fixed with screw eyes placed one or two inches apart will also serve as a lure holder.*

on. One way to keep all of this from underfoot if there are no storage compartments on the boat is to carry and place in a corner of the stern a small, lidded plastic trash container. This will hold all the extra gear and is waterproof. If the lid won't lock on, use shock cord from handle to handle to hold it in place.

If you fish where the temperature or climate changes rapidly during the day, and you are constantly changing in and out of raingear, sweaters, light jackets, and so on, rig a three-foot-long clothing hammock along the gunwale or in back of or in front of a seat. Make sure that the bottom of the hammock is above the deck, which can become wet, when full of clothing.

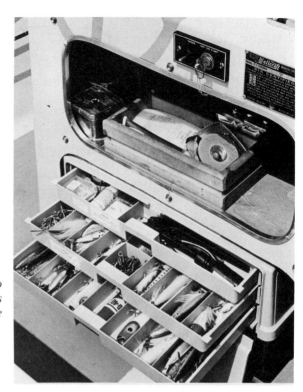

*Pull-out tackle boxes such as this Plano 747 often fit beneath center consoles offering adequate lure storage while remaining out of the way.*

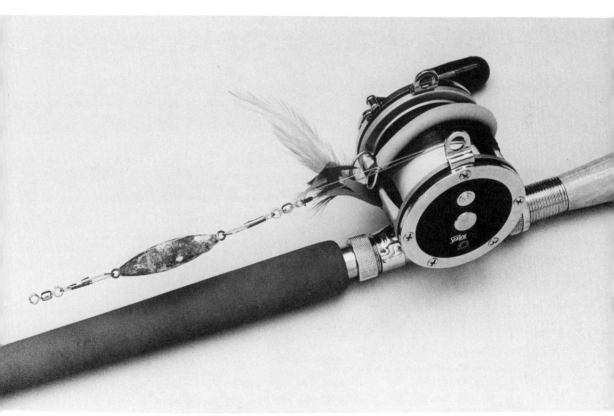

*Trolling outfits using 30-foot leaders between in-line sinkers and the lure can be stored effectively by wrapping the leader around the reel and hooking the lure into a reel pillar.*

*Gaff storage on a small boat, showing the racks and bungee cord holding the gaffs securely but ready for instant use. Note the spring-type point protectors; rubber tubing will also serve as a point protector.*

*To store leaders used with planers, wrap the leader loosely around the planer and secure with a rubber band.*

# 17
# Storing and Handling Tackle on Trips

Tackle handling on trips requires forethought and attention to detail with respect to what tackle to take along and how to take it. In a car there is little problem provided you use tackle boxes and store rods in individual cases or travel rod cases. Uncased rods can easily be broken in car doors, windows, and by the cross springs in a car trunk.

Airline travel is frought with greater danger to tackle. On a recent week-long trip to Bristol Bay Lodge in Alaska, two of the guests in our party arrived in Anchorage from New York with all seven rods in their hard travel case crushed. While there is no way to prevent all damage, there are ways to pack tackle to minimize the risk of damage.

## CAR TRAVEL

Pack rods in rod cases and keep tackle in tackle boxes. Boat bags in several sizes or duffle bags are ideal to hold accessory gear such as raingear, extra clothing, spare reels, lure and plastic-worm boxes, short gaffs, fishing vests, and rod belts.

If you carry your fishing rods with reels and lures on, use a car rod rack to minimize damage. If you place rods in the trunk of a car, case them. Never place loose rods in a car trunk where they can shift and become broken or scarred.

Station wagons or vans are ideal since rods can usually be carried fully assembled with interior racks. Types of racks include:

- Two horizontal bars across the van on which to support the rod at the handle and just above the ferrule. However, this type of rack is suitable mainly for traveling short distances on smooth roads because the rods, which are not held down, can slide.
- Use the above system, but with shock cord spiraled around the rear bar. This way, the rod handles can be slipped under the shock cord to hold the rods in place.
- Use a shock cord spiraled around the rear bar with a forward holder made of PVC or ABS pipe or golf-club tubes. This way, each rod is slipped into a tube for ultimate protection of the blank and the guides. This is the system we use.
- J-shaped hangers of wood or metal, across the top of the van or wagon or along the sides will also hold several rigged rods. Usually the best way to hold any racks or hangers close to the top of the car is with a wooden or aluminum bar that stretches from one side to the other.

*How not to pack a station wagon or car. Rods are thrown in, and no thought has been given to efficient organization of ice chest, gas cans, seat cushions, duffle bags, or boat bags.*

*The patented Sto-A-Way by Burke Products holds rods securely in cars or on boats.*

## AIRLINE TRAVEL

The first consideration in airline travel is packing rods. An easy route to take is to use telescopic or multipiece pack rods that will break down into sections that will fit in a suitcase. Outdoor writer and travel consultant Buck Rogers does this for all of his travel throughout South America. He likes the system and it works well for him while reducing by one (a rod case) the pieces of baggage he must carry.

Multipiece pack rods are available from many manufcturers in fly, spinning, spin-cast, and casting-rod models. A few saltwater models are available. Telescopic rods are available, but at this writing are usually found only in less expensive models and not in a full range. The state of the art of making rods is such that it is only a matter of time before more multipiece and telescopic rods become more available.

Another alternative to get the rods that you currently have or want to use into a standard-size suitcase is to have a qualified custom rod builder, thoroughly familiar with the making of glass-to-glass or graphite-to-graphite ferruling systems, cut your rods and ferrule them for your travel needs. If you go this route, remember to measure the inside dimensions of the suitcase and to give this information to the rod builder. He must know this, especially since the ferrules will add some length to the shortened rod sections after they are cut.

If you don't like the idea of cutting down your rods or buying a new assortment of multipiece or telescopic rods, the other alternative is to buy a travel rod case. Travel rod cases come in several different styles, as follows, each with advantages and disadvantages.

**Plastic, nontelescopic.** These are usually light plastic with plastic end caps. Some open in the middle and others at the end. Most have about 3½- to 5-inch diameters, and will hold about 10 to 15 light freshwater rods. The advantages of this case are light weight, relatively good protection, and low cost. Disadvantages are that they can't be adjusted for different lengths of rods and they are relatively fragile for extensive use.

**Plastic, telescopic.** Similar to above, except that some of them will take rods up to eight-feet long. This is fine, except that when you go over about six-feet long, you risk not getting it past the ticket agent and onto the plane. Also, the longer it is the more risk in getting it on and off the plane undamaged. These rod cases, in spite of the pins that keep them positioned at a certain length, *can* be telescoped from a sharp blow on the end, and this will break rods inside. Once, one of our rod cases of this style was telescoped on a flight, breaking the tips on two rods and stripping the guides off of four more. This rod case had an *extra* pin in the side to provide additional protection against such an accident.

Also, many cases like this have the handle fixed at one spot on the case. An adjustment of the handle position can't be made to carry the case easily when the case is extended. The big advantage is that you can adjust the length for any length of rod for any fishing trip. You can add a handle at the balance point by making one of nylon or canvas strapping secured with filament shipping tape or large hose clamps.

**Metal, round cases.** These are similar in length, diameter, and construction to the plastic cases. The one disadvantage is that the aluminum cases won't bounce back from a blow as will a lightweight plastic case.

**Metal, rectangular cases.** These are rectangular or square in cross section and hinged at the long axis as is a suitcase. As a result, they are far easier to pack with rods. The one big advantage of all rectangular cases is that the rods can be arranged after being placed in the case so guides are clear when the case is closed. Because the whole interior of the case is exposed when opened, you can also pack it with other items if the rods don't fill it up. However, be sure to pack only light items so that they don't damage the rods or guides. Raincoats, fishing vests and light jackets are ideal "stuffers."

**Round versus square travel rod cases.** Everything else being equal, the square cross-section case is better. It won't roll as will a round case, and in the hinged style described above can be loaded and unloaded more easily. Also, for the same diameter, the square case has more room. A 6-inch diameter round case, for example, has a cross-sectional area of 28¼ square inches, while a 6-inch square case has a cross-sectional area of 36 square inches—almost 33 percent greater than the round case.

Airline representatives tell us that if there is a choice of color, don't pick a case that is light grey, silver, or a metallic color. They also suggest that if you have an aluminum case, paint it a bright color, or add some brightly colored stripes of self-adhesive tape to the outside in several spots. The inside of the cargo holds of all commercial aircraft are aluminum and they have a number of struts and supports that resemble a rod case in size, color, and configuration. If the case is not a bright color or lacks stripes of brightly colored (preferably fluorescent) tape to mark it, there is a higher risk it will not get off the plane when you do.

An alternative to rod packing is to use the standard aluminum cases (1⅝-inch diameter for fly rods, 2-inch to 2½-inch diameter for most spinning rods) to case your rods (sometimes by reversing handles you can get two rods in each case). You can strap several cases together into one bundle. Use a strong filament tape or duct tape, mark the cases so that they won't look like part of the airplane, and add your name and address to each case, to protect against losing a case in the event they become separated. Be sure to take along enough tape to repack the bundle, should you have to take the bundle apart while on your fishing trip.

A final possibility, if you have no more than two to three rods for a trip or if you have some extras that you want to be sure of getting there, is to take the bagged rods (no hard-plastic or metal cases) onto the plane as cabin baggage. You should check into this thoroughly before leaving, since all airlines vary in their policy on cabin baggage such as this. Often you can place the bagged rods alongside a window seat, under the seat, or best, in the special compartments for carry-on clothing bags. Some airlines have "businessmen special" planes with racks for small suitcases, where bagged rods will also be safe.

A travel rod case must be packed right to provide maximum protection for the rods during the handling that they will receive from airline and airport baggage crews. Use a bag for each rod or roll all the rods up together in one large piece of cloth. We like a soft flannel for this. Use a piece three feet wide and about twice as long as the average length of rod section. To pack your rods, lay the cloth out on the floor and spread the rod sections on the cloth. Fold over the two ends and roll up the cloth. This assures that each rod section is protected by a wrap of the cloth and that it does not come in contact with the other rod sections. When the bundle is complete, wrap it with several rubber bands or tie it loosely with cord.

For maximum protection, individual rod bags should also be taped or tied together before being placed in a travel rod case. If using a telescopic rod case, keep the case at least two inches longer than the longest rod section. This will prevent rods from being broken by a sharp blow to the end of the case. We have even had telescopic cases become telescoped several inches without damage to the rod using this method.

After rods, there are reels, lures, and accessory equipment that must be taken on any trip. One method, but one that we don't like, is to pack everything in a large tackle box, lock it, and check it in as baggage. Unfortunately, everyone knows that tackle boxes contain tackle, which makes them a prime target for theft. The airlines will reimburse you for the loss later, but this doesn't make up for the inconvenience of arriving at a prime fishing spot without tackle.

Another distinct disadvantage is that luggage seldom stays right-side-up throughout a flight and airport handling, and a rolled or upside-down tackle box can spill and mix lures and tackle enough to require several hours of re-sorting at your destination.

We prefer to store all lures in polypropylene lure boxes. Many tackle companies make them and the polypropylene boxes are tough. A second choice would be the butastyrene boxes. They are tough and have the added advantage of being almost clear (a light amber smoke color), so that you can see the contents. Do not use the plastic tenite boxes, such as those often sold in discount, hardware, and ten-cent stores. Even in a suitcase, they can shatter with the rough handling that airlines give baggage.

The lure boxes, along with the reels, spare spools, fishing pliers, fishing cap, sunglasses, and other gear needed for the fishing trip are all packed in a small, hard suitcase. Use plenty of fishing clothes to separate the contents. It also helps to pack the reels and spare spools in socks, which will serve as reel bags. Before packing reels, be sure to fold down any parts to make them more compact and less prone to damage. On many spinning reels, for example, you can fold down the handle and the bail. See the manufacturer's specifications and instructions for such features on your reels.

An alternative is to use duffle bags for travel. These are an advantage when weight is a consideration. Use the above packing methods, but make sure that there is plenty of padding around all the sides and ends to protect the gear inside. Since the soft duffle bag may subject the gear inside to more blows and shifting, make sure that there is plenty of padding between each hard piece of equipment. You will probably develop a system for your clothing and equipment that best suits you, but we like the following, which has worked well during thousands of miles of travel with no damage to tackle.

**Bottom of duffle bag.** Waders or hip boots (if needed for the trip) and heavy raingear. This will protect the clothing should the duffle bag be placed on a wet runway or in a wet boat.

**Ends of duffle bag.** Tennis shoes, wading shoes, wading sandals, all with soles out. These, or similar items, will protect inner contents.

**Sides of duffle bag.** Any soft clothing such as pants and shirts.

**Center of duffle bag.** Lure boxes, reels, and other accessory equipment, properly padded for protection.

**Top of duffle bag.** Sweater, light raingear, shirts, light jacket, and so on to protect contents if a trunk gets dropped on top of the duffle as a plane is loaded or unloaded.

This packing arangement applies only to the horizontal type of duffle bag. Vertical (military) bags are more difficult to pack this way.

We also carry as hand luggage a small kit bag filled with miscellaneous items needed for the trip. Upon reaching the fishing camp, the lure boxes and other accessories go into the kit bag, which in essence becomes the tackle box. Airline bags, small lightweight nylon boat bags, and similar bags are fine for this.

*Protect spare spools for casting, spinning, and fly reels by carrying them separately in a bag.*

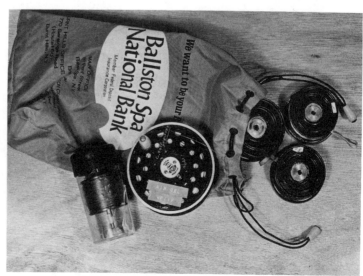

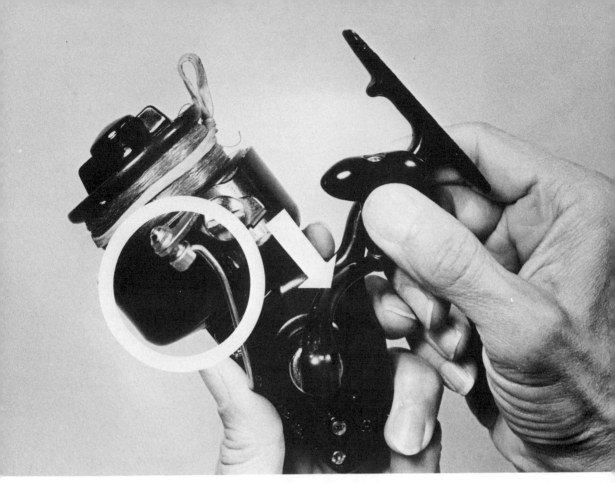

*To store reels compactly for travel, fold down any parts possible. On this spinning reel, the bail can be folded down and the handle reversed to fold next to the reel body.*

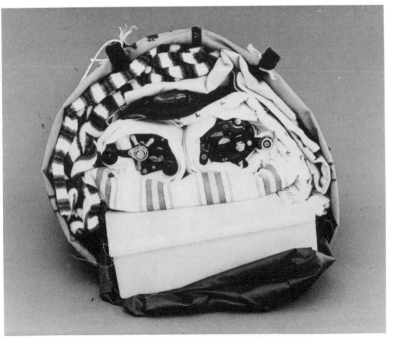

*This cross section of a duffle bag shows proper packing: rain gear on the bottom followed by lure boxes and reels protected by layers of clothing.*

Make sure that all checked-in luggage, including duffle bags and rod cases, is properly marked with your name, address, and telephone number. Airline regulations now require this, and even on the small bush flights where this might not be required, it is necessary if you are to regain any lost luggage. Also, we find it helpful to write our names in large letters on the top, sides, ends, and bottoms of all luggage. You'd be surprised at how duffle bags can look alike when you are going into a fishing camp with other anglers at the same airport. The labeling makes it easy to retrieve yours quickly and also helps prevent theft. Your name and address should always be included *inside* all pieces of checked luggage as well as on the outside.

Where possible, note your luggage going onto the initial plane, at all flight changes, and coming off the plane at the end of the flight. At many airports this is impossible, but in the smaller, less-regimented ones, it helps to count your luggage at each change.

Loose hooks present a unique storage and handling problem. One of the best ways to handle this problem is to use a small, multicompartment box in which you can store the sizes that you use. Label each compartment so that you can find what you need when you need it. Other alternatives are to use the plastic 35-mm film containers to hold hooks of one size. If you only need a few hooks, consider placing them between strips of scotch tape, or threading them by the eyes on a safety pin. Similar methods can be used for storing and handling swivels, snaps, snap swivels, or any other small piece of terminal tackle.

Flies for trout, salmon, bass, and panfish can be stored in the regular fly books or boxes of your choice. Similar containers can be used for the smaller saltwater flies, however, many of the long saltwater flies are more difficult to keep without bending the hackle or wing. One method is to place each fly in a small cellophane or plastic envelope and store the envelopes in a lure box with long compartments.

Once on the fishing grounds, saltwater flies used for certain species of fish present another problem because they are used with a wire or heavy monofilament shock leader. Since rigging these shock leaders is time consuming, flies must be rigged beforehand and stored so they are accessible for rapid connection to the fly-line leader. One method is to use a commonly available tubular snelled-hook holder that holds the hook at one end while the snell fits into a slot in a round rubber ring at the other end. The same method can be used with flies, holding the fly in the hook holder and the monofilament or wire leader in the snell holder. Another method is to use a board that holds the fly, prerigged with shock leader, tippet section, and connecting loop. This arrangement keeps the shock leader and fly straight, is quite easy to pack for travel, and aboard the boat it makes changing flies a quick and easy process.

Leader storage and handling can be another problem. Most leader material, whether monofilament or wire, is packaged on small spools. some have self-locking devices to prevent the material from unwinding. If your brand doesn't have one, or if the device doesn't work, use a wide rubber band over the spool to catch the end. Eight-millimeter movie-film reels are also ideal for storing leader material.

One easy way to keep together all the spools that you need is to loop them on a cord. Keep them in order so that you can easily locate the size leader material that you need. Then you can carry the looped spools in a fishing-vest pocket, tackle box, or boat bag without fear of losing or misplacing one.

If you change the selection of spools of monofilament or wire that you use for various types of fishing, use a short length of chain with a large key ring at one end. Run the chain through the spools in order of size, and finish with a large fender washer. (A fender washer, available in any good hardware store is a very wide washer with a relatively small hole.) Put a simple overhand knot in the chain to keep the washer in place.

Another method is to make and use a leader box. Any small box will do, although we have been using this method with a Tupperware plastic celery crisper, which will hold up to about 20 spools one-half-inch wide and three-inches in diameter. Place the spools

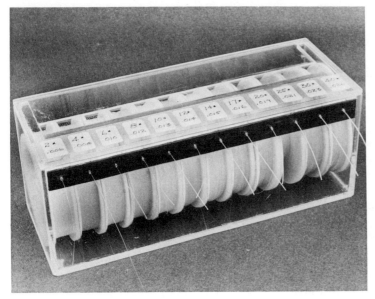

*A leader box file made of Plexiglass. The rubber strip glued to the front of the box maintains tension on leader material.*

that you wish to carry in the box and mark the center position of each spool on the side of the box. Remove the spools and drill or punch a one-eighth-inch-diameter hole at each spot. Replace the spools and run each leader through the appropriate hole. Place the lid on the box and place a large rubber band or one-inch-wide section of inner tube around the sides of the box covering the holes in the side. Leave the ends of each leader sticking out under the rubber band. When you need a section of leader, pull that strand and clip off the needed length. The rubber band will keep the rest of the spool from unwinding. To make selection easy, use a tape printer or permanent felt-tip marker to label each leader size. This box is particularly handy for boat use, where space is not an important consideration but quick access to many leader sizes is. Up to 118-mm film spools can be carried the same way in a 3-by-5 index-card box.

## CHECK LISTS

Check lists are simple, inexpensive insurance against forgetting something on a fishing trip. While they are helpful for all anglers, they are particularly useful for anglers with busy schedules—those who must sandwich fishing trips into taxing work schedules, those taking exotic foreign trips, and those fishing for a wide variety of fish under widely varying conditions. Different anglers use different lists in different ways.

Outdoor writer Lefty Kreh uses a list that he has copied (instant-printing shops can run off 100 copies for a few dollars) and then keeps them in his home office. When he plans for a trip, it is easy to grab one of the sheets, run a line through those items that will not apply, and use the rest of the list to check off against. An all encompassing list such as Lefty uses is ideal, since it covers all possibilities that might come up. By printing up a number of lists, he is able to use one list for each trip, discarding it after use.

Another method is to use a master list, place it between clear plastic covers, and check off with a grease pencil or washable felt-tip marker those items that you need. It can be wiped clean and reused indefinitely, but it can become messy and smeared if you don't handle it carefully.

Separate lists can be made up to cover float trips, ice fishing, big-game offshore fishing, surf fishing, and so on. The important thing is to make your list or lists workable for all your fishing. Three lists follow to provide examples.

# LEFTY KREH'S TRAVEL AND FISHING PACK LIST

*passport*  
*tickets*  
*camera customs slips*  
*letters and phone numbers*  
*reading material*  
*shaving kit*  
*notebooks and pencils*  
*medical kit*  
*suit*  
*dress belt*  
*tie*  
*dress shoes*  
*sneakers*  
*hiking shoes*  
*dress shirts*  
*light summer shirts*  
*warm shirts*  
*pajamas*  
*dress socks*  
*heavy socks*  
*underwear (shirts and shorts)*  
*light summer pants*  

*warm pants*  
*two fishing hats*  
*sunglasses*  
*down jacket or vest*  
*raingear (full parka or jacket and pants)*  
*waders and/or hip boots*  
*Sun Guard*  
*insect repellent*  
*field glasses*  
*rod and reel repair kit*  
*film*  
*camera/camera case*  
*light meter*  
*flies*  
*lures*  
*reels*  
*spare spools for reels*  
*rods*  
*lines (extra lines and shooting-tapers for fly rod)*  
*leaders*  
*tackle box or boxes*  
*rod case*  

If you are planning many foreign trips, it might be well to note international health card (not normally needed in most areas now) and any visas required by the country to be visited.

Customs slips, to prove purchase of an item in this country, are necesary to avoid the possibility of having to prove domestic purchase by other means. Failure to do so can mean that the Japanese camera or Swiss watch that you bought here might be considered by customs to have been bought abroad, requiring a duty to be paid on it. You could later prove by receipts that it was purchased here, but in the meantime there would be a great deal of trouble, delay, and possible expense for you.

Also, it doesn't make any difference if the country visited and the country of origin of the equipment are different, since many countries (Panama, for example) have very low duties on their imports, and items from all over the world can be purchased in such countries. Thus, customs slips should be carried for foreign-made cameras, watches, fishing rods and reels, tape recorders, radios, and so on.

Customs slips are obtained by taking the equipment and filling out slips with the equipment name and serial number at your nearest customs office. Customs offices are located in all major airports with international traffic.

If you must, you can fill out slips between domestic and international flights at most airports, but be sure to allow extra time between flights for this purpose. An alternative is to carry with you original receipts for all equipment, listing the equipment and the serial number.

Letters and telephone numbers of contacts for the trip should be carried, even if you have firm reservations and confirmations. This could save a hassle in the event that something goes wrong on the other end of the trip. It is especially important on international trips.

A small medical kit for field treatment of medical emergencies should be included. This can be a simple kit of such things as adhesive bandage, aspirin, and antacid pills, or it can be a medical kit of prescription drugs for treatment of various illnesses that might be encountered on a fishing trip. The latter kit is described in the section on first aid.

Two fishing hats are a good idea in case one blows off and is lost in the water. Lack of a hat, particularly for those with sensitive eyes or for anyone fishing under bright conditions, can cause eyestrain, eye fatigue, and make an otherwise good trip unpleasant.

Sun Guard is a sunscreen designed to block ultraviolet rays and prevent sunburn. It is a must for those with fair skin or for those fishing in tropical areas.

The rod and reel repair kit is designed by the authors and described later in this section. It is a simple kit containing tools, lubricants, and spare parts for fishing rods and reels. It is a good idea on any trip where a tackle store is inaccessible for the duration of the trip.

# ADRIFT ADVENTURES PACKING LIST
(for wilderness fishing trips)
**Bag #1**
> 1 sleeping bag
> 1 air mattress or foam pad
> 1 nylon tent
> 1 warm jacket
> 1 wool sweater
> 1 pair tennis shoes for the raft
> 1 pair camp shoes for hiking or evening wear
> 2 pairs wool socks
> underwear
> jeans and/or shorts (minimum 2 pairs, 1 pair long)
> shirts or blouses (minimum 2, 1 long)
> Toiletry: toothbrush, toothpaste, Kleenex, comb, biodegradable
> soap, towel, washcloth, shaving gear
> fishing gear (collapsible required)
> flashlight with extra battery

All of the above will not be available during the day. To pack, place items inside a large plastic garbage bag and then place inside a vertical duffle bag (army style).

**Bag #2**
> swim wear
> rain jacket or poncho
> camera and film
> insect repellent
> sunscreen lotion
> suntan lotion
> sunglasses (tie-strap recommended)
> wide-brim hat (tie-strap recommended)
> tobacco items
> matches
> candy and gum
> bandana
> Chapstick
> canteen or water botttle

Bag #2 will be available during the day. To pack, place items inside a small plastic garbage bag and then place inside a day pack.

(This list is used by Adrift Adventures, who run wilderness fishing trips, to insure that patrons are properly outfitted.)

# IRV SWOPE'S TRAVEL CHECK LIST

*tickets*
*passport (or voter's registration card or*
*birth certificate)*
*vaccination record*
*customs slips*
*cash money*
*checkbook*
*credit cards*
*fishing tackle*
  *rods*
  *reels*
  *lines*
  *lures*
*spare tackle*
  *rods*
  *reels and reel spools*
  *lines and leader material*
*wading staff*
*Sportmate pliers*
*small Vise-Grip pliers and file*
*tackle-repair kit*
*WD-40*
*fly jacket*
*chest-high waders*
*hip boots*
*tackle bag*
*surf bag*
*Tac-a-pac (over-the-shoulder tackle pack)*
*masking tape*
*nylon reinforced tape*
*old towel or rag*
*waterproof watch*
*raingear*

*fishing clothes*
  *hats*
  *shirts and pants (or shorts)*
  *shoes and/or sneakers*
  *pants for wet wading*
  *light and/or heavy jackets*
  *sweater*
*Polaroid sunglasses and spares*
*spare eyeglasses*
*Snuggers (eyeglass strap)*
*binoculars*
*hand warmer and fluid*
*sunscreen*
*Chapstick*
*insect repellent*
*snake-bite kit*
*motion-sickness pills*
*first-aid kit*
*flashlight (throwaway)*
*travel clock*
*underwear, socks, handkerchiefs*
*bathrobe*
*traveling clothes (shirt, pants, shoes, and*
*outer garments)*
*toilet articles*
*camera (lenses, filters, flash unit, gunstock,*
*tripod, and other accessories)*
*film (with X-ray protection)*
*camera bag*
*plastic trash bags*
*notebook and pen*
*fish-identification handbook*
*luggage identification (inside and outside)*

# 18
# Tackle Maintenance

Tackle manufactured today is finer than it has ever been. New materials for rods, improvements in reels, and constant innovations in lures and lines have given modern anglers tackle that would have been undreamed of 20 years ago. But to keep tackle working as it should requires regular maintenance and annual checkups.

## REGULAR MAINTENANCE

This consists of checking and cleaning tackle everytime you return from a trip. This is the best time to remove grit, grime, or saltwater residue, and to make sure that your tackle will be ready the next time you leave to go fishing.

**Rods.** After every trip, wash down the rod to remove grit and pay particular attention to the inside of the guide rings. Grit here will wear both the guide and the line. If fishing in saltwater, we find the best method is to take the rods in the shower with you and wash them off with a soapy washcloth, rinse, and leave to dry in the shower. When dry, check each of the guides for cracks and check the guide wraps for possible wear that could cause them to unwind.

If necessary, replace the guides or add a coat of varnish or epoxy finish to the wrap to protect it against wear and eventual unwrapping. If guides need further cleaning, use an old toothbrush, typewriter brush, or gun-cleaning brush to get out the grit.

Use a pipe cleaner if necessary to clean out any grit from metal or glass-to-glass or graphite-to-graphite ferrules. A bit of sand here can score a metal ferrule and weaken the glass or graphite ferrule such as those found on modern rods. Use a brush or pipe cleaner and lighter fluid to clean out the threads on locking reel seats if required.

If using rods with a glass-to-glass or graphite-to-graphite ferrule, coat the male section of the ferrule with candle wax to lubricate it and give it a good fit. If a ferrule is loose (either between the two parts of a metal ferrule, or between the metal ferrule and blank itself) remove it and reglue or replace it or have this done by a qualified repair shop.

**Reels.** When you return home, back off all the drags if you haven't already done so. Drags kept tight will lose their resilience and effectiveness. If the reels have been used in salt water or scummy or algae-filled fresh water, or if they have otherwise become dirty, remove the spools (on spinning and fly reels) and place them in a basin of warm water to soak. Scrub lightly with a washcloth or soft brush.

Some anglers do not like soaking reels, but instead flush them with water from a faucet. If you use this technique, scrub softly first with soap and water to remove any salt residue and do not use the high force of a garden-hose nozzle, which will drive any dirt or salt deeper into the reel. Use small brushes or pipe cleaners to remove any dirt from cracks and crevices. Areas to pay particular attention to include the bails and rollers of spinning reels and the pawls and level wind of casting reels.

Remove from the water, allow to dry, and spray with a demoisturizer such as WD-40, CRC, LPS-1, PennsGuard. Follow the manufacturer's instructions with respect to oiling and greasing and pay particular attention to such parts as spool shafts, level winds, bails, and bail rollers. Check to be sure that all screws are tight and check especially the thumbscrews on the removable side plates of casting reels. Store the reel in a clean, dry place; and out of the sun to protect the line that is on the reel spools.

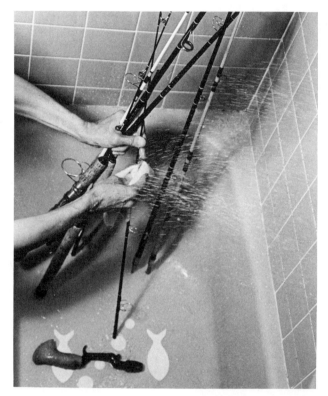

*Proper maintenance includes washing down tackle after each trip.*

*Remove spools from spinning and fly reels and soak reels in water after use in salt or dirty fresh water.*

*To protect reels after cleaning, spray exposed surface wth a de-moisturizing agent.*

CRC, LPS-1, PennsGuard. Follow the manufacturer's instructions with respect to oiling and greasing and pay particular attention to such parts as spool shafts, level winds, bails, and bail rollers. Check to be sure that all screws are tight and check especially the thumbscrews on the removable side plates of casting reels. Store the reel in a clean, dry place, and out of the sun to protect the line that is on the reel spools.

**Lures.** If using lures in salt water, be sure to rinse them off after each trip to keep the hooks from corroding. Also, if you in some way soaked a fly box, be sure to open it up immediately after the trip and dry the contents and the box in the sun or under a hair dryer to prevent the hooks from rusting and ruining the flies. The same applies to lures. Check lures for possible hook damage, breakage, broken barbs, and replace or bend back into shape if possible. Repaint or touch up if necessary. Soft plastic lures require little care, but when returning them to your tackle box, make sure that you keep them separate from the hard lures and that soft lures are kept in tackle boxes or lure containers labeled as "worm proof." The plasticizers in the soft plastics will react with some hard-finish lures, with older tackle boxes, and some plastic containers to cause the hard plastics to soften or melt. The finish on hard-plastic lures will soften and come off after prolonged contact with soft lures, making the hard-plastic lure unusable until it is cleaned and repainted.

**Lines.** After each trip, check the last 10 feet of your monofilament or braided line for wear. If worn, cut it off. Also, this should be checked several times a day while fishing, cutting off several feet at a time when the line is abraded.

Clean fly lines with a manufacturer-recommended cleaner and allow to dry before replacing on the reel. Modern lines, whether braided nylon, Dacron, fly lines, or monofilament are almost troublefree, if guides and reel spools are kept clean. The one big danger to fly lines is contact with solvents that will break down their plasticizers and cause them to become brittle, cracked, and useless. Gasoline, insect repellents, and suntan lotions are examples of such solvents. Fly rodders applying suntan lotions, sunscreens or insect repellents should be particularly careful in this regard and wash their hands carefully after application and before handling their tackle.

## ANNUAL MAINTENANCE

All of the above applies to annual maintenance, except that it should be done more carefully and with more attention to detail. Also, this is the time to repair any damaged

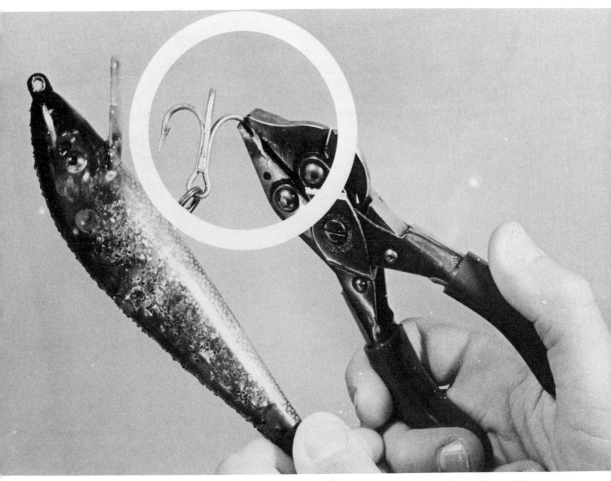

*Check tackle frequently and, when necessary, straighten out hooks or replace them if required.*

tackle that has been neglected or temporarily repaired to get through the fishing season.

**Rods.** Check carefully as in regular maintenance, and replace any guides that are broken, grooved, or bent. We also find that a lot of repair work can be kept to a minimum with rods if you will take the time at the end of each season to add a coat of rod finish to the wraps. Often during hard fishing trips, the finish will become worn and ultimately expose the threads. If this happens, it is only a matter of time before a thread is cut or frayed, requiring replacement of the entire wrap. An annual coat of rod finish prevents this and keeps the rod looking new.

**Reels.** After cleaning reels as you do after each trip, take the reel apart to check the grease content and for any worn parts inside. To do this, consult your owner's manual for proper disassembly, and use the proper tools. Use an egg carton, biscuit tin, or any compartmentalized box to hold each part as you remove it. This makes it easy to replace parts in order. After all the parts are removed, clean if necessary in a solvent such as kerosene, lighter fluid, or mineral spirits.

*Do not* clean any plastic parts this way, since they will often react with the solvent and can become soft or deformed. Clean plastics with soap and water, dry, and replace. Once all the parts are clean, check for wear. Reel parts that wear include the pawl and level wind on casting reels, the roller, roller bushings, bail spring on spinning reels, and drag washers and plates on all reels. Replace if necessary. Grease and oil all parts as per the manufacturer's instructions, and reassemble the parts in order.

**Lines.** Line is the most inexpensive link between you and fish. It doesn't pay to skimp on line and try to make it last forever. Replace it each season (with the exception of fly lines, which should last several seasons) with a top-quality brand of line. Hard fishing may require replacement several times per year.

**Lures.** Check carefully and replace or sharpen hooks as necessary. Touch up any scarred finishes. Jigs and bucktails often become chipped. Repaint any worn jigs and repaint or otherwise coat the thread wrapping that holds the tail in place. Polish all spinners and spoons, using metal polish. To protect from tarnishing, use a protective finish, such as the clear spray G-96 Rod Wrap Epoxy.

## ROD AND REEL REPAIR KIT

One of the most useful items an angler can carry for long trips to fishing camps, to foreign countries, or even on short boat-fishing trips is an emergency tackle-repair kit. Such a kit is easy to make, costs little, and carries those items that you will specifically need for repairing your rods, reels, and lures. It takes up little space and can save the day by repairing tackle that otherwise would be useless for the remainder of a trip. We keep such a kit in a Vlchek M-606 lure box.

This six-compartment box will hold almost anything that you need for a quick repair and makes it possible to separate items by categories. While your needs, box size, and contents might differ slightly, we find the following to be adequate.

**Compartment 1:** various oilers, tubes of lubrication, grease, and so on for reels. Carry those recommended by the manufacturer or get the small sets of hypodermic-type injection lubes for grease and oil. For protection against leaking, wrap each piece in a separate plastic bag.

**Compartment 2:** glues, including Pliobond, Duco Cement, stick ferrule cement, candle wax (for lubricating glass-to-glass and graphite-to-graphite ferrules), five-minute epoxy for gluing such tackle as broken and cracked plugs. Store each in a clear plastic bag.

**Compartment 3:** fly-line cleaner, in cans or packets, and fly dressing.

**Compartment 4:** the tools that are supplied with each fishing reel. We carry one for every type of reel that we own so that we have all repair tools regardless of the type or quantity of tackle that we take on a trip. Most of these wrenches are small, flat, and lightweight.

Also include split-ring pliers, a four-inch adjustable wrench, and a set of small screwdrivers. The best screwdriver sets are those that have blades from about one-eighth- to one-quarter-inch width rather than the sets with smaller blades for precision jeweler's work. Also include an ignition file for touching up any parts that might be worn or tight as well as for sharpening small hooks.

**Compartment 5:** parts for reels and rods, including bail springs, reduction or high-speed gears, spare handles, spare spool washers, antibacklash weights for casting reels, spare pawls for casting reels, spare rollers for spinning-reel bails, and other such parts. Carry those parts that are most likely to break down in the field.

**Compartment 6:** miscellaneous items and parts for repair of lures, including treble and single hooks, wrapping thread (for rewrapping bucktails, rod guides, and so on), hook hangers, screw eyes, spinner-bait skirts, split rings, and other such items. Often lures can be put back in service quickly with the proper part and Sportmate pliers or split-ring pliers.

When you make up such a kit, make sure that you label it as such so that it can be distinguished from similar lure containers. Secure it with heavy rubberbands to keep it from opening up.

*Vice-Grip pliers will hold hooks securely while you sharpen them before each trip.*

*A tackle-repair kit as described in the text includes tools, spare parts, lubricants, glues, and accessories for repair of rods and reels in the field. All items fit into small six-compartment Vl-chek box.*

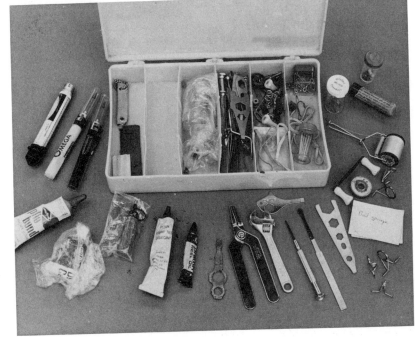

# PART FIVE

# 19
# Dealing with the Sun

Most of the time that we are out fishing, it is sunny. That makes the fishing pleasant most of the time—certainly more pleasant than fishing in rain, sleet, or snow. But the sun presents some dangers to the angler that must be dealt with.

Being members of a nation of sun worshippers, many fishermen often discard caps and shirts or wear short pants to cash in on the tanning effect of the sun while they are fishing. This is fine provided that it is done in moderation. Too much sun has a number of short- and long-term bad effects. The immediate short-term effect is sunburn, while the long-term effects, according to the American Cancer Society, can be prematurely aged skin, wrinkles, loss of the skin's elasticity, and scaly gray growths and dark patches called keratoses. These keratoses are often precancerous. The effects of the sun in sunburn and premature aging of the skin are strictly esthetic. Skin cancer is a far more serious condition, and one that must be considered just as seriously by the high-mountain Colorado trout fisherman, the surf angler at Hatteras, the offshore fisherman at the Baltimore Canyon, the San Diego party-boat fisherman, and the bonefish stalker on the Florida flats as by the bikini-clad sunbather in the Bahamas.

According to the American Cancer Society, almost all of the 300,000 cases of skin cancer that occur annually in Americans are sun caused or sun related. Fortunately, early treatment usually results in a complete cure.

Skin cancer does have early warning signals as follows:

- A sore that does not heal rapidly and promptly.
- A change in the size or coloration of a wart or mole.
- The development of any unusual or new pigment area on the skin.

These signs do not always mean cancer, but any angler noticing any of these signs should consult his doctor. Skin cancers found early enough can be removed with little trouble and with little or no scarring.

Your complexion will determine the amount of risk you run from the sun, both in terms of sunburn and skin cancer. The damage from the sun comes from the ultraviolet rays. Blacks are relatively safe because of the darkened pigment of the skin (although blacks will sunburn slightly, the degree depending upon the darkness of the skin), while fair-skinned blonds and redheads are most susceptible to skin damage from the sun. Olive or dark-skinned Caucasians are somewhere between these two extremes. As a basic rule, your degree of protection from the ultraviolet rays is directly proportional to how easily you tan without burning, blistering, or discomfort.

Fishermen are outdoors all the time during their sport and will be exposed to a great amount of sun under most fishing conditions. Other factors that influence the effect of the sun are:

- Certain drugs used temporarily or habitually can make the skin more susceptible to burning. Antibiotics, antibacterial agents in medicated creams and soaps, barbiturates, and birth-control pills can increase the danger of burning.

- Some perfumes, suntan lotions, and insect repellents can cause a sensitive reaction in some people.
- You won't be fully protected even under a boat canopy, umbrella, or in other shade. Canvas boat canopies will only deflect some of the ultraviolet rays. Additional rays will bounce at you from all directions off the water, sand, beach, or boat deck.
- You can also get badly burned on cloudy days. Seventy to eighty percent of the harmful ultraviolet rays will penetrate the cloud cover.
- If you are susceptible to burning, take extra care if you are wearing a light shirt that becomes wet from surf or boat spray. The wet shirt (T-shirts are especially bad in this regard) will cling to your skin and the water will help transmit at least 50 percent of the ultraviolet rays directly to your skin.
- Take extra care in high altitudes. High-mountain areas have less atmosphere to filter out the ultraviolet rays, therefore the sun will be more damaging there than at sea level. Also, high-mountain areas are often still snow covered in early summer and snow can reflect up to 85 percent of the sun's rays back to you to cause additional burning.
- There is a greater incidence of skin cancer in the southern and southwestern portions of the country than elsewhere. If you live or fish in these areas, take appropriate measures to protect yourself.

## PROTECTION FROM THE SUN

This chapter assumes the worst: that you are fair, highly sensitive to the sun, and need maximum protection from its harmful ultraviolet rays while fishing. Thus, you will find listed here the maximum practical protection that fishermen can use. Adjust or modify for your fishing conditions and individual requirements.

**Sunglasses.** The best glasses for fishermen have polarizing lenses. There are two reasons for this in addition to the protection such glasses offer from the sun. First, if you are fishing flats or other waters where you want to see the fish, polarizing lenses will cut the surface glare and allow you to see the water to spot the fish. Second, the polarizing effect of the glasses will reduce the glare off the water and lessen eyestrain during a long day of fishing.

If you don't wear prescription glasses, you have a wide choice of sunglasses from which to choose. Pick glasses that have a flat lens, since the flat lens will have less possibility of distortion of any image. Choose glasses with a large surface area to give your eyes maximum protection. The frame should be large and preferably dark. Avoid large, bulky metallic frames that might reflect light into the glass. Make sure that the nose piece fits well, without undue pinching, and that the temple pieces are the right length to hold the glasses on even when you become sweaty.

If you wear prescription glasses, you have several alternatives. First, you can often get prescription polarizing glasses. But they are expensive, and also some complex prescriptions prevent their use. Clip-on polarizing lenses are available but are often too small to completely cover regular glasses to give you the type of protection that you need in the field. They are easy to carry and add little extra weight to the regular glasses. Some clip-on glasses make it possible to keep the polarizing glasses on yet flip them out of the way when not needed. There are also some polarizing glasses that are designed to fit over regular glasses, but these are generally heavier when combined with the prescription glasses that still must be worn.

To prevent glare reaching your eyes from the side, choose glasses that have side shields if posssible. Most glasses don't, but at some optical stores you can buy slip-on side shields of lightweight, dark-green plastic. If these aren't available, you can make your own from scraps of tinted plastic that can be glued, slipped on, or riveted to the temple piece. Ideally, these should be D shaped and large enough to run from the top of the frame to the bottom of the glass and as far back as your temple to prevent glare from the side.

(If you are using polarizing sunglasses you must remove them before taking photographs with a polarizing filter on the front of the camera lens. The effect of the two polarizing lenses would be to darken the image seen through the camera, though it will not affect the set exposure.)

**Cap or hat.** A cap or hat is important in protecting your head from sunburn, preventing eyestrain from the glare of the sun, and protecting your neck from the rays of a high summer sun. Caps are lightweight and often preferred by fishermen, but they do not provide any neck protection. One exception to this is the "Florida guide's cap," which has a brim around the side and back in addition to a bill at the front. The brim can be raised for breezes or lowered to provide neck protection from the sun. On any cap, it is important to choose one that has a dark (black, dark green, or dark blue) undersurface of the brim. A light underbrim color will only  bounce the rays of the sun reflected off the water into your eyes, circumventing the glare protection that you want and expect from a cap.

Broad-brimmed, lightweight straw hats are also good and provide full protection from the sun. Get one that is a fairly tight weave, so that the sun won't pass through to cause burning and to provide some glare protection by the forward brim, even though the underneath will be the natural straw color. If you wish, you can color the underbrim with spray paint or a permanent felt-tip marker. The one disadvantage of broad-brimmed hats for boat anglers is that they will blow off easily while running.

*The rear sunshade on a Flordia type guide cap can be lowered to protect the neck and tops of the ears from excessive exposure to the sun.*

*The side shields on these sun glasses prevent glare early and late in the day when the sun is low. Sun screen on the cheeks gives further protection.*

**Shirt.** Best are the long-sleeve lightweight sport shirts, preferably in a light color that will reflect heat. Cotton will be most comfortable but will also be heavier and tend to stick to you if wet from perspiration. You can wear an undershirt to absorb perspiration, but will probably be cooler if you wear only the lightweight sport shirt. Choose the shirt carefully, however. Slip-over types of cotton often have a crew-neck collar that can cause pain everytime you turn your neck if your neck gets sunburned. If you choose a button-front shirt, make sure that you keep all but the top buttons secured, and that you use ample amounts of sun-block lotion at the exposed v of skin above the second button. Several years ago, one of us was fishing the flats in Florida under an unbearable sun, and loosened the second and third buttons to take advantage of any slight breeze. In spite of a broad-brimmed straw hat that kept this area in shade, reflected glare burned the chest area severely.

Long sleeves are best for protection of your arms from the sun. If you have a long-sleeve shirt, you can always roll the sleeves up if you want. Fair-skinned anglers in particular should use sunscreen on the backs of hands.

**Pants.** Lightweight, light-colored pants are best to reflect the sun. Wear long pants to protect your legs.

**Socks.** Some fishermen new to southern waters remove socks for comfort while wading, boat fishing, or shore fishing. Often the result is a badly burned instep. Keep socks on for sun protection or use a sun-block lotion on this sensitive area. White socks are best to reflect the sun.

**Shoes.** Keep shoes on to protect your feet from the sun. In addition, beaches, boat decks, and docks can be hot enough in the summer to burn the bottoms of your feet badly.

**Kerchief.** A kerchief, rolled and knotted loosely around your neck, will help to prevent sunburn of that area and will also absorb perspiration.

**Hands.** Use light cotton gloves, if necessary, or a sun-block lotion.

## LOTIONS AND CREAMS

Liberal use of suntan lotions, sunscreens, and sun blocks provide the best way to protect those areas of skin that can't be covered by clothing. It is important to use any product according to the manufacturer's directions and recommendations. Most suggest that you keep them away from your eyes and mouth, and that you use them on dry skin, preferably before going out into the sun. Sweating or getting wet from boat or surf spray will wash off most lotions so that liberal reapplication will be necessary. Apply to all exposed areas, even if they are covered by the shade of a hat or cap. Cover your face, neck, (including the upper chest if you have an open shirt), your ears, backs of hands, forearms (if your sleeves are rolled up), and your instep and ankles (if you are not wearing socks).

Products available can be broken down into several general categories:

- Suntanning products: these will promote rapid but safe tanning and are primarily of interest to sunbathers interested in getting a year's tan on a two-week vacation. Various degrees of protection are offered, usually based on the type of skin that you have. They give some protection, but not enough for a desk-bound angler on his first day-long fishing trip of the summer.
- Sunscreens: these provide more protection and usually contain varying amounts of para-amino-benzoic acid (PABA). These will absorb some of the ultraviolet rays and will allow gradual tanning along with the protection. Most should be applied about 30 to 45 minutes before exposure to the sun, and like other preparations should be reapplied if you become wet or if you sweat excessively. Some manufacturers are now using a numbering system to indicate the degree of protection that you get from their products. Thus, you can choose for the amount of protection and tanning aid that you want.

The numbers are standard among manufacturers and the higher the number, the greater the protection. Number 15 gives maximum protection. The number also refers to the number of hours that you can stay in the sun and get no more of a burn or tan that one hour without protection. A number 4 lotion will give you the same tan or burn in four hours that you would get without it in one hour; a number 8 lotion would give you eight hours in the sun with no more danger than one hour; number 15 will block out all (for practical purposes) of the sun and give you the maximum protection. (The sun blocks mentioned below are equivalent to number 15 protection.)

- Sun blocks: These allow no tanning at all, completely deflecting the ultraviolet rays. They are good. Some sun blocks are creamy while others are clear and watery. One well-known sun-blocking agent is zinc oxide, an opaque white ointment best for the nose, lips, ears, and other highly sensitive areas. A creamy solution of sulisobenzone, available under several brand names, is also good and is used by many fishermen.

 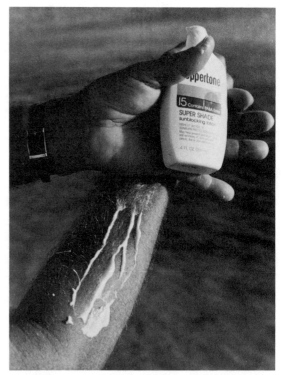

*Apply sun tan or sun screen lotions with the back of your hand not the palm, as they repell fish when accidentally touched to line or lures and might harm plastic fishing tackle. Also, note the number 15 on the bottle; this denotes the relative sun-screening protection of the product—lower numbers provide less protection, higher numbers provide more.*

# 20
# Dealing with the Heat

Dealing with the heat is important when fishing to prevent heat stroke, heat exhaustion, fatigue, and general discomfort. And, as the saying goes, it's often not the heat, but the humidity. When you are having fun fishing, bodily comfort sometimes gets sidetracked; however, heat does present difficulties that must be dealt with.

In coping with the heat, you want to do just the opposite of coping with the cold. With the cold you try to retain body heat by adding insulating clothing; with heat, you want to promote rapid and continued evaporation to keep your body temperature as cool as possible while replacing lost fluids regularly. The ultimate might seem to be fishing in a nudist camp, but protection from the ultraviolet rays of the sun is equally important as cooling the body. You will have to compromise with clothing that will be loose enough to allow for rapid evaporation yet at the same time protect you from the sun's rays. Here are some suggestions on what to wear.

**Hat.** If you are in the sun, follow the suggestions included in the preceding chapter for choosing the best types of fishing hats. If you are fishing in the shade but still in high-heat conditions, as when under a Florida bridge, in a Louisiana swamp, or in a Central American jungle, you might want a hat that you can dip into the water to help cool your head. In this case, the terry-cloth hats often worn by golfers are ideal, since they can be soaked, wrung out, and worn without the water dripping onto your glasses or down your neck. They provide maximum cooling over a relatively long period of time. The worst type of cap for this cooling effect would be the synthetic mesh type of cap often used as promotion by various companies. They won't hold enough moisture to do the job, although their favorable attribute is that they allow passage of cooling breezes through the mesh.

Lacking a hat, you can get the same cooling effect with a large, cotton handkerchief or bandana knotted at each of the corners to keep it on your head. It will do the job and make fishing far more comfortable. Stay away from the synthetics, since they won't hold water well or for very long.

**Kerchief.** Some anglers like a wet kerchief around their necks for the same cooling effect that a wet hat will give. Others, however, find that kerchiefs are annoying and add to heat build-up. If you do decide to try it, knot the kerchief lightly, otherwise if you wet it, it will be difficult to untie later. Keep it loose around your neck for comfort.

**Shirt.** Cottons tend to be loose weaves, allowing evaporation quicker and providing less of a chilling effect than synthetics of polyester or nylon when the shirt is wet and plastered to your skin. Personally, we don't like the clinging T-shirt styles, which seem to hold in the heat, and instead opt for the button-front, loose, regular-style shirt in either short or long sleeves.

Make sure the shirts are large enough to provide air space all around your torso for maximum evaporation and cooling. And if a choice exists, pick shirts with a loose weave, but not loose enough for the sun to penetrate and cause a burn. For obvious reasons, do not wear an undershirt, but protect the area around your neck and where the shirt is open in front with a sun block if you haven't previously built up a tan.

**Pants.** Pants should be lightweight, a loose weave, and roomy enough to prevent clinging and excess sweating. We like very lightweight synthetic khakis in a light tan that will not absorb heat. White is good also, but they can look awfully dirty quickly. Shorts are ideal in shade conditions or if you protect your legs from the sun with a sunscreen.

**Socks.** Wear lightweight socks, not the heavy wool or athletic type that you will want for spring, fall, and winter fishing. Pick white to repel heat.

**Colors.** Black and dark colors absorb heat, and white and light colors reflect heat. Whenever possible, pick hats, shirts, pants, and even sneakers and shoes that are light in color. You are on the inside of that clothing and any dark clothing will absorb heat and transmit it to you.

**Diet.** Most of us automatically adjust our habits for summer heat by eating a little less than usual and also eating lighter foods. It seems that the lighter foods and less food makes you feel more comfortable, less bloated, and less likely to feel slightly queasy or drowsy.

Since the high heat puts a strain on all your bodily systems, it is especially important during sultry fishing days to keep your eating habits before, during, and after fishing on the light and bland side, rather than chancing an unpleasant time on a fishing trip with food quantities and quality that might be risky. All of us are different in this regard, and what might make one person queasy, another could digest with ease and never pause between casts. Usually it gets back to avoiding those foods that, as the saying goes, "we like them, but they don't like us."

**Drinks.** There is no question that high heat causes copious perspiration and loss of body fluids. Some authorities have suggested that under high-heat conditions (desert or jungle) and with a person working or under steady exertion, up to one-half gallon of fluid is lost per hour through perspiration. It is necessary to replace this fluid on a regular basis, but the choice of the replacement is important to prevent other problems. If you like beer or soft drinks, instead of a steady diet of such beverages, alternate them with plain water, a fluid-replacing drink such as Gatorade, unsweetened tea, or other unsweetened drinks.

It is equally important to replace salt lost through perspiration, so many anglers use salt tablets when they are going to be all day in a boat, offshore fishing, on a foreign trip south of the border, or otherwise in a situation where salt replacement will be required. Salt tablets are available at most drug stores, but a person with high blood pressure or a heart condition or using any type of medication should consult his doctor before using. Some persons feel nauseous after taking salt tablets. If you find this to be the case, try extra-heavy doses of salt on all meals instead of the tablets, or a light snack taken with each salt tablet.

# 21
# Dealing with Precipitation

Rain does more than get you wet. It chills you, causing you to lose body heat, and if it soaks your clothing it will reduce any of the insulating effect and make the clothing useless for retaining body heat.

All raingear in some way comprises an outer shell, and raingear can include waders, hip boots, ankle-high rubber boots, rain pants, rain-proof bib overalls, wader-height jackets, waist-long jackets, three-quarter-length jackets, and full-length jackets. Under a hard rain or under heavy-spray conditions, raingear should include head-to-boot protection. A three-quarter-length parka that protects you down to the knees but lets your legs and feet get wet and chilled still leaves you miserable.

Raingear fabric should be completely waterproof. In the raingear industry this causes much discussion, since a fabric might be waterproof under a light rain but not under a heavy rain or when sitting on the fabric (as in rain pants) where the tendency is to push the water through the fabric pores. Some fabrics might be waterproof, but able to stand only 12 to 30 pounds of water pressure per square inch.

Some fabrics, such as Royal Red Ball's Flexnet fabric (their name for a polymer-coated, elasticized, cotton-knit fabric used in many of their outdoor parkas and raingear), will withstand 170 pounds of pressure per square inch according to the manufacturer, and thus is advertised as completely waterproof.

One of the problems with raingear, especially in warm climates, is that it will hold in moisture just as readily as it keeps it out. Perspiration builds up to cause a clammy, chilling, uncomfortable effect that is almost as bad (and sometimes worse) than getting wet from the rain or spray. It would be ideal to have clothing that would keep all the rain out yet let perspiration escape or dissipate. But as you gain one feature, you loose the other. As a general rule, completely waterproof fabrics don't breathe at all.

One exception is the very expensive, breathing, waterproof rain suits in which the fabric permits body vapor transmission while resisting water of up to 70 pounds per square inch of pressure. The one disadvantage of this type of suit is that the fabric can't be permanently bonded and all pieces must be stitched. If this step is not very carefully done with overlapping seams, there is the likelihood that in time the garment will leak at the seams.

The best solution is to get a suit with an inner lining of cotton or nylon (cotton is best) that will absorb some of the moisture from your body and clothing. To help in vapor dissipation, some garments have open grommets at spots where the rain can't enter easily, such as under the arm, on the back (protected by a storm flap), and high on the chest (also protected by a storm flap).

The only other solution to this problem is to try to open the garments at the neck,

*Foul-weather gear is a must when boating to remain comfortable when rain threatens your fishing. This angler would be more comfortable if he had foul weather pants to go with his ¾ length parka.*

*C.B.P. dressed for February bass fishing in Delaware with a waterproof parka to cut the wind and a knit watch cap and gloves for added protection.*

*Waterproof pants and parka such as this angler is wearing provide good protection against the cold and wind of early spring and late fall even when the weather is clear.* Converse

sleeves, legs, and front whenever possible, and to take them off immediately after the rain stops unless they're needed for wind protection.

Most rain suits and parkas have zipper fronts. Make sure that the zipper is brass, or better yet, plastic, especially if you are fishing around salt water where corrosion is a problem. Storm flaps over the zipper are a must, and they should button or snap in place to keep the zipper as protected as possible.

A hood is a necessity, but should be large enough to go over other headwear, including some of the heavy down or knit caps used in winter fishing. A drawstring around the hood is also good for those times in heavy rain, boat spray, or surf conditions when such a closure will reduce or eliminate the amount of water driven down your neck. Similarly, elastic cuffs on the sleeves, along with an overhanging storm cuff are a help in keeping rainwater from running down to your elbow when your hands are raised, as in fly-casting or rigging lures. Flap pockets are equally important if you carry pliers, cigarettes, clippers, or other items that you want to keep dry.

Seams on all rain clothing should be welded if possible, or if only stitched, should be covered with a tape or sealant.

Where possible, especially in sunny climates, raingear should be light colored to reflect heat. This is especially important where raingear is worn as protection against wind. Finally, raingear should be as lightweight and thin as possible, especially for traveling anglers. Weight and bulk are costly to ship and difficult to pack and carry, so the lighter the gear, the less nuisance and expense.

One aspect of raingear often overlooked is its ability to cut wind in addition to protecting from rain. If the water can't get through, neither can air. As a result, raingear is a must for any angler to carry at all times. If a light wind comes up or if the temperature drops, the addition of a rain parka and/or rain pants will retain body warmth.

For the fisherman or outdoorsman who might get into a survival situation, the Vexilar Radar Jac is an excellent item. It is a six-ounce jacket that comes in its own pouch, fits

*A survival type parka which includes U.S. Coast Guard approved flotation and a gold-metallized mylar coating for radar detection and warmth. A hood is recessed in the collar of this Vexilar jacket.*

over flotation equipment and PFD's, provides insulation, and is rot proof, waterproof, nonporous, and heat reflecting. But the great advantage over many similar jackets is that the Radar Jac utilizes a material that is a high-strength, metallic-gold, polyester film chemically bonded to a tear-resistant fabric to make the jacket highly visible and radar reflective. Small pieces of the fabric tested in the Gulf of Mexico and Lake Ontario have been spotted by radar by sea- and air-rescue units as far away as 40 miles. With aircraft alone, a man floating with a PFD and using only a hood made from the reflective material has been spotted from a 5,000-foot altitude. The waterproof and heat-insulating properties make it a worthwhile though expensive jacket for fishing trips with the added bonus that should such an emergency occur, it can easily be spotted at sea by search units.

# 22
# Dealing with the Cold

There are a lot of opportunities to get cold while fishing. Wind, boat spray, surf, cold water, rain, sleet, snow, and temperature drops during a day's fishing all contribute to making you cold—and you don't have to be ice fishing, nor do you only get cold in the middle of winter.

Proper dress for the cold can be nothing more than a light jacket or sweater thrown in with your gear against the possibility of a temperature drop, increase in wind, or overcast sky in the summer. For these situations, we like to use light nylon jackets. They are easy to fold up, take up almost no space and add almost no weight to a kit, come in bright colors, have one or more pockets, often have a hood, usually have elastic cuffs to keep out the cold, are inexpensive, come lined or unlined, and are available almost everywhere.

Sweaters are just as good for this purpose unless there is a high wind, in which case the open weave of the sweater can't hold the warm air and keep you warm for prolonged periods. You might wish to carry both a sweater and a lightweight nylon jacket—the sweater will give you warmth and the jacket over it will keep the warmth in. And you will have the option of using one or the other as conditions dictate. This is an example of "layering," in which articles of clothing can be added or subtracted from the body to provide just the right degree of warmth for the weather and the amount of activity.

While we often speak of clothing as being "warm," clothing itself has no intrinsic thermal properties. What clothing does is to retain varying amounts of body heat so that the body is bathed in its own layer of heat from the constant heat loss through the skin. Retaining a dead-air space of warm air is accomplished by clothing. More clothing holds in more of the heat, less clothing holds in less of the heat—and some types of clothing hold in more heat than others. It's as simple as that.

While layering isn't thought of much in light-clothing situations, it is a must for cold-weather fishing. When cold-weather fishing, proper choice of clothing layers is a must. With some exceptions, layering can be accomplished from head to foot.

**Feet.** The saying that you are comfortable if your feet are comfortable applies especially when you are fishing. Warmth is the key to comfort and there are several ways to get it short of battery-operated socks. First, pick the right socks. Use the layering technique here by choosing a light pair of cotton socks to wear next to the skin, and an outer pair of heavy wool socks for warmth if needed.

If wearing hip boots or waders, the two layers of socks will allow less slipping and more comfort in the boot as well as providing more warmth when you are in the water. Make sure that the socks are large enough to provide enough dead-air space to conserve body heat and keep you warm, but not so large that they will be loose and chafe you as you walk. The Royal Red Ball insulated Bama socks are excellent as are wick socks, which allow passage of moisture to an outer sock and keep your feet dry.

If you are going to be out all day doing a lot of walking, wading, or other activity, you might want to consider taking an extra pair or set of socks for a midday change, whether

*Clothing needed for cold-weather fishing includes,* top: *outer jackets, parkas, and sweaters;* center; *insulated and net underwear and pants;* bottom: *hats, gloves, and socks;* left: *dickeys, scarfs, and kerchiefs;* right: *various types of boots.*

or not your socks are wet from sweat. It will make your feet warmer and more comfortable.

Boots are equally important for proper warmth and comfort while fishing in cold weather or under chilly conditions. In some cases, part of the choice will be made for you by the type of fishing that you are planning to do. For example, if you are going to be wading a trout stream in early spring or late fall, you will be wearing hip boots or chest-high waders. Under these conditions, the best choice would be the boot-foot waders rather than the stocking-foot waders. The boot-foot waders will compress less in the water and will help to hold dead air space around your foot (and also around your leg).

There is also a choice of insulated or noninsulated waders. Generally, if you are in a temperate climate and/or only plan to use your waders or hip boots during moderately cold weather, and if you can stand some cold, you will be best off with the noninsulated waders or hip boots. They will be better for mild or warm-weather wading and you can add an extra pair of heavy socks to wear during particularly cold-weather wading and fishing. If you live far enough north or do enough cold-weather fishing to warrant the insulated boots, use them. You should still add two layers of socks for additional comfort and warmth.

For boat or shore-line fishing, there are a number of boot choices that are more a matter of personal preference than anything else, although you should avoid sneakers, light jogging shoes, canvas slip-ons, and low shoes of any type when you require warmth. You could wear a moccasin-style boot, a bird-shooter's boot, insulated boots, rubber boots or pacs. Moccasin or bird-shooter's boots, six- to eight-inch height, are a fine compromise for most fishing and give comfort with warmth, provided that you add the socks first as outlined above. If you are going to be fishing from a boat that is likely to take on a little water or if you will be fishing from shore where you know that you will probably have your toes in the water in an effort to get the last foot of distance out of a cast, then pick something that will be both waterproof and insulated. Good choices here would be the moccasin or insulated boots that are guaranteed waterproof (available now from a number of companies), fully waterproof rubber boots, the L.L. Bean Maine hunting boot (with a waterproof rubber bottom and leather top for comfort), or pacs, consisting of a waterproof shell that fits over an inner liner of felt that provides insulation with comfort. For extremely cold conditions, the snowmobiler's boots are ideal provided that you don't have to walk long distances. They are waterproof, provide the ultimate in warmth for long days in the cold, but are bulky and heavy and not made for hiking.

It is extremely important to pick the right size boot for your fishing. If possible, buy your boots in the evening when your feet will be slightly swollen or larger and take to the shoe store the socks that you will be wearing in the field. Try the boots on with the socks before purchase and make sure that there is enough room in the boot without it being sloppy on your foot. Too tight a fit will not only prove uncomfortable, but will also reduce the amount of dead-air space around your foot and lessen the amount of insulation. For waders and hip boots, you will probably take one-half to one size larger than your street shoe, while lighter moccasins worn with light wool socks may be your street-shoe size or one-half size larger.

*For maximum foot comfort in cold weather, use two pairs of socks, starting with a pair of light white cotton socks over which is worn heavier wool socks.*

*Boots for cold-weather fishing can include hip boots* (rear), *rubber boots for shoreline fishing* (right foreground), *and leather boots for boat fishing* (left foreground).

**Underwear.** Good layering insulation in the field starts with underwear. You have several alternatives to choose from, based partly on personal preference and partly on the degree of warmth and protection that you will need in the field. First, for moderately cold conditions in which you will be wearing heavier-than-normal, wind-resistant pants, you might want to wear your regular underwear. You won't feel quite as bulky as you would with long johns or other styles, but you will be wholly dependent upon the outerwear for the dead air space and warmth that you require.

Standard long johns are ideal for maximum warmth, preferably in wool, which will stay warm even if it becomes wet. Unfortunately, wool is itchy for most of us, so some manufacturers have responded with two-layer long johns (an inner layer of cotton for comfort and an outer layer of wool for warmth). Ski-type underwear and ski-type pajamas of flannel have knit cuffs at the wrist and ankle and as a result are particularly good when wearing other loose outer clothing since they will help to prevent gusts of wind going up the legs and arms. They are also a little lighter and looser than the standard long johns and as a result don't feel as confining.

Quilted underwear is even heavier and bulkier than other types, but does have that one plus of providing the maximum of dead-air space required under extremely cold situations. Choose this with care, however, since it is ideal only for those situations where you will be relatively inactive, as when ice fishing or boat fishing. If you move around a lot and start to perspire, you will soak the quilt and reduce or eliminate the insulation, in turn chilling you and perhaps leading to hypothermia.

The Norse net underwear is also good in that the coarse-mesh netting provides the necessary dead-air space required for insulation. Fish-net underwear for this reason is best when covered with a cotton undershirt, long johns, ski pajamas, or similar wear that retains the pockets of dead air created by the mesh next to the skin.

**Pants.** Choice of pants will be dictated in part by the presence or absence of long johns or other underwear protection from the cold. If you have long johns or similar underwear for warmth, your prime concern with pants will be wind and water resistance, plus whatever warmth the fabric helps provide. When you are active, heavy khaki's are fine in moderate cold worn alone or over long johns. Jeans might provide the same wear with a little more warmth, while wool pants will provide warmth even when wet.

*Insulated underwear, or flannel pajamas make good insulating underwear for cold-weather fishing.*

Hunters' brush pants will provide the ultimate protection from the wind (short of the completely waterproof rain pants), but are cold against the skin unless you are moving to provide constant leg warmth or unless they are worn over an insulating layer such as long johns or ski pajamas.

**Shirts.** Shirts should have long sleeves and long tails (for kidney and back protection and warmth) with a collar that you can turn up against the cold if needed and a top button to keep the cold from your neck when required. Synthetics are lightweight and while they look good and drip dry, they provide little in the way of protection against the cold. Cotton is better, flannel better yet, while wool is the best for warmth. Wool shirts are often available in several weights, ranging from a lightweight soft shirt, to those that are almost heavy enough to be a jacket. Choose according to your needs.

**Outerwear.** Under this category comes the vast array of garments designed to provide warmth in the field, including but not restricted to sleeveless sweaters, long-sleeved sweaters, down vests, down jackets, wool vests, lambskin vests, and light fiberfill jackets. Personal preferences may be exercised here, but for our money, the best combination of weight, insulation, ease of movement, and comfort is found in the wool, long-sleeved pullover sweater, the down vest, or the down jacket.

**Shells.** While the down and the wool sweaters will provide good protection on a calm day, they have no ability to hold your body heat on a windy day. Shells of outer jackets, parkas, rain jackets, and so on allow the other layers to retain the body heat that you build up. (Some heavy down jackets do have heavy, windproof outer shells of rip-stop nylon or similar material.)

For fishing where spray or mist is a problem, the best protection will be a rain parka or a three-quarter- or full-length rain jacket. The jackets are best in a boat if stationary, but not so good when you have to move around. Both parka and jackets will repel the rain as well as the wind.

Rain jackets don't last well in heavy brush for stream-trout fishermen, and a hunter's brush jacket or a down jacket with an outer covering of heavy rip-stop nylon or similar tear- and scratch-resistant fabric might be a better choice. Nylon parkas, such as those worn by and popularized by mountaineers, are hip length, made of rip-stop nylon, have plenty of pockets and a hood. They are ideal. They come in a variety of colors and are loose enough to fit comfortably over most down jackets or vests.

*Jackets, sweaters, and down vests needed to keep warm by the layering technique.*

Additional features to consider in choosing any outer shell are:

- A high collar or a hood that can be used as a collar. Heat rises so it is important to keep your body heat in with a good collar.
- Zippers are ideal for outer-shell closure, but often the cold or wind can seep in through the zipper. Storm flaps that cover the zipper with button or snap closure help to strenghten this weak link in the warmth chain.
- A bottom-opening (double) zipper on three-quarter- and hip-length rain jackets and nylon parkas will allow you to keep your shell zipped up but open slightly from the bottom to provide more leg room while walking and comfort while sitting, and also allow you to get into your pants pockets.

**Accessories.** Gloves, hats, and kerchiefs are necessary when the weather gets very cold. Tests have shown that as much as 50 percent of your body heat can escape through your head and neck area. The warmest and best protection are the down caps with ear flaps that can be raised or lowered as needed. Second best are knit watch caps that can be worn on top of your head or pulled down around your forehead, ears, and neck for maximum warmth. They come in all colors and several different knit thicknesses. There are some knit caps that also have a slight brim in front to provide additional protection

*Outer wear useful in cold-weather fishing includes,* left to right: *hunter's brush jacket, nylon-shell down jacket, down sweater, and nylon parka shell.*

*Baseball-type caps* (rear) *are poor choices to keep your head warm during cold-weather fishing. Good choices include watch caps, knit berets, or tam o' shanters.*

against glare off the water that is just as harsh in the winter as in the summer.

Following the above are the regular dress hat (preferably in a heavy fabric for warmth) or a heavy-fabric hunter's cap with a brim that can be folded.

Equally important as a hat is a kerchief or dickey to provide protection for the neck and upper-chest area. You can use a regular bandana knotted around your neck for slight protection, a wool scarf or a knit dickey (basically a collar with a front and back flap to fit inside your shirt for chest and back protection.

Gloves present an awkward problem for fishermen since hand and finger freedom are needed for using fly, spinning, spin-cast, and casting gear as well as handling rigs, tackle, fish, and tying knots. By the same token, if your hands are too cold to move without gloves, you can't fish effectively. Wool gloves are best, but there are gloves made specially for outdoor sports that work well to provide protection and still allow you to fish easily. Hunter's gloves with a slit to expose the index finger work well for spin fishermen and allow you to pick up the line for each cast, although you might have to take them off to tie knots or rerig. Millarmitts, available from specialty outdoor-clothing mail-order shops are English gloves with a wool-knit back and hard-knit palm, but lacking the finger tips. As a result, they provide protection for the bulk of your hand, while leaving all the finger tips exposed to allow you to tie knots, cast, thumb a casting reel, and so on.

Cheap, easily made alternatives to the above include taking an old pair of gloves and removing the thumb (for fishermen using casting tackle) or removing the index finger

*A dickey* (left) *provides maximum neck, chest, and back protection in cold weather. Scarfs* (center) *and cotton kerchiefs* (right) *also provide protection.*

*Millarmitts (center) provide warmth for your hands while allowing your exposed fingers to tie knots, rig tackle, etc. Inexpensive gloves (left) can have the fingertips cut off to produce the same effect. For spinning, a pair of gloves with the index finger cut off will allow you to cast while giving maximum warmth to the rest of your hand (right).*

(for fishermen using open-face spinning tackle) or removing all ten finger tips for the most functional style.

## USE OF LAYERING

The importance of all these layers of clothing is to allow you to add or subtract clothing as necessary during a day of fishing to adjust for changing weather conditions or extremes of activity. You might start out in the morning—usually the coldest part of the day—completely bundled up for warmth. As the sun rises and warms the air and water, you might want to remove an outer shell. Later on, a wind can freshen and you might want to remove the sweater to keep from overheating, but wear the outer shell for protection from the wind. By late afternoon if the sun continues and the wind ceases, you may want to remove both outer shell and sweater or down jacket. Then as evening approaches, the wind rises, and the sun drops behind some clouds, you can bundle up again in all the layers.

The point is that you should carefully watch your activity and weather conditions. Just because you have several layers of clothing doesn't mean that you have to wear them all the time. Just as it is important to keep your body from becoming initially chilled, it is equally important to keep it from becoming overheated, causing you to sweat, which wets your clothing, and reduces its insulating ability. Layering, sensibly used, allows you to adjust for almost any condition that the weatherman predicts and to be comfortable in the face of the worst or best.

The importance of cold-weather protection while on the water is becoming increasingly recognized. Some state and federal agencies are sponsoring workshops on cold-weather survival for boaters and commercial fishermen as a way of educating those who will be working in cold weather and providing information to the public about cold-weather protection. For information on such workshops in your area, consult the United States Coast Guard, your state department of conservation or natural resources, or the Red Cross in your area.

## WIND-CHILL INDEX

Some of the best fishing is in early spring or late fall when the temperatures will be chilly at best. Ice fishermen throughout the northernmost part of the United States fish during the coldest times of the year. Unfortunately, when you get up in the morning to dress for a day's fishing in cool or cold temperatures, you can't rely wholly on the reading of an outside thermometer, unless the weather is dead calm and will stay that way throughout the day where you will be fishing. Temperature is one cause of loss of body heat, but the wind is a second cause. The wind strength is a very important factor in figuring out how much to wear outdoors to prevent loss of body heat.

The loss of body heat from the combination of temperature and wind has been studied for some time. The first facts on this subject began to emerge from studies by Paul Siple who accompanied Admiral Byrd to the Antarctic. During and after World War II, both the Quartermaster Corps and the Medical Research Laboratory of the United States Army conducted research in this area, also. As a result of this continuing research, tables have been formulated that help determine how cold you will feel with various combinations of temperature and wind speed. It's important to understand that wind can cause extreme chilling at temperatures that otherwise might be considered mild. The result, usually called a wind-chill index, makes it easy to dress according to these two variables.

There are other factors that will affect these charts, such as individual metabolism, state of nourishment, clothing, and body weight. Wind-chill indexes will vary sometimes with the company or agency distributing them. Continuing research might modify them slightly, but most come close to the following, prepared by the National Oceanic and Atmospheric Administration.

# WIND CHILL TABLE

### F. Dry-bulb Temperature

(EQUIVALENT TEMPERATURE) - Equivalent in cooling power on exposed flesh under calm conditions

| WIND M.P.H. | 35 | 30 | 25 | 20 | 15 | 10 | 5 | 0 | -5 | -10 | -15 | -20 | -25 | -30 | -35 | -40 | -45 |
|---|---|---|---|---|---|---|---|---|---|---|---|---|---|---|---|---|---|
| calm | 35 | 30 | 25 | 20 | 15 | 10 | 5 | 0 | -5 | -10 | -15 | -20 | -25 | -30 | -35 | -40 | -45 |
| 5 | 33 | 27 | 21 | 16 | 12 | 7 | 1 | -6 | -11 | -15 | -20 | -26 | -31 | -35 | -41 | -47 | -54 |
| 10 | 21 | 16 | 9 | 2 | -2 | -9 | -15 | -22 | -27 | -31 | -38 | -45 | -52 | -58 | -64 | -70 | -77 |
| 15 | 16 | 11 | 1 | -6 | -11 | -18 | -25 | -33 | -40 | -45 | -51 | -60 | -65 | -70 | -78 | -85 | -90 |
| 20 | 12 | 3 | -4 | -9 | -17 | -24 | -32 | -40 | -46 | -52 | -60 | -68 | -76 | -81 | -88 | -96 | -103 |
| 25 | 7 | 0 | -7 | -15 | -22 | -29 | -37 | -45 | -52 | -58 | -67 | -75 | -83 | -89 | -96 | -104 | -112 |
| 30 | 5 | -2 | -11 | -18 | -26 | -33 | -41 | -49 | -56 | -63 | -70 | -78 | -87 | -94 | -101 | -109 | -117 |
| 35 | 3 | -4 | -13 | -20 | -27 | -35 | -43 | -52 | -60 | -67 | -72 | -83 | -90 | -98 | -105 | -113 | -123 |
| 40 | 1 | -4 | -15 | -22 | -29 | -36 | -45 | -54 | -62 | -69 | -76 | -87 | -94 | -101 | -107 | -116 | -128 |
| 45 | 1 | -6 | -17 | -24 | -31 | -38 | -46 | -54 | -63 | -70 | -78 | -87 | -94 | -101 | -108 | -118 | -128 |
| 50 | 0 | -7 | -17 | -24 | -31 | -38 | -47 | -56 | -63 | -70 | -79 | -88 | -96 | -103 | -110 | -120 | -128 |

Wind speeds greater than 40 mph have little additional chilling effect.

There are also two factors that fishermen must consider in checking any wind-chill indexes before dressing for a day of fishing. First, most fishing is on open water where wind can often be more severe, with high gusts or more sustained winds than might be found outside your front door. High buildings in cities and the hedge rows and trees in the suburbs and country tend to break up the wind and reduce its force—but the wind will be fully felt while fishing. As a result, always plan on the wind being a little stronger when fishing than it is at your home.

Second, consider any fast movement made while fishing that will increase the wind-chill factor. For example, if you go boat fishing in a dead calm when the temperature is 20 degrees Fahrenheit, but then run your boat at 30 miles per hour, the wind chill while you are running will be -18 degrees F. The same will apply if you are out on a windy day and run your boat into the wind, which is a likely possibility. For example, fishing at 35 degrees with the wind at 10 miles per hour will result in a wind-chill factor of 21 degrees F. But if you run your boat at 25 miles per hour into this wind, the combined force will be a wind of 35 miles per hour and a resulting wind-chill factor of 3 degrees F. Plan accordingly for your fishing trips.

# HYPOTHERMIA

Just a few years ago, neither medical textbooks nor outdoor guides and survival texts included the word hypothermia. Today the word is widely known and the problem is more widely understood. Hypothermia is basically the constantly increasing loss of body heat that, if not treated, can result in coma and death. The cause is the loss of body heat faster than the body can replace it. Once this happens, hypothermia has begun. As the body temperature begins to drop, physiological changes begin that must be reversed if the victim is to survive.

The victim begins to shiver and volutarily begins to exercise in order to keep warm and to build up body heat. But as soon as the exercise is stopped, heat production instantly drops by about 50 percent. The body begins to make involuntary reactions to preserve the normal temperature of the important body organs. At this point the body will begin to slow blood circulation to the arms and legs, keeping the warm blood for the organs and preventing the blood from going to those areas of the body (the extremities) where it will be cooled rapidly. As the blood temperature continues to drop, it affects the brain (which uses about 20 percent of the body's supply of blood). Thinking becomes confused, irrational, slowed. The heart and brain continue to cool with the spiraling effect of the body chilling. If not reversed at this point or before, coma and death will soon result. Death can occur as quickly as 1½ hours after the onset of shivering if nothing is done.

It is easy to understand that hypothermia can happen in the winter or when falling into the water in early spring or late fall, but it is a dangerous myth to think that it can happen only at such times—hypothermia can occur in temperatures as warm as 40 to 50 degrees Fahrenheit. Fishermen are in an especially dangerous situation, with the possibility of getting soaked by falling into a stream or out of a boat, by the spray of a running boat in rough water, or by a sudden rainstorm that they can't escape.

Soaking is especially bad, since it immediately chills the body through evaporation and makes it almost impossible for the body to regain lost heat. The result is the spiraling loss of body heat and the shivering that is the first sign of hypothermia.

Wet clothes lose about 90 percent of their insulating properties and become almost useless for retaining body heat. Wind, as shown in the wind-chill index, also robs the body of heat and could initiate or accelerate hypothermia.

Hypothermia can also be caused by the slight, insidious chilling that comes about when the temperature drops below what you anticipated or prepared for (both mentally and with extra clothing), when the rain gradually trickles down your neck, and when clothing allows high or gusty winds to pass through to cool your torso. Admittedly, many of us who have spent more than one season outdoors can usually recall days like this, when one or more of these factors—cold, moisture, or wind—have made the day uncomfortable. Usually we shivered a little bit as we slipped on an extra jacket, or added raingear or foul-weather gear. Even though we were able to stop it, or stop fishing to get out of the weather, we were suffering the first signs of hypothermia.

The only difference between shivering and being able to cope with it and shivering to end up in a coma near death is the degree of chilling and the ability to stop the spiraling drop in body temperature.

Symptoms of hypothermia are various and include slight shivering, violent shivering, muscular stiffness and rigidity, slurred speech or difficulty in speaking and communicating, slow and/or irregular pulse, drowsiness and grogginess, lack of muscular coordination and use of hands and legs, stupor, incoherence, complete exhaustion or collapse, paleness of the skin (particularly in the extremities), and slow and/or labored breathing. Not all of these symptoms may occur, and they occur usually at different body temperatures. Just what you can expect and how severe it is can be generalized as follows:

- 98.6 to 96 degrees Fahrenheit: shivering begins and becomes violent, coordination and ability to perform simple tasks become slowed or impossible.

- 95 to 91 degrees Fahrenheit: the skin begins to get pale (the body is trying to conserve the warm blood for the torso and vital organs and the circulation to the extremities is reduced and shunted to deeper circulation systems in the arms and legs). Shivering becomes definitely violent, speech communication is slowed, reduced, or impaired.
- 90 to 86 degrees Fahrenheit: limbs beome stiff and rigid; it is difficult to perform tasks, thinking becomes dulled or confused.
- 85 to 81 degrees Fahrenheit: victim becomes irrational and may drift into stupor or unconsciousness. Pulse is slow.
- 80 to 78 degrees Fahrenheit: unconsciousness occurs, reflexes cease to function.
- 78 degrees Fahrenheit and below: condition probably irreversible, death is imminent.

**Hypothermia prevention.** Prevention of hypothermia is relatively simple, except for accidental chilling as outlined above. First, dress warmly not only for the temperature, wind, and precipitation that are present when you start a trip, but also any that you might expect during the course of the fishing trip. Use the outdoorsman's adage that before you go out, figure that it will be warmer than you think, colder than you think, and that it is sure to rain. Dress in layers, and on especially cold and raw days, use wool underwear that will retain some body heat even when soaked. Carry extra jackets, a parka, sweater, down vest, and so on in a waterproof stuff bag or keep handy in your boat, recreational vehicle, car, or another place that allows you to get to the items in a hurry if you need to. Always carry sufficient raingear, either a parka or a combination of pants (or bib overalls) and a covering jacket with a hood.

**Curing hypothermia.** What to do about hypothermia depends upon how severe it is and what facilities and help you have at your disposal. For slight shivering (the first sign of hypothermia) adding clothes, buttoning up, adding raingear to cut the wind-chill factor, and so on will all help to reverse the trend of losing body heat. Beyond this first stage, however, victims become slowed in thinking and speech and even though they might protest that they are all right, they should be given treatment as follows.

The main initial concern is to stop the loss of body heat and help to regain some of that heat. Unfortunately, some of the experts differ in advice given, so we are concentrating on those areas of agreement or general consensus, realizing that further research might modify some of the current findings and theories. First, call for medical help if possible, or plan to get the victim to the hospital as soon as temporary first aid is given. Any wet clothes should be removed and replaced with warm, dry clothing. If the victim is conscious and able to eat and drink, give high-energy foods such as nuts, raisins, chocolate, and warm tea laced with sugar or honey. Have the victim lie down in a comfortable place, protected from wind and rain, and warm if possible. Begin warming the victim immediately, but concentrate on the torso and head. Do not try to warm the legs and arms. Do not massage the victim. Keep him conscious or awake if at all possible.

The reason for not warming the arms and legs immediately is due to what is now being called an "after-drop" effect. As mentioned earlier, arms and legs become cool with reduced blood flow in order to preserve the warm blood for the brain and vital organs of the chest and abdomen. Thus, warming the arms and legs immediately after rescuing a victim will cause the blood flow to increase in the arms and legs, and will return chilled blood to the torso. This chilled blood will prevent vital organs, notably the heart and lungs, from functining properly, with death the possible result. In fact, many cases reported as "heart-attack" prior to the late 1960s, when Dr. L. G. Pugh of Glasgow University in Scotland did some of the initial research into the cause and effect of hypothermia, might well have been due to this after-drop effect.

Get the victim into warm clothing and/or a warm sleeping bag. If you are camping, make a fire and use warm rocks wrapped in towels or clothing to serve as a heating pad. If you have warm water at your disposal, get the victim into a tub, small dinghy, or rubber life raft, but keep the arms and legs outside initially to avoid the danger of the after-drop effect. Use water temperatures that are warm, but not hot or scalding. Lacking anything else, if you are camping and have a sleeping bag available, have the victim strip and get into the bag with one or, preferably, two persons who have also removed their garments. Two "warmth donors" can help to warm the victim by skin-to-skin contact on both front and back of the victim's body. Get the victim to medical help, or medical help to the victim, as soon as possible.

# 23
# Seasickness

Seasickness is nothing more than motion sickness initiated by an unstable platform or irregular movement. It is caused by various balancing organs of the body becoming mixed-up due to the conflicting signals they receive. When you are on dry land or a stable platform, the otoliths of the inner ear work as a carpenter's level to help your body realize when everything is level or when you are at an angle. Eyesight always records a fixed horizon to help maintain balance. The semicircular canals (three of them, each on a different plane) relay information when the head moves in relation to the body, and help to keep the body at balance. All three systems send signals to the brain to help it maintain balance and equilibrium. The deck of a moving boat causes these signals to get mixed-up and relay seemingly contradictory information to the brain, which in turn causes the usual reaction of nausea and vomiting. In addition to the conflicting signals going to the brain, seasickness can also be caused (or more likely accentuated) by smells of food, fuel, engine exhaust, or the misplaced kidding of anglers not so affected. Typical symptoms are an uneasy feeling in the stomach, nausea, a pale, clammy look, and vomiting.

Seasickness can affect anyone, and no one can consider himself completely immune. Experienced Naval and Coast Guard officers and 20-year enlisted men will often become seasick on the first few days of a long voyage. Seasickness was probably a contributing factor in the loss of the Spanish Armada to the British in 1588, when the Spanish admiral was too ill from seasickness to stand on the deck of his flagship and give orders. Lord Nelson, a master seaman of his age, is reported to have become sick on the first few days of every long voyage. Unfortunately, there is no cure or first aid but there are preventative measures that can be taken and some tactics that can be used on boats to help prevent or reduce its effects. Ironically, persons with inner-ear damage are not susceptible to seasickness.

## PREVENTING SEASICKNESS

There are two tactics to prevent seasickness if you are susceptible. One is by pills and the other is by proper habits before and during a trip. First, before going on any trip, get enough sleep and avoid any foods that might cause you difficulty on dry land, since the effects will be accentuated on the rocking deck of a boat. Avoid excessive drinking of alcoholic beverages before and while on the boat. Avoid greasy foods, fats, and overeating. If possible, eat a little less than normal on the day or night before to avoid stomach distress.

If you are at all susceptible or think that you are susceptible to seasickness take one of the preventative drugs available without prescription or see your doctor for a prescription. For their cost, such pills are inexpensive insurance against ruining a trip.

For years Dramamine was the most widely known drug for motion sickness. Today, there are a number of available drugs, including Dramamine, Dramamine II, Tripton,

Bonine, Marezine, Trav-Arex, and Dimen. Different drugs will affect different people differently, so you might have to experiment to find that drug that is most effective for you and causes the least side effects. Side effects can include drowsiness, which can reduce some of your fun fishing and also make it dangerous if you have to operate the boat or drive home while some of the drug is still in your bloodstream.

It is important to take these nonprescription drugs at the right time. If you wait until you are feeling uneasy, it is too late. The best time to take them is before or with breakfast, before you get onboard (about half an hour before boarding), and to take them thereafter according to the manufacturer's recommendations.

New drugs are constantly being developed and several that are now in the experimental stage offer even more effectiveness than those currently on the market. Most of the currently available drugs are about 65 to 70 percent effective, while some of the ones now being tested are reported to be about 75 to 90 percent effective.

Once on the water, there are other precautions that you can take, based on the experience of long-time deep-water fishermen. First, the worst thing that you can do is to retire to the cabin of a large boat and lie down. Here, you will be in a closed area with no fresh air and with the possible presence of oil, diesel, gas, or exhaust fumes. All this will just accentuate any feeling of sickness that you might already have. Instead, stay out of the cabin and stay in the aft cockpit or on the bridge or flying bridge. If on a charter boat or party boat, ask the captain before entering his domain, and if necessary, explain your reasons.

We also find that it helps to nibble on something all day long. Often, instead of waiting until noon and eating a large meal, we'll start eating 30 to 90 minutes after leaving the dock. Often we'll hold off until noon for a sandwich or two, but will nibble on cookies, crackers, candies, and so on both before and after lunch. Crackers are the best since they aren't excessively sweet and won't cause you problems that might result from a long string of sweet snacks. This, along with an occasional soft drink, helps most anglers to keep from getting seasick.

Another factor, strictly psychological, is easier said than done. Don't think about getting seasick, about the motion of the boat, about how rough the sea is, or other such things. If possible, move around, talk about the fishing, the tackle, anything, but keep your mind (and the mind of other anglers who might be susceptible, even if you are not) off the possibility of motion sickness. Avoid rigging or watching the mate rig ballyhoo or other trolling baits if you are queasy about such things.

A lot of seasickness is olfactory, visual, and in many cases psychological. Regardless of its cause, it is a terrible feeling. The old saying is, "that first you are afraid you will die, and then you are afraid that you won't!" Proper precautions, however, as outlined above, can eliminate or reduce seasickness to a minimum in almost all cases. But it is not a matter that should be treated lightly, so consider it before any boat trip.

# 24
# Dealing with Insects, Ticks, Spiders, and Snakes

The insects that sportsmen have to deal with include mosquitoes, blackflies, deerflies, no-see-ums, chiggers, ticks, bees, wasps, and hornets. All are bad, and some are worse than others. All have the ability to annoy or disable fishermen.

## MOSQUITOES

These are common throughout the western hemisphere, particularly around still or stagnant water. They are prevalent around beaches, sand dunes, lakes, ponds, and low depressions that collect rainwater and become stagnant. They are particularly active at dawn and dusk, which makes it hard on the fishermen since these times are usually quiet and still and often provide the best fishing. Mosquitoes are least active on sunny days or when a breeze is blowing to prevent their flying.

Only the female mosquito bites, and the worst period is from spring through midsummer, although they continue into fall in many areas. Dark clothing seems to attract them, perhaps because dark colors are warmer, and warmth attracts mosquitoes.

Protection against these insects includes using repellents and wearing light-colored clothing, long-sleeved shirts, and long pants. Smokers sometimes smoke a little more heavily in an effort to keep them at bay. Alcohol, Listerine, and analgesic rubs and sprays applied to bites will keep them from itching.

## BLACKFLIES

These are small insects, but related to the larger deerflies in the way that they attack and the type of damage that they do. Both sexes bite, and they bite as soon as they land. Most anglers don't feel the insect or the bite until it is too late and blood is running off their wrists, face, ankles, or neck, which are the favorite areas for the blackfly to attack.

Blackflies are found near running water for the most part, which makes them an especially vexing problem for the trout or river smallmouth-bass fisherman. They are prevalent in Canada and throughout the northern part of the United States. Like mosquitoes, they are most active and prevalent from early spring through midsummer but can also be found later on in the year. Hot, calm days are the worst times for them, and a breeze will keep them at bay as will cold weather. Blue clothing seems to attract them more than any other color.

Prevention includes the liberal use of repellents, elastic-cuffed nylon jackets, long pants with the bottoms tucked into long, thick socks that blackflies can't bite through. Wear light-colored clothing, a brimmed hat or cap to help prevent bites at the hair line, and a repellent-treated kerchief to keep them off your neck and the back of your head. For those allergic to the bites or for those in heavily infested areas, a head net fitted over a hat might be the only solution.

The bites bleed immediately and often become swollen and itchy. The bites may exude fluid or become infected. Some people are allergic to blackfly bites and experience severe swelling. Alcohol, Listerine, and nonprescription analgesic sprays and solutions will help to reduce the itching and swelling. For more cures, see your doctor.

## DEERFLIES

These are like blackflies but bigger, some of them up to one inch long, and like blackflies they are most prevalent in Canada and the northern United States. The exposed areas of the body—ankles, wrists, neck, head, and face—are bitten most frequently. Prevention includes the same repellent and clothing suggestions given for blackflies, but be prepared for deerflies to bite right through lightweight clothing. Use alcohol or analgesic salves to reduce the swelling and itching from bites.

## NO-SEE-UMS

These tiny insects are common in brackish-water areas, near salt water, in swamps, marshes, and any quiet waters where they can breed. They are common in the Everglades as well as on the Canadian border. Unlike blackflies, you instantly feel a no-see-um's bite, and the flies are small enough to get at you anywhere—through screens, tent netting, head nets, and clothing. Breezes and sun will keep no-see-ums away. Watch out for them on hot, muggy, overcast days and at evening and dawn.

Prevention can include liberal applications of repellent. Tight clothing and head nets might help some, but they can't be relied upon. One thing that we noticed is that the no-see-ums seem to be attracted to the highest part of an individual. Thus, you can get some relief, for brief periods and as long as your arms hold out, by holding your hands above your head. This keeps most of them away from your face and you can swat at them until you get tired.

## TICKS

Any fisherman fishing woodland streams or going through brush and fields to get to a lake, pond, or river has a chance of picking up ticks, which are relatives of spiders and are not insects. There are 300 species worldwide, with the wood tick and the Rocky Mountain spotted tick most prevalent in the United States. The Rocky Mountain spotted tick can cause Rocky Mountain spotted fever, the most serious danger from these creatures that feed on blood and can bloat up to several times their normal size.

They drop onto your skin or clothing while you walk through infested areas, and they can walk all over before deciding upon a spot to bite through the skin and suck the blood. Often the only way that you will feel them is when you are at rest and feel one walking on your skin, or long after one has broken through the skin you might feel it. There are no repellents that you can use, and since they will hitchhike on clothing until they can get to your skin, the tight wrist and pants technique won't work. It is important to strip completely at the end of every fishing day in tick country, and to check your body carefully, using a mirror to look for ticks.

If you find a tick on your body, don't try to pull it off with your fingers. The tick might break off and leave the head in the skin, which may cause infection. The best way to get a tick off is to touch the back of it with a lit cigarette or cover it with nail polish. You can also touch them with alcohol, turpentine, gasoline, or a liquor with a high alcohol content. Usually the tick will back right out of the skin after one of these treatments, and then it can be removed and disposed of. Dress the wound with an antiseptic.

## CHIGGERS

These insects are also called jiggers, red bugs, and chigoes. There are hundreds of species of chiggers; in the United States they are most prevalent in the South. Only about 50 species attack humans, and when they do they usually lodge around the waist where clothing is tight. They cause redness and severe itching. Protection includes liberal application of insect repellent and avoiding mossy, damp wood, thick grasses, and Spanish moss—such areas can harbor chiggers.

## BEES, YELLOW JACKETS, WASPS, AND HORNETS

These insects, unlike the other insects considered in this chapter, will leave you alone if you leave them alone. The danger of being stung comes when you disturb or get too close to their nest, which will bring swarms of insects ready to attack.

The best prevention is to avoid any areas where you see a lot of activity by these insects, since it might indicate a nearby nest or hive. Bees will hive in the ground, in rotten logs, or in the crotch of a tree. Yellow jackets will frequently nest in a hole in the ground, making it particularly dangerous for barefoot anglers but also a danger for anyone who crosses or steps on their nest area. Hornets have football-size, paperlike nests either high or low in trees.

Since these kinds of insect stings can be serious, treating them is covered in the section of this book on first aid.

## SPIDERS

While all spiders carry a poison that would be toxic to man, almost all spiders are too small to inject any amounts that could cause problems. But spiders seldom bite; they are shy and will retreat in the presence of man.

The two spiders that can cause problems when they bite are the black widow and the brown recluse. While it is true that both spiders will bite and both can and have caused death in humans, the possibilities of a bite in the first place and a serious bite in the second place are extremely rare. However, it does occur. A survey of black-widow bites in the United States from 1726 through 1943 showed that there were conservatively 1,291 bites of which 55 proved fatal. There are thought to be three subspecies of the black widow and it is not known if there are differences in the toxicity, venom, or severity of bites by these subspecies.

The brown recluse has been the subject of such concerns only in recent years, but it is known to have caused deaths as well. Both spiders, however, are shy and tend to avoid human contact. The most common places to get bitten are outside privys or outside plumbing in rural areas or around old dumps or trash piles. You may also get bitten by trapping a spider in your shoe when getting dressed in the morning while camping.

The best protection against bites is to avoid those areas where black widow and brown recluse spiders might reside, and not touching spiders or webs in those areas. Generally, even the black widow will not bite unless molested, so the best advice for anglers is to leave spiders alone and avoid their habitats.

Bites from black widows cause immediate pain culminating in severe pain in about 30 minutes and with pain gradually moving into the stomach area and limbs, causing nausea or even a coma. There is no established first-aid treatment for black-widow bites, and you should seek medical attention as soon as possible. Brown-recluse bites do not cause immediate pain, but within hours a mottled, red, painful area appears at the bite site. Do not attempt first aid but seek medical attention.

## SCORPIONS

Scorpions are eight-legged arachnids, related to spiders and mites, and they possess a whiplike tail tipped with a stinger, or telson, by which they can inject a poison. They can and have caused death. There are over 600 species and those found in the Western Hemisphere are located in the South, mostly in the Southwest but with some throughout the Gulf states and Florida. The typically publicized scorpion bite occurs when the victim traps one in a shoe in the morning while getting dressed, or it occurs when working around rubbish or debris, where the creatures live.

Thus, prevention consists of shaking out clothing and shoes each morning or whenever changing clothing to dislodge any scorpions.

If you feel something crawling over your body in the dark in scorpion country, brush it off. Do not try to swat it since this will almost guarantee being stung. If you are dislodging debris or lumber while looking for bait wear heavy gloves. Before picking up lumber, look under it to check for scorpions.

First aid is not applicable in the case of a scorpion bite. Get to the hospital or get the victim to a hospital. In some cases cooling has been reported to be beneficial, but must be started at once, preferably by placing the stung area (usually a hand or foot) into a bucket of ice water while going to the hospital. However, cooling such as this, sometimes also used for snake bites, should not be continued for long periods of time. Prolonged cooling can in some cases create the need to amputate fingers or toes. While there is controversy in the medical profession about this, the safest advice for the present is short cooling. Prolonged cooling (more than 15 minutes) should not be done. If you can, kill the scorpion and take it to the hospital for identification that might help the doctors in medical treatment.

## SNAKES

The four poisonous species of snakes in this country are the rattlesnake, water moccasin (or cottonmouth), copperhead, and coral snake. The first three are pit vipers with basically hemotoxic poison (attacking the blood); the coral snake is a member of the cobra family with neurotoxic poison (attacking the nervous system).

While snakes are more a problem to hikers, campers, and hunters, fishermen do come in contact with them and should take pains to avoid them. Basically, snakes will avoid most well-used or frequently-walked trails and roads. The only places in which you might have problems are in truly wild areas: when walking from camp to boat or from your car to a trout stream, always look where you're walking; don't step over a log or into a brush pile without checking first; use a stick or wading staff to scare out any snakes that might be present. Similarly, in canyon areas frequented by fishermen, don't climb up rock ledges using your hands above your head: more than one angler has done this to find a dozing snake. When in snake country, create lots of movement; throw sticks and stones—keep in mind that snakes smell and feel vibration but have no ears. Snakes are more afraid of you than you are of them and will get out of the way if given advance notice.

When fishing southern waters, small-boat fishermen should be particularly wary of overhanging tree limbs and brush, which might harbor cottonmouths. Avoid these areas if at all possible and proceed slowly and carefully if you must navigate through them.

# SNAKE-BITE FIRST AID

The first thing to do when bitten by a snake is try to determine whether or not it was poisonous. Dr. Hobart M. Smith, in his excellent book *Snakes as Pets,* offers the following as a sure method of identification:

Any snake of this country can be identified as being venomous if (1) it is marked with *complete* rings of red, yellowish-white, and black, the yellow rings bordering the red on either side ("Red against yellow will kill a fellow; red against black a poison lack"); or (2) it has a rattle at the end of the tail; or (3) it has a deep pit on the side of the head between the nostril and the eye.

The coral snake can be identified by the color of its rings, but be aware of imposters; there are numerous nonvenomous species that resemble the coral snake but do not have its complete color bands or have colors in the wrong sequence: the scarlet kingsnake is frequently mistaken for the coral and causes many people much undue panic.

The other three venomous species—the cottonmouth, copperhead, and rattlesnake—are, as mentioned before, pit vipers and will have that distinctive pit on the side of the head.

If the snake is nonpoisonous then the wound can usually be cleaned with antiseptic and dressed, although the bite of any snake over 2½ or three feet can be painful and somewhat severe and might require tending by a doctor.

In regard to the bite of a poisonous snake: some authorities believe in the old Boy Scout "cut and suction" method, while others argue that chilling the wound area decreases the toxicity of the poison, others insist that the antivenin-injection kits (available only with a doctor's prescription) are the best sure treatment, and still others argue that the best treatment is to clean the wound and get the patient to proper medical treatment as rapidly as possible. It's difficult to recommend a definitive treatment.

We side with the latter method of cleaning the wound and getting the victim to a doctor or hospital rapidly, provided that this is possible. In most parts of the country, even wilderness fishermen can quickly contact state rangers, game wardens, state police, paramedic teams, or med-evac units for help.

The injection units are only available by prescription and only valuable to those who will be far away from help and are familiar with injection procedures. However, if the patient hasn't been tested for serum sensitivity, don't use it, since the injection alone could kill.

The chilling method is pretty well discredited now, in spite of the fact that chilling *will* reduce the toxic effect of snake poison. The problem is that the prolonged and severe chilling necessary to do any good can also lead to frostbite and tissue death or damage, leading to finger, toe, and hand amputations.

The cutting method is suitable only if immediate help is not available. Use the blade supplied with the kit, or sterilize a knife blade in a flame. Make "X" cuts about ½ inch long and ¼ inch deep parallel to the axis of the limb. Add the suction cups to remove the poison as much as possible. *Do not* cut on the backs or palms of hands, on the backs of feet or toes, or around the face or neck. In these areas, arteries, veins, nerves, and muscle tendons lie close to the skin and could be irreparably damaged without proper knowledge of how and where to cut. Cutting a radial artery near the base of the thumb, for example, would lead to severe bleeding that would have to be treated by direct pressure and would only add another life-threatening problem.

If you plan to fish in areas where snakes are prevalent, check with your local Red Cross office or doctor for current, up-to-date information on snake-bite treatment, and use their suggestions, based on your needs, your first-aid knowledge and the potential danger.

# PREVENTING PROBLEMS WITH INSECTS

**Diet and personal habits.** There is some evidence that vitamin B12 helps in repelling many of the biting insects such as blackflies, mosquitoes, and no-see-ums. But few of us would like to continue taking massive vitamin doses on the possibility of decreasing insect problems. However, it is easy to avoid certain substances that are known to attract insects: perfumes, colognes, deodorants, scented hair sprays, and scented soaps. Ironically, fresh, clean people seem to attract insects more readily than those in need of a bath. Some anglers find that smoking cigarettes, pipes, and especially cheap cigars is helpful in keeping insects at bay.

**Clothing.** Wear a hat or cap that will provide the maximum coverage of your head and neck area. A good hat is the Florida guide cap, which is like a cloth baseball cap with the addition of a flap around the back to cover the back of the neck and the ears. Sprayed liberally with insect repellent, such a hat will repel most insects and keep them from the face, head, and neck region.

There is also clothing available that repels insects. But it is not the clothing, but the repellent in which it is soaked that repels insects. These are mesh jackets designed to be lightweight and cut full to cover any other clothing that you might be wearing. They work, but are relatively expensive, somewhat smelly, and a nuisance to fool with. However, they are sometimes the only solution in insect country.

To avoid attracting bees and yellow jackets, avoid brightly colored or flower-pattern shirts and clothing when in the woods or fields since a bee might take bright colors and flower patterns for flowers.

**Repellents.** Over the years, man has tried a number of likely and unlikely substances as insect repellents. They include straight and mixed solutions of camphor, balsam oil, oil of bay, pennyroyal, allspice oil, anise oil, garlic, hemlock, lavender oil, and pine oil among the natural repellents. Man has also tried various chemical compounds, including ethyl-hexanediol, dimethyl phthalate, dimethyl carbate and N,N-diethyl-meta touluamide. Most of the commercially available repellents, such as Off, 6-12, Black Flag, Mosquitone, Camper's Lotion, and Skram include one or more of these ingredients. Most of them have heavy concentrations of N,N diethyl-meta touluamide (abbreviated DEET), with some small percentages of the other natural and chemical repellents. Many are available in several forms, including aerosol sprays, lotions, and creams. Almost all of the many repellents tested over the years have fallen short of the effectiveness of DEET, now the prime ingredient in most repellents. DEET has proved safe for use on clothing and the skin and could be used in a 100-percent concentration, although it is most frequently diluted in commercial preparations. In tests, even at 50 percent dilution, DEET gave full protection for 3½ hours to all volunteers, significantly better results than those shown by any of the other repellent chemicals. In other tests in Panama, in which volunteers were placed in heavy concentrations of insects with a biting range of 26 to 39 bites per minute, DEET gave full protection for 24 hours when used in a 100-percent concentration.

Thus, when you purchase an insect repellent for your personal use, check the content of DEET in the small print on the bottle or can. Manufacturers are constantly changing and improving their formulas for better results, but most of the commonly available preparations have concentrations of DEET of about 15 to 50 percent. Deep Woods Off, Cutter's, 6-12, Mosquitone, and others are all good, but Muskol (with a 95-percent concentration of DEET) stands out as the best based on the above tests and current surveys. Muskol is odorless and 100-percent safe on skin.

If there is a disadvantage of DEET it is that it will chemically attack plastics. It is necessary to wash your hands after applying DEET in strong concentrations before handling plastic fly lines, monofilament line, tackle boxes, fishing lures, or plastic parts on fishing reels.

One way that you can lessen the possibility of causing damage to plastics in your fishing kit is to spread the repellent on the back of your hand, and use the backs of your hands to spread the DEET on your face, neck, hairline, arms, around your ankles, and any other exposed area. While it is a little awkward and time consuming, we like it since we feel that we can fish without worrying about a tackle box developing a soft spot, fly lines cracking, or plastic plugs losing their shape as a result of contact with DEET.

To use any direct-application repellent, follow the manufacturer's instructions and apply to dry skin. Avoid the lips and eyes, but apply over all other exposed areas, including the often-neglected ear area. Do not overapply, since this will just waste the repellent and may possibly cause softening of any synthetic fabrics that come in contact with these areas.

While Muskol comes only in the direct-application bottle at this writing, most of the other commercially available substances come in spray or aerosol cans for application to clothing. These are ideal either as an addition to the direct lotions for skin application or as a substitute for those times when the insects aren't too thick and when the sprays are sufficient to repel them. The sprays are similar to the lotions in that they contain the same active ingredients, except that they contain a propellant for spray application.

Some researchers have suggested the possibility in the future of building up systemic poisons in the body that will naturally repel insects while not harming humans or human metabolism. Some research has indicated that among the natural repellents available, eating large quantities of garlic builds up a natural insect repellent. Research has also shown that mosquitoes are attracted to some elements in human perspiration, while repelled by other ingredients. Thus, whether or not you are mildly or strongly irritated by insects might depend upon your metabolism and factors controlled by heredity. Currently, however, the best way to keep insects away is with insect repellent.

**Electronic repellents.** There are several electronic mosquito-repellent devices on the market. These are battery operated, about the size of a small calculator, and are generally worn around the neck on a cord to keep insects away. The electronic repellent is reputed to work by emitting a buzzing sound. One such product is advertised as emitting a sound that resembles the buzzing of a male mosquito and thus is designed to chase away the female mosquitoes, which are the ones that bite. Some anglers have reported success with these, while others have reported no success at all. Electronics might be the ultimate answer to repelling insects, but the evidence doesn't seem to support that conclusion yet.

# 25
# First Aid

Fishermen are subject to the same dangers in the field and on the water that accompany others in the outdoors. Since all outdoor activities are often away—sometimes far away—from immediate medical help, it is important to have at least a rudimentary knowledge of first aid. First-aid courses are available through local chapters of the Red Cross, local hospitals, fire departments, high-school and community-college night classes, and through similar agencies and institutions. Increasing emphasis is placed on cardio-pulmonary resuscitation (CPR) courses, since heart attacks remain very high on the list of killers of adults and often occur during recreation and strenuous activities outdoors. The importance of such courses can't be overemphasized for active fishermen who spend much of their leisure time in the outdoors.

As we have tried to point out previously in this book, often the need for first aid can be avoided by following simple rules, common sense, or by organization of tackle and equipment. Fortunately, when first aid is required due to minor accidents, it usually is simple and does not adversely affect the long-term fun of a trip. Some of the common difficulties are discussed below.

## SUNBURN TREATMENTS

Most sunburn treatments are local anesthetics in a gel, cream, or spray that desensitize the skin. Follow the manufacturer's instructions exactly for as much relief as possible, and stay out of the sun or use proper protection if you must stay in the sun. If the burn is severe, use a sunburn treatment immediately, and seek medical advice as soon as possible.

## CUTS

Cuts can occur while fishing from a variety of sources including knives, hooks, gaffs, oar locks, wire line, monofilament line, metal boats, and the gills, spines, or teeth of fish. In the case of cuts, treat them as you would any cut received at home. Wash the cut thoroughly, remove any foreign matter, and treat with iodine, first-aid cream, or Mercurochrome and cover with a suitable bandage.

There are two additional dangers from fish hooks or fish-inflicted cuts. First, fish hooks may be rusty so that the possibility of tetanus can't be overlooked. For this reason, try to promote bleeding from any small cut inflicted by metal of any type to remove any foreign matter. Second, cuts from fish hooks or from fish will often contain residues of bait or mucus or slime from the fish that could cause infection. Here, too, promote bleeding to prevent infection. Treat with an antiseptic and cover with a bandage.

# HOOK PENETRATION

The barb on a fish hook makes a hook highly dangerous when it penetrates the skin. Fortunately, not all hooks penetrate this deeply. For those that stop short of the barb, it is easy to back them out. Since this is a puncture wound, try to promote bleeding. If the penetration is in the finger or hand, swing your arm in a wide arc to force blood to the area. Milk the area toward the finger tips to force blood to the wound and promote bleeding to discharge any material that might cause an infection.

When the hook goes in past the barb, the skin will close behind it and it can't be backed out. If possible, and if you are near a medical center, it is best to have a doctor remove it. In fact, in the case of deep penetration of large hooks or penetration beyond the barb of large hooks, this is a must. Also, *do not try to remove any fish hook that has become stuck into the side or forward part of the neck or anywhere on the face. Remove any terminal rigging tied to the hook and seek immediate medical help.*

In the instances where medical help is not available and where you have determined the hook can be removed safely, here are three methods for doing so.

The time-honored way, still used, but least effective in most cases (and certainly more painful) is to grasp the hook with fisherman's pliers, and following the bend of the hook push it through the skin past the barb and cut off the barb. If you try this method, make sure before starting that you have pliers sufficiently strong enough to cut through the hook. The only ones that we know of that will do this without bending the hook in the process (and causing severe pain) are the compound leverage cutting pliers such as those made by Sportmate or G-96. Once the hook shank is cut below the barb, removal is accomplished by backing the hook out. Then treat as a puncture wound. While this method has been reported in enough outdoor books and magazine articles to make it well known, it lacks a lot in terms of patient comfort, ease of operation, minimizing tissue damage, and increased possibility of infection. Unless there are no other options, one of the following methods is better.

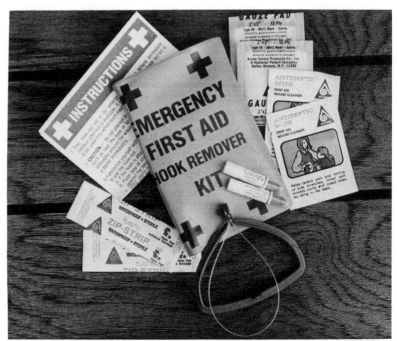

*A first-aid hook-remover kit includes items necessary to remove hooks from skin using the loop method as described in the text.*

A method that has gained recognition and popularity involves rapidly pulling the hook out through its entrance path. But there are tricks to this method that reduce trauma and pain in almost all cases. First, to be done right, it requires another person's help.

Take a shoelace, a loop of strong fishing line, or another such cord and tie the two ends together. Then loop it around the bend of the fish hook. Use the thumb of your other hand to press down on the shank of the hook so that the barb of the hook is depressed in the channel that the hook point made upon entering the skin. With a sharp jerk on the loop of line, pull the hook out of the skin. Pull in a direct line with the plane of the shank of the fish hook. The result is little trauma, little pain, and little bleeding.

If you are particularly worried about the possibility of hooking yourself or others, the Fisherman's Friend Emergency Hook Remover, sold by Sports Aid, includes all that you need to accomplish the above operation. The hook remover is strong nylon attached to a plastic handle, and the kit also includes methiolate swabs, antiseptic swabs, gauze bandages, plastic Band-Aids and comes in a soft plastic pouch with instructions.

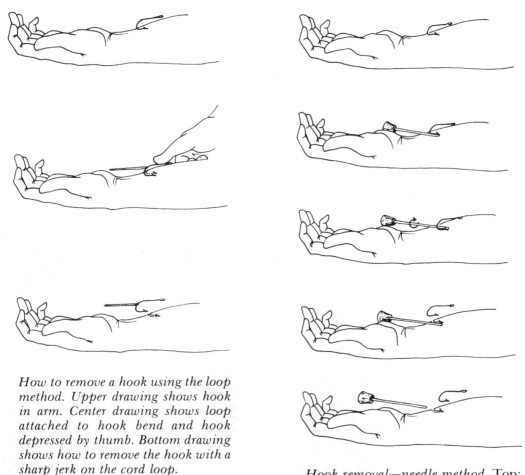

*How to remove a hook using the loop method. Upper drawing shows hook in arm. Center drawing shows loop attached to hook bend and hook depressed by thumb. Bottom drawing shows how to remove the hook with a sharp jerk on the cord loop.*

*Hook removal—needle method. Top: 1. hook in arm; 2. run blunt darning needle down path of hook; 3. rotate needle until it is on barb side of hook; 4. back out hook using needle as protection against catching flesh with barb; 5. back out needle.*

However, some doctors do not like this method. They feel that its use in areas of the body where muscles, nerves, and small blood vessels run close to the skin can cause muscle, nerve, arteriole, tendon, or ligament damage. Areas to consider carefully before using this method would include the backs of the hands and insteps of the feet

Another method of hook removal involves the use of a blunt needle to hold open the channel made by the hook and allow easy removal of the hook barb back out through the skin. The idea of this method is to open the channel made by the hook point and to allow the barb to back out of the channel without catching on the flesh. Choice of the needle is important. Most needles have sharp points, and are difficult to run into the same hole without going off course, making a new hole, and causing more pain. Some of the darning needles with a dull, rounded point are ideal, however. File the point off a darning needle and carry several different-size needles for different-size hook wounds. Run the needle down the outside of the hook point until it reaches the end of the hole, at the point of the hook. Then rotate the needle 180 degrees until the needle lifts the flesh above the barb on the inside of the hook. Hold the needle in place with one hand and carefully slide the hook out with the other hand. Once the hook is clear, remove the needle and treat the wound as a puncture wound with antiseptic and a bandage dressing.

It is easy to make up a small kit of a needle or two pressed into the bottom of an iodine or methiolate bottle cap, so that the needle is always sterile and ready to use.

## TETANUS SHOTS

Since anglers are constantly around fish hooks, bait-cutting knives, and fish that can cause cuts and scrapes, tetanus shots are highly recommended. Booster shots will keep the tetanus immunizations in effect, and should be received on a regular basis as recommended by your doctor (every several years, usually). Since tetanus shots are easy to obtain from a physician, hospital, or medical clinic, are inexpensive, and cause little local reaction, it only makes sense to get innoculated and keep it effective. This is especially important for those anglers taking trips to out-of-the-way areas where medical help might be distant and where a language barrier might create problems.

## INSECT AND SPIDER BITES

Poisonous snakes get the bad publicity, but insects kill far more people and are far more dangerous to most of us when outdoors. In deaths recorded in the United States from 1960 through 1969, 105 occurred from snake bites (rattlesnakes, water moccasin, copperhead, and coral snakes), but 211 deaths were recorded from insects and arachnids. Fortunately, however, for most of us, insect bites are only a painful annoyance that only slightly mars a day outdoors. If stung, take the following action.

First, remove the stinger if the insect has left it in you. Bees have barbed stingers and usually die in the process of stinging. Don't try to pick the stinger out with your finger. If the poison sac is there, you may only succeed in pumping more poison into the wound. Instead, use the flat blade of a pocket knife to scrape the stinger and the poison off.

Once the stinger is out, make a paste of water and baking soda (carry some in a first-aid kit, if possible) and apply it directly to the wound.

Then chill the area. This will reduce the chemical activity of the poison and reduce the spread of the toxin to surrounding tissues. Use ice and cold water held in a sandwich bag and changed frequently. Any amount of chilling is helpful, but take care not to overchill, which might cause frostbite. In most cases, anglers anxious to get back to fishing will not have this problem, and will probably err on the side of too little chilling than too much.

Some people (9 out of every 1,000) are highly sensitive to insect bites and may suffer a severe reaction, called anaphylactic shock. If you know you suffer this, take extreme care around any insects and if stung, get to a doctor as soon as possible. In the meantime, follow the above recommendations. If you have no past history of problems, but experience shortness of breath, swelling around the wound area, wheezing, stomach cramps or pains, uterine cramps or pain, fainting, or shock, you may be suffering anaphylactic shock and must get to a physican as soon as possible.

If you know that you have reactions to insect stings and plan to fish actively where you might be stung, consult your physician about desensitizing or carrying rapid-acting sprays of antihistamine and/or epinephrine. Consult your doctor for the best treatment or prevention in your particular case.

Some doctors (notably Dr. Claude Frazier, an Asheville, North Carolina, allergist) are recommending a "sting kit" for persons who are allergic to insect stings and who are outdoors a lot. The kit would cost only a few dollars and would contain a premeasured dose of Adrenalin in a hypodermic syringe. Adrenalin is the only effective treatment for shock from an allergic reaction and dropping blood pressure.

Recently researchers at Johns Hopkins Hospital in Baltimore have determined that the whole crushed bee extract (traditional treatment for those with allergic reactions to bee stings) is relatively useless, but that an injection of the poison secreted by the bee to stimulate the body to produce a blocking antibody, is highly effective. It is now commercially manufactured, and should be available at most hospital emergency rooms for bee-sting victims.

## JELLYFISH STINGS

Jellyfish range from the small jellyfish occasionally found in quantities in coastal waters to the large and dangerous man-of-war found primarily in tropical and southern temperate waters. Stings can come while saltwater surf fishing, flats fishing for bonefish, or from handling line and bottom rigs that have come in contact with jellyfish in heavily infested waters.

If stung, first remove any parts of the jellyfish from the skin. Since the "jelly" might adhere to the skin, use sand, mud, a towel, or similar item to remove it as rapidly as possible. If you use a towel, don't use it later on, since it will still contain the jellyfish toxin (you can clean it by washing as usual).

Then, from your first-aid kit, sprinkle some Season All, Accent, household ammonia, or Adolph's Meat Tenderizer on the afflicted area. Any of these will conteract the toxin of the jellyfish and reduce the pain and itching. Meat tenderizer comes in small, handy, shaker containers that are easy to carry in a first-aid kit or tackle box.

## BURNS

Burns can be inflicted through contact with a hot exhaust muffler on an engine, through friction from thumb or finger contact on a reel spool when a big fish is taking out line, as well as from campfires and so on.

Burns are classified into three different types, depending upon the severity. First-degree burns are those that cause only a reddening of the skin and slight pain. Second-degree burns cause blistering as well, usually within minutes of contact. Third-degree burns are those that result in the destruction and damage of deeper tissues and are very serious.

First- and second-degree burns are those most often experienced, while third-degree burns are very serious, requiring qualified medical treatment.

For first- and second-degree burns, chill the area with ice or immerse in cold fresh water. Keep it in the cold water or chilled with ice for 15 minutes to reduce local trauma and pain. Treat with a burn ointment or salve, and cover with a loosely fitting gauze or adhesive bandage. A paste of baking soda and water also works well as a burn treatment.

Avoid using the burned area and, if at all possible, avoid breaking any blistered areas of second-degree burns, since this could promote secondary infection.

# STINGRAY PUNCTURES

Stingrays inject a neurotoxin into the puncture wound that they inflict. The best immediate first aid is to immerse the wounded area into water as hot as the victim can stand. Unfortunately, this may only be possible if you are near a fishing camp or other facility where hot water is or can be made available. Keep the wound in hot water for about 45 minutes. This will help to dilute or detoxify most of the poison and eliminate or help to eliminate the possibility of paralysis, always a danger in a stingray wound. Similar treatment is recommended for stings from other toxic fish, such as wounds from the spines of anglerfish, midshipmen, and spiny dogfish, especially if the victim is sensitive to bites and stings.

# POISON IVY

Poison ivy, the climbing vine or upright shrub with three smooth leaves, causes a skin reaction from a volatile oil called urushiol. The oil is present in all parts of the plant, and some persons can even become poisoned by contact with third parties or things, such as dogs, clothing, tools, or camping gear, and from the smoke of the plant burned in a fire. You can get it year-round, so it can be just as much of a problem to winter ice fishermen as to summer trout anglers.

The best prevention is to avoid the readily distinguished plant. Some desensitizing shots are available but these are not as popular with physicians as they once were, and are questionable as to their effectiveness. If you must fish in areas where the plant is prevalent, wear long-sleeved shirts and jackets and long pants. When you are finished with your fishing trip, wash all clothing and wash your body thoroughly with a laundry soap (bar soap such as lye soap or Fels Naptha). Work up a good lather, and allow it to stay on for a few minutes before washing it off. Alkali soaps are the best, and washing is most effective if done within 20 to 30 minutes of contact.

If you are in the field and come in contact with poison ivy, you might try to locate some jewelweed to reduce the itching and stop the spreading. Crushed leaves of jewelweed applied directly to the affected skin will help. Look for jewelweed around the edges of streams and ponds.

If you get poison ivy, try to avoid scratching, and use a nonprescription cream lotion or gel of your choice to reduce the local pain and itching. Calamine lotion is the old standby, but there are some new products on the market that are less messy and work just as well. In severe cases of poison ivy or any poisoning around your eyes consult your physician.

# 26
# First-Aid Kits

Because anglers are often far from direct medical help, first-aid kits should be carried on all trips. A wide variety of first-aid kits is available from reputable manufacturers, or you can make up your own. Some of the popular ones for fishing include those that are made and promoted as first-aid kits for boats, camping trips, backpacking, and other outdoor activities. They often vary in items included. The backpacker's first-aid kit is often minimal for space and weight requirements, while those for boats are larger and more complete.

If you buy one, first examine the contents to make sure that it has those items that you will need. In some cases, you will have enough extra space in a commercial kit to add those few items that aren't included yet might be necessary.

You can easily make your own kit, buying individual components that you will need on your trips and including sufficient quantities of each item to take care of any emergency.

As a minimum, you might want to make up a kit similar to one that one of us put together for some week-long backpacking hikes. Since both weight and space were at a minimum, the kit included only the following:

- several Band-Aids of different sizes
- two gauze pads
- small roll of one-half-inch adhesive tape
- small ampule of iodine
- small ampule of first-aid cream
- small ampule of burn ointment
- small pack of baking soda
- small ampule of ammonia
- small ampule of sunburn cream
- six aspirin
- six stomach-acid pills
- small pad of moleskin (for blisters)

Add a darning needle or loop of cord for hook removal and seasickness pills and the same kit would make a good angler's field kit for trips of up to several days duration. And packed right the whole thing would fit into any fishing vest, tackle box, small boat emergency bag, surf bag, or the glove compartment of a car, recreational vehicle, or beach buggy. Obviously, such a skeletal kit would only suffice for one angler should an emergency arise, so groups that fish together or stay together should plan on enough of each item to suffice for the size of the group.

Larger homemade kits will fit well in plastic freezer or Tupperware containers, such as the T-10 Stow-N-Go, a small container with a separate inner tray and an airtight lid. The box measures 10 inches by 7 inches by 2½ inches.

Avoid the temptation to get a large, complete kit. While it might solve any problem that you might encounter in the field or on the water, it will also usually be the one left at home, in the car or motor home, or elsewhere. And if you don't have it when you need it, you might as well not have it at all. This can't be over emphasized. If you don't have it, you can't use it.

Where you keep a first-aid kit will often depend upon the type of fishing that you are doing. For example, it might be all right to leave the kit in a vehicle if you are trout fishing a small stream and will only be a few hundred yards at most from the vehicle. The same would apply to surf anglers fishing from a beach buggy. If you are a boat fisherman and own your boat, keep it on board at all times. If you rent boats, the best spot for it is in the bottom of a tackle box, accessory-kit bag or box, or some similar place in a container you know will be carried along on every trip.

If you are going out of the country to fish where medical help will be limited, you might consider carrying a second medical kit of prescription drugs in addition to the small kit of nonprescription items listed above.

As outdoor writers and photographers who travel frequently to out-of-the-way places, we have made up such kits with the advice of our doctors, following the lead of outdoor writer Mark Sosin, who put together his kit with help from a physician. Such a kit contains pills for pain, sinus congestion, cough, infection, diarrhea, gall-bladder or digestive-tract problems, poison-ivy irritation, ointment for cuts, scratches, and bites, and ointment for fungal infection and eye infection. Obviously, you would want to include any prescription or nonprescription drugs that your physician feels would be necessary for your personal health needs.

Since a box of prescription drugs could present problems going through customs, we had our physician write a signed letter listing the need for such a kit, the drugs contained in each vial, and a telephone number at which he could be reached 24 hours a day for verification or consultation about the kit. We carry the original letter along with three or four copies in case local customs officials would need to closely examine or keep a copy for their records. While we still carry the copies and will continue to do so, no customs official has yet requested to see a copy of the letter or required a copy for their records. A copy of our letter follows for your physician's guidance should you desire to make up such a kit. We are not endorsing any of the following drugs, but list them only for guidance. Consult with your doctor for his recommendations and advice.

[*date*]

TO WHOM IT MAY CONCERN:

This attached medical kit was prepared by myself for Mr. C. Boyd Pfeiffer's personal use. He is an outdoor writer and makes numerous trips in and out of the United States. As his personal physician I have authorized that he carry the following items in his kit:

Vial #1: Fiorinal Capsules #18, one every four hours as needed for pain.

Vial #2: Dimetapp Extend Tabs #36, one every twelve hours as needed for sinus congestion.

Vial #3: Hycodan Tab #48, one every three to eight hours as needed for cough.

Vial #4: Erythrocin #20, one tablet every six hours as needed for infection.

Vial #5: Lomotil #36, 2.5mg tablets, two immediately, then one or two every six hours as needed for diarrhea (severe diarrhea).

Vial #6: Donnatol Capsules #24, one or two every six hours as needed for gall-bladder or digestive-tract symptoms.

Vial #7: Valisone Cream, to be applied sparingly to the skin four times daily for poison ivy and similar irritations.

Vial #8: Mutiple unidose packets of Garmycin ointment to be applied liberally many times daily to skin infections (cuts, scratches, bites, and so on).

Vial #9: Halotex Solution, 4cc's, apply sparingly twice daily to skin and mucous membranes fungal infection. Not for use in the eye, or mouth, or genitalia area.

Vial 10: Neosporin Opthalmic Ointment, one tube. This is to be used to apply to the eyeball directly four times a day as needed for eye infection. This will cover most needs in this department.

In clearing U.S.Customs or foreign customs, there should be no problems with the contents of this kit. If any problems arise, I am available day or night for telephone consultation regarding this. Call [*telephone number*], my answering service will put you in touch with me.

[*signed*]

Such a kit is best kept in a small container. There are three ways that you can package your medicines to keep them handy and compactly stored. One way is to buy from a regular medical supply house a doctor's leather pill case (your doctor can probably get one for you if you don't have a medical supply house near you). Several sizes are available to carry from 10 to 20 different types of pills. The case is zippered, contains glass or plastic vials in elastic straps, and is first-class quality. The price, however, is high.

A cheaper and just as reliable way to go if your needs are small both in terms of quantity of pills per prescription and total number of pills required, is a similar case sold by a number of the novelty and home-need catalog houses. These cases are lower both in quality and price, but will work fine for sportsmen.

The least expensive way to go is to make your own case, using 35-mm plastic film containers and a Vlchek Plastic Company M-606 lure container or a similar item from other tackle-box and lure-container manufacturers. The advantage of this Vlchek box is that it is made of polypropylene and is very tough. Each of the six compartments will hold three Kodak 35-mm plastic film canisters perfectly.

To keep the pills from contact with the plastic containers, which are not manufacturered for food or drug storage, wrap them in the corner of a plastic sandwich bag. Cut off the excess plastic but leave enough to twist the top shut. Keep each prescription in a film container and label the outside of the container with the appropriate vial number to correspond with the listing your doctor gives you. Numbering is better than using only drug names since it removes possible confusion between similar generic or specific prescription labels.

Paste a list of the contents, by vial number, on the inside top of the case and carry the original and copies of your doctor's letter in an envelope inside. Often this case will be large enough to store your nonprescription medication, as well.

# 27
# WILDERNESS
# SURVIVAL KIT

If you are planning to go far off the trail while river or surf fishing, you might want to consider a mini-survival kit, such as the one suggested by Joyce MacDuffie, a consultant to and active member of the National Rifle Association. Items in her mini-kit for survival for short periods (statistics indicate most lost persons are found within three days and virtually all are found within five days) includes the following:

- A small metal container such as Sucrets box to contain all the survival items. A plastic box of nonbreakable butastyrene or polypropylene could also be used, provided that it is small. The box can be used to melt snow and also to mix small quantities of soup, instant coffee, or tea. Glue a small mirror to the inside lid to use as a signaling device for searching aircraft. If using a plastic box with a slip-on lid, include a thick rubber band to hold the lid in place. Alternatives, should this be too small for the following, include plastic cigarette cases and similar boxes.
  - Matches, waterproofed by dipping in paraffin, or commercially-available waterproof matches.
  - One foot of heavy, loosely woven cotton string, dipped in paraffin and sealed in a small piece of aluminum foil, to use as tinder for starting a fire.
  - Steel wool of 00 or finer to use as a hot tinder for fire starting. This burns quickly, so it would be used with the cotton string or other tinder (pine sap, pine needles, small twigs, or other such items) to sustain the fire starting.
  - Two snelled fish hooks, preferably with the bait-keeper barbs on the shank, each a different size to use with string or a leader to catch fish. (Obviously, as an angler, you will have fishing tackle with you, so you might want to omit this item. However, if you lose your tackle, or discard it to travel light, or have only hooks for large species that won't work on the small fish usually caught for survival food, you might want to include it anyway.)
  - Coil of picture-hanging wire to use as a snare, or to help erect a simple shelter.
  - Coil (as much as will fit into the box) of 20-pound-test monofilament leader to use with a hook for fishing, to use with a needle for repairing clothing and equipment, or to help lash together a rudimentary shelter.
  - Four small finishing nails to be used for making a snare, to help erect a shelter, or for a light sinker when lashed to a fishing line.
  - Instant-soup mix, coffee, or tea—any or all in small packets that will fit into the box. Mix with water in the box for refreshment and quick energy.
  - Vitamin pills (one-per-day type) for metabolic balance. Persons on any type of medication should carry one week's supply, and keep it up to date so that it is effective when you need it.
  - Razor blade, single edged, to make fuzz stick for starting fire, to clean and skin

small animals or fish caught for food, to cut up or modify belt or clothing, and other such functions.

- Salt, small packets such as those available with carry-out food, or a small amount wrapped in foil.
- Water-purification tablets, in small container or wrapped in foil to use when there is any doubt about water purity for drinking.
- Antibiotic ointment, a small sample tube, usually available from your doctor, for any infections, scratches, or cuts.
- Adhesive bandages in different sizes for covering small cuts or abrasions.
- Plastic electrician's tape, red or yellow, in a length of four feet. Use to seal and waterproof survival-kit container, repair equipment, use small pieces to mark trail or make "help" sign.
- Large-eyed needle to remove splinters or use with monofilament leader for sewing.
- Safety pins to replace button, fasten torn clothing.
- Small whistle to call for help. Three blasts is a recognized distress signal.

# Bibliography

## FISHING

CHIAPPETTA, JERRY. *Modern ABCs of Fishing*. Harrisburg: Stackpole Books, 1966.

DUNAWAY, VIC. *Baits, Rigs and Tackle*. Miami: Wickstrom Publishers, 1979.

———. *From Hook to Table*. New York: Macmillan Publishing Co., 1974.

EVANOFF, VLAD. *Surf Fishing*. New York: Harper & Row, 1974.

FALLON, JACK. *All About Surf Fishing*. New York: Winchester Press, 1975.

KREH, LEFTY. *Fly Fishing in Salt Water*. New York: Crown Publishers, 1974.

KREH, LEFTY, and SOSIN, MARK. *Practical Fishing Knots*. New York: Crown Publishers, 1972.

McCLANE, A. J. *McClane's New Standard Fishing Encyclopedia*. Edited by A. J. McClane New York: Holt, Rinehart and Winston, 1974.

OBERRECHT, KENN. *The Practical Angler's Guide to Successful Fishing*. New York: Winchester Press, 1978.

PFEIFFER, BOYD. *Tackle Craft*. New York: Crown Publishers, 1974.

SOSIN, MARK. *Angler's Safety and First Aid*. New York: Popular Science Publishing Co., 1971.

———. *Practical Light-Tackle Fishing*. New York: Nick Lyons Books, 1979.

SOSIN, MARK and DANCE, BILL. *Practical Black Bass Fishing*. New York: Crown Publishers, 1974.

WISNER, BILL. *How to Catch Salt-Water Fish*. New York: Doubleday and Co., 1973.

WOOLNER, FRANK. *Modern Saltwater Sport Fishing*. New York: Crown Publishers, 1972.

## BOATING

AMERICAN NATIONAL RED CROSS. *Canoeing*. New York: Doubleday and Co., 1977. Excellent book covering all aspects of canoeing techniques, equipment, safety, rescue, camping, fishing, etc.

ANGIER, BRADFORD, and TAYLOR, ZACK. *Introduction to Canoeing*. Harrisburg: Stackpole Books, 1973.

BOTTOMLEY, TOM. *The Boatkeeper's Project Book*. New York: Motor Boating and Sailing Books, 1972. Ideas for modifications and improvements on all types of boats, but applies mostly to larger power and sailing craft.

———. *Boatman's Handbook.* Compiled and edited by Tom Bottomley. New York: Motor Boating and Sailing Books, 1971.

———. *The Complete Book of Boat Trailering.* New York: Association Press, 1974.

CHAPMAN, CHARLES F. *Piloting, Seamanship and Small Boat Handling.* Revisions by Elbert S. Maloney. New York: Motor Boating and Sailing Books, 1972. An extensive and definitive book for boaters on all types of boating, both power and sail. Highly recommended for serious fishermen running larger boats and offshore sport fishermen.

DRUMMOND, A. H., JR. *The Complete Beginner's Guide to Outboarding.* New York: Doubleday and Company, 1974.

DUFFETT, JOHN. *Modern Marine Maintenance.* New York: Motor Boating and Sailing Books, 1973. Excellent on all types of caulking, sealing, and repairs to all types of wood, fiberglass, and metal boat hulls.

GIBBS, TONY. *Powerboating.* New York: Sports Illustrated book, by J. B. Lippencott Company, 1973.

KENDALL, DAVE. *The Complete Book of Boat Maintenance and Repair.* New York: Doubleday and Company, 1975.

MARTENHOFF, JIM. *The Powerboat Handbook.* New York: Winchester Press, 1975. Brief and to the point, but complete on the selection, operation, and maintenance of small boats for all water sports.

MILLER, CONRAD. *Your Boat's Electrical System.* New York: Motor Boating and Sailing Books, 1973.

NATIONAL MARINE MANUFACTURERS ASSOCIATION. *You and Your Boat, A Guide to Power Boat Ownership and Operation.* Chicago: 1979. Available free in single copies from the National Marine Manufacturers Association, Dept. OM, North Michigan Ave., Chicago, Illinois 60611.

RICHEY, DAVID. *The Small-Boat Handbook.* New York: Thomas Y. Crowell, 1979.

WALLACE, BILL. *The Golden Guide to Power Boats.* New York: Golden Press, 1961.

# WEATHER

BACON, THORN. *Weather For Sportsmen.* New York: Motor Boating and Sailing Books, 1974.

GUDEBROD BROTHERS SILK CO., INC. *Guide to Better Fishing with Gudebrod Fishing Tackle and How to Forecast the Weather.* Free with a self-addressed, stamped envelope from: Gudebrod Brothers Silk Co., Inc., 12 South St., Philadelphia, Pennsylvania 19107, or from your fishing tackle dealer.

LEHR, PAUL E.; BURNETT, R. WILL; and ZIM, HERBERT S. *Weather.* New York: Golden Press, 1965.

LONGSTRETH, T. MORRIS. *Understating the Weather*. New York: Collier Books, 1962.

RUFFNER, JAMES A., and BAIR, FRANK E. *The Weather Almanac*. New York: Avon, 1979. Wealth of information on storms, lightning, hail, tornadoes, hurricanes, and how best to prepare for them.

WATTS, ALAN. *Instant Weather Forecasting*. New York: Dodd Mead and Company, 1978.

# FIRST AID

ANDERSON, GAIL V., M.D.; HAYCOCK, CHRISTINE E., M.D.; and ZYDLO, STANLEY M., M.D. *AMA Handbook of First Aid and Emergency Care*. New York: Random House, 1980. An excellent paperback book with easy-to-read itemized instructions on symptoms and first-aid care for all common emergencies including many which could involve fishermen.

ARNOLD, ROBERT E., M.D. *What To Do About Bites and Stings of Venomous Animals*. New York: Collier Books, 1973. Complete coverage of the subject. Excellent for those allergic or suspected to be allergic to such dangers.

CARAS, ROGER A. *Dangerous to Man*. Harrisburg: Stackpole Books, 1977. Thick, comprehensive book on animals of all types which are dangerous to man. Of interest to anglers will be the section on reptiles, amphibians, fish, invertebrates, and appendices on snakebite and cigutera poisoning by eating of reef fishes.

GALTON, LAWRENCE. *Outdoorsman's Fitness and Medical Guide*. New York: Harper & Row, 1966.

GREGG, JAMES, O.D. *The Sportsman's Eye*. New York: Collier Books, 1971. On vision and improving your vision for outdoor activities, including fishing, boating, water sports, etc.

# SURVIVAL

There are many such books on the market and all cover the basics of map and compass, survival kits, survival attitudes, edible wild foods, fire and warmth, emergency shelter, signaling for help when lost, weather considerations, traps, snares, fishing, hunting, water, camps, and equipment. In addition to the following there are also good specialized survival books available through surplus stores of the government printing office that are compiled especially for the navy, army, air force and marines. Consult current listings if you are serious about this subject. All of the following are good and complete.

ACERRANO, ANTHONY J. *The Outdoorsman's Emergency Manual*. Chicago: Stoger Publishing Company, 1977.

ANGIER, BRADFORD. *Survival with Style*. Harrisburg: Stackpole Books, 1972.

BERGLUND, BERNDT. *Wilderness Survival*. New York: Charles Scribner's Sons, 1974.

DAIRYMPLE, BYRON. *Survival in the Outdoors.* New York: Outdoor Life, E. P. Dutton, 1972.

SHOCKLEY, ROBERT O., and FOX, CHARLES K. *Survival in the Wilds.* New York: A. S. Barnes and Company, 1970.

TROEBST, CORD CHRISTIAN. *The Art of Survival.* New York: Doubleday and Company, 1965.

WHELEN, COLONEL TOWNSEND, and ANGIER, BRADFORD. *On Your Own in the Wilderness.* Harrisburg: Stackpole Books, 1958.